How to Develop an Exceptional Memory

MORRIS N. YOUNG, M.D.
AND
WALTER B. GIBSON

1976 EDITION

Published by
Melvin Powers
WILSHIRE BOOK COMPANY
12015 Sherman Road
No. Hollywood, California 91605
Telephone: (213) 875-1711

Copyright © 1962 by Morris N. Young, M.D., and Walter B. Gibson
First Edition
All Rights Reserved
Designed by William E. Lickfield
Published in Philadelphia by Chilton Company,
and simultaneously in Toronto, Canada,
by Ambassador Books, Ltd.

Printed by

HAL LEIGHTON PRINTING CO.
P.O. Box 1231
Beverly Hills, California 90213
Telephone: (213) 983-1105

Library of Congress Catalog Card Number 62-16638
Manufactured in the United States of America

MORRIS N. YOUNG, M.D.

is a practicing ophthalmologist in New York City and holds degrees from M.I.T., Harvard, and Columbia University College of Physicians and Surgeons. With his wife, Chesley V. Young, he maintained a collection of 12,000 items on Illusion Practices which they donated to the Library of Congress in 1955. They have also established a special library on the subject of mnemonics (the art of improving the efficiency of the memory), the largest known private holding of this nature and of world-wide reputation. Dr. Young is the author of numerous books and articles, including *Houdini's Fabulous Magic* which he wrote with Mr. Gibson. He also authored *Bibliography of Memory,* the most complete book on the subject ever published. Both books were published by the Chilton Company.

WALTER B. GIBSON

has, himself, a vast memory and the ability to retain a multitude of facts, which have played a role in establishing him among America's greatest living free-lance writers. He has authored many books on magic and psychic subjects as well as in the fields of science fiction and mystery fiction. Among his most notable works are *The Shadow* novels which appeared in *The Shadow Magazine* under the pen name of Maxwell Grant. With Dr. Young, Gibson compiled and edited *Houdini on Magic* and *Houdini's Fabulous Magic,* which latter book was published by the Chilton Company (1961).

Contents

PART I. FUNDAMENTALS

PART II. ADVANCED AND VARIETY

PART III. BRILLIANCE AND FLAIR

Part I · Fundamentals

Section A · Paving the Way

1. GENERAL THEORY OF MEMORY; NATURAL MEMORY; ARTIFICIAL MEMORY

Memory is a highly important function of the human mind. Without it, all brain work could be wasted, for there would be no other way within itself of utilizing past experience. Indeed, life or consciousness can be looked upon as basically a series of memory impulses in which learning and memory are either simultaneous or synonymous.

Often, someone will speak of a person who constantly encounters trouble: "He just never will learn." Usually, the situation could be phrased more properly: "He doesn't remember." Learning itself has a dual function of absorption and application of ideas, with memory bridging the gap between.

It is the efficient and skilled co-ordination of these factors, their proper balancing, which brings results that we attribute to "great minds" or may even regard as the expression of genius. All memory *training,* all efforts to develop an effective memory, should be aimed toward such a goal.

At the same time, it should be noted that a "good memory" is by no means always a valuable asset, if restricted to one narrow field to the virtual exclusion of all else. The lives of many persons have been limited by their memories, or the distorted character of such. Child prodigies are sometimes capable of putting on fantastic exhibitions of memory in certain lines, yet are unable to put that ability to practical use. Some have been actually handicapped by their freak memories; and there are on record cases in which amazing power of memory is accompanied by feeble-mindedness.

In contrast, there are some persons whose whole key to success lies in memory and little else. Many famous political figures have risen to power through this one great faculty—their ability to remember their constituents, both passingly and where favors are concerned, has contributed extraordinarily to their popularity. True, they have also developed the ability to say the right thing at the right time, thus preventing party breaks; but that, too, is usually simple memory of a formula that worked before and therefore should work again.

Orators, actors, even writers, go through similar phases, which they attribute to artistic or creative genius, although it is largely the application of things well learned, often by mere rote. In poetry, there is a much closer link than might be supposed between the doggerel verse uttered singsong fashion by a child and the effusions of a poet laureate.

Proof of this is seen in the vast amount of "in between" material, in the form of verse that has been turned out daily for newspaper columns, the words of popular songs, and many other catchy forms of rhythm that have gained mass appeal. Literary quality often resolves itself into a rejection of the commonplace because intellectual readers, whose memories are abnormally large, recognize it as too familiar. Less sophisticated minds, however, welcome hackneyed rhymes and platitudes as they would old friends. That is because such things stir their recollections and give them a sense of passive achievement, as though they were responsible for the rhyme or the saying. New writers frequently put forth expressions that they have often heard or read, considering their work to be original rather than the imitative outgrowth of a cumulative memory.

2

Incentives are necessary to the development of natural memory. Without incentives, there would be no urgency to remember anything, and much that goes on about us could be totally ignored. But since we require things in life, we look for ways to obtain them and we remember the methods that succeed.

Wild birds learn to hop on perches of automatic feeders that deliver seed. Animals have been taught to press levers that open cages, so that they can obtain food. Seals are fed fish after they have done their tricks and the memory of that pleasant climax encourages them to go through the act again.

Human beings are seen to follow similar behavior patterns. Infants cry for food because this continues to bring results, and they soon learn to recognize the people and the objects that represent the things they want. Their urge to talk is directed toward the same purpose, but, as their minds grow, they develop broader desires than those of sheer necessity and utilize their memories toward reaching new and complex goals.

Interest becomes a prime factor where the memory is turned into difficult or unusual channels. Without interest, there is no desire to learn. Without learning, there is nothing to remember. But once an interest has been fully roused, or pushed beyond ordinary expectations, it stirs the memory processes to a degree where they frequently produce phenomenal results.

Typical interest rousers include attainment of popularity, improvement of position, overcoming of limitations, or the fulfillment of a task and the upholding of prestige. These often resemble the simpler or more primitive desires—even sheer necessity where certain individuals are concerned—but usually a choice is involved with interest.

The youth who seeks popularity may decide to learn to dance or recite poems or try out for an athletic team at school. Immediately he applies interest to that subject, sometimes at the expense of others. He wants to learn and also wants to remember what he has learned.

The young man or young woman who enters business soon becomes interested in advancement and sets an eye on a job higher up. This requires learning the workings of that job, and even more important, remembering them, because only through display of such knowledge can an applicant qualify for the higher position should it become available.

The salesman interested in his product gets to know its fine points so well that he can outsell a rival who depends only on a glib, high-pressure spiel. The veteran athlete, long interested in the game, uses his memory of tight situations to win out in a pinch, where speed or strength might fail.

A man elected or appointed to high office realizes that he must remember facts and faces to accomplish his mission or maintain his prestige. Many owe their success to early recognition of such interest; others have gained it and purposely applied it. Certainly, everyone will find such interest to his advantage, one way or another.

Interest may be developed at a very early age. The children of acrobats or actors often take up those callings because it seemed almost like play to them. The factor of heredity figures in many cases, but not in all. In America, from the days of the pioneers onward, opportunity has shaped many choices of occupation, along with existing needs.

Stores, industries, vast transportation systems have been established by persons with little or no background in such fields. These enterprises have often been carried on by successive generations or by persons who, like the founder of a business, entered it by chance. But they all developed one factor in common: interest in the business or the results it produced; otherwise, they would have branched out into other fields.

An early interest has many ramifications. If a boy has a hobby, his interest in it may be an index to the career path he should pursue. Often, it may rouse his interest in things of greater importance. Effort should be made, therefore, to create interest in worthwhile subjects on the chance that they, too, will open new vistas.

Since interest exerts such a strong influence in learning and memory development, ways must be found to give an interesting touch to material that an individual finds drab and purposeless. If it can be tied in with an existing interest, fine. A person interested in astronomy, for example, might overcome an aversion toward mathematics upon learning that this subject is necessary in studying the stars.

When interest still lags, the reward factor may be introduced. This may even involve a penalty: until certain things have been learned and memorized, other and more pleasant pursuits must be postponed.

Attention. While some interest is required to apply attention, it is significant that interest, no matter how intensive, will accomplish little or nothing unless accompanied or followed by attention.

Often, you meet people whose enthusiasm for various subjects is literally overwhelming until the superficial stages and comments have been exhausted; then they become deflated balloons where further knowledge is concerned. They have pursued their interest only to the point where strict attention was required; then they have dropped it for something else.

Observation is the keynote of attention. It is essential to learning, with memory a major goal. Hence, every factor, every faculty, should be marshaled and arrayed to command one's own attention and put powers of observation to full use.

Good health, a mind free from distraction or worry, a relaxed mood, physically and mentally—all favorably affect the memorizing process and are therefore conducive to proper attention and observation. If these conditions are not obtainable, begin to blame them, not your memory, if the latter lags.

Often people go to a lecture after a heavy meal; they also attempt to do business over a lunch table; or they hold conferences at a late hour after a tiring day. With such handicaps and distractions, it is not surprising that they find it hard to remember what went on. Concentration is a factor in attention and observation, just as it is invaluable to intensive study.

In reading or studying a subject, choose conditions suitable to holding the attention. Avoid places that are noisy or where interruptions may occur. Be wide awake and try not to be too comfortable. More scholars have succeeded while seated stiffly at a desk than when lounging in the depths of an easy chair. Often, walking about or changing position is a help.

Observation makes use of all the senses. Sight is important in art, hearing in music, but the sense of touch is also required with these. In cooking, taste and smell also play a part. In many forms of work, a sense of balance, motor memory, and other factors are vital. In acquiring skills, the various senses are combined wherever and whenever possible or helpful. Hence, the same plan should be used with memorization.

If you picture an avalanche, immediately the roar of crashing rock springs to mind, followed by a deep silence. The thought of a fire in a fireplace suggests not only the flicker of flames but also the accompanying crackle and finally the smell of the burning logs. Hence, in reading, in study, in talking about various subjects, every phase of observation should be called upon or otherwise applied to produce a fuller dimension and, with it, a more lasting impression.

In study, itself, some persons favor the visual process, as the reading of a book, while others prefer the auditory, as hearing a lecture. These can often be combined to good advantage but they offer supplementary helps as well. A person who is uncertain about the spelling of a word often writes it out and thereby can tell whether it is correct. That is a simple example of a visual aid to study and memorization.

Often, the drawing of a rough map or diagram, the charting

6

of certain factors in their relative positions or importance, will clarify or simplify a complex subject. Later, in recalling the subject itself, the simplified chart will come to mind and help form the complex. Many such visual aids are found in modern textbooks and should be utilized in full.

Foreign languages may be acquired through auditory aids, such as recordings, and also through visual aids, in which pictured objects are named. These two elements have been combined in the modern audio-visual method in which spoken words are correctly pronounced on records, while the student looks at a picture connected with the statement. Reading and writing are later tied in with the same words and pictures, adding the final touches to this mode of language study.

Retention is the aim of memorization and it is strengthened by such factors as interest, attention, observation, association and repetition. In a sense, there is no limit to one's memory capacity; an aphorism has it that something once noted or experienced is never forgotten. But it is as good as forgotten if it can't be remembered. It is like the farmer's son, who asked, "Dad, is a thing lost when you know where it is?" To that the father replied, "Why, of course not." Relieved, the boy announced, "Then the key is down the well."

Many things that we are sure we know, often are swallowed in a vast, forbidding well of memory that threatens to engulf every waking thought. Then, people think that they are trying to remember too much, whereas they are not memorizing properly to begin with. The more keys we have to memory, the less it matters if we lose one.

The mere act of learning a subject so that it can be recalled a few times after short intervals, is not sufficient for good retention. This is gained through "overlearning" which is simply another name for "practice and more practice." In acquiring a difficult skill, everyone knows that the achievement of the goal is just the beginning. The juggler who can toss four balls at once does not stop practicing the trick as soon as he acquires it. He continues, hoping to retain and improve his skill.

The same applies, in proportionately less degree, to some slighter skill, or the simple memorization of facts. They must be practiced, rehearsed, reviewed, and in some cases even relearned, if they are to be remembered properly. In short, learning itself includes a certain amount of overlearning. Until retention has been tested, it is difficult to tell whether something has been learned thoroughly.

So it is better to go beyond than to fall short. Putting facts once learned into regular use also strengthens retention. This, in turn, introduces the factor of repetition.

Repetition. The mere fact that a bad fault or habit is difficult to correct is proof of how important repetition is to natural memory. Often, a thing learned wrong requires more time in its correction than it would to have learned it right in the first place. The advantage of repetition is that some things can be learned to the point where they automatically take care of themselves.

Going back to the juggler, once his hands have learned to toss the four balls, he can turn his attention to balancing a plate on his forehead at the same time. This applies to other fields, mental as well as physical. Often, in learning facts, statements or verse, repetition may take the form of rote, which is often gone over and over, with little regard as to meaning.

There are times when rote may be helpful. Many children have been taught a verse listing the days of the months before they had any special use for the calendar. To them, "Thirty days hath September, April, June and November——" may have been meaningless jargon, but, in later years, the rapid recollection of those opening lines is a key to the number of days in any month.

Likewise, many proverbs and slogans have been learned as pure rote, only to be quoted or applied when their significance became better understood. Often, the principles of rote are used in learning something quickly, though not necessarily permanently, or as a reenforcement to something already learned.

Throughout the entire memory process, there is one dominating factor:

ASSOCIATION

The famous 18th-century philosopher, David Hume, characterized association as a "gentle force," developing from what he termed "original qualities of human nature" and "pointing out to everyone those simple ideas which are most proper to be united into a complex one."

Given any single idea, the mind instinctively associates it with something else. Just as a photograph of a runner catches him in a momentary phase of a continuous action, so does the expression of an idea represent an instantaneous portion in a chain of thought. In physical action, the body moves from place to place; in mental action, the mind moves from idea to idea.

Consistent with this view, memorization itself can be regarded as a series of associations, being nurtured by such fundamentals as interest, attention, observation, and repetition. The more ideas that the mind attaches to a single idea, the more easily that one idea may be remembered. Each association then leads to the thing to be remembered. The stronger or more vivid the link, the better the association. The formation of such associations thereby develops a better memory of the idea.

In natural memory, these associations are logical. They lead sensibly from one to another, so that the mind can later run over the same course like the runner on a track. It is only when the mind begins to encounter hurdles and obstacles that the process must be forced.

New facts must be observed to keep some point in mind. The very size of the job, the number of things to be remembered, may prove discouraging. Unfamiliar paths must be gone over and over, even in rote fashion. If the natural and logical associations

9

fail, those of an unnatural, illogical type can be introduced as artificial aids.

The line of demarcation is hard to define because the switch from logical to illogical associations is very slight at first. But as the need becomes more complex, the difference is more striking. First and perhaps the simplest of artificial aids is the grouping method.

Grouping Method

When the mind is given too many items to memorize, the natural course is to lessen the burden. With a shopping list of, say, twenty items, a person might decide to break it into two or three, each pertaining to a different store. That simply means more but shorter lists, with separate memorization, still under the head of natural memory.

But if the items are grouped according to size, price, or some other odd similarity, an artificial aid has been introduced. One way would be to group any items beginning with the same letter of the alphabet, as:

Candy, celery, cereal, cheese, coffee, crackers.

Talcum powder, tea, toothpaste, tomato juice, turnips, towels, toaster.

With these thirteen items disposed of in two separate categories, the memorization of the remaining seven-odd items would be much easier.

Such grouping of "letter ideas" has been used often to remember special things from much larger groups. For instance, the "Three R's" once represented the chief subjects of elemental schooling: "Reading, 'Riting and 'Rithmetic."

In the early days of automobiling, the "Three P's" were touted as the best cars: Packard, Peerless, and Pierce. Students of British colonial history classified the "Three B's" as having a similar type of government: Bahamas, Barbados, Bermuda.

While many of these resemble accidental dodges, they are a

10

form of artificial arrangement that is very frequently applicable in every-day memorization.

Numerical Method

Here, things are grouped and remembered by the *number* in each category. This is as old as the *Ten Commandments,* one of the earliest examples. It has had many modern applications: During World War I, President Wilson proposed his "Fourteen Points," and during World War II, President Roosevelt presented the "Four Freedoms." Each of these requires memorization of the individual items, but the fact that there is a *specific number* serves as the key.

This artificial aid can be applied in many ways: for example, each word in CENTRAL AMERICA contains *seven* letters and there are just seven states or political divisions in that section. Knowing the total makes it easier to memorize them.

Alphabetical Arrangement

Putting items in alphabetical order, and trying later to recall them from their first letters, is another artificial aid. It can be somewhat helpful in memorizing fairly long lists, but usually an added system is required. One is given in the next chapter, showing how strong associations are made by planned exaggerations and distortions.

Topical Systems

In this type of system, the word "topical" refers to "place." What the memorizer does is put things to be remembered in specific places, which he already has in mind, as mental pigeon-holes. These can be the rooms of a house, or objects about a room, as will be detailed in the following chapter.

These systems lend themselves to excellent exaggerations, such as an elephant seated in an easy chair and other fanciful notions.

Size, proportions, can be distorted to any degree, making their recall all the easier.

Topical systems date back to ancient times, Cicero having utilized such a method in the memorizing of some of his famous orations. From "topical system" has come the expression, "In the first place" as appropriate to the division of a speech.

Chain System

Natural associations provide many words that link logically, particularly in pairs, as *cat* and *mouse; hat* and *coat; land* and *sea; night* and *day*. Efforts were made in early memory systems to extend such links as well as to pair up unrelated items.

For example: starting with *salt* and *pepper,* it would be reasonable to link *knife, fork, table, chair, carpet,* and so on. All these spring naturally to mind, but they are of little help in remembering less closely associated objects. The chain weakens if it goes on with bed, safety razor, hatbox, light bulb, mousetrap.

All these are things about the house, but that makes them even more difficult to recall in sequence, since other items begin to intervene. This is where the artificial method can be applied, using illogical—even senseless—associations to form the chain.

Take these objects: clock, duck, piano, socks, stepladder, suitcase, bird feeder, helicopter, electric mixer, ashtray, tape measure, camera.

First you would picture the *clock* as very big. It would be a cuckoo clock, calling the hour, but instead, a *duck* would fly out and start playing the *piano*. At that, the piano would kick its legs, which would be wearing *socks*. These would fly all over the steps of a *ladder,* which would collapse so that you could pack it in a *suitcase*. Someone would hang the suitcase on a *bird feeder,* which would fly up like a *helicopter,* but come down buzzing as an *electric mixer,* pouring its contents into an *ashtray*. A *tape measure* would emerge and roll into a *camera,* which would suddenly click and open up, revealing the *clock* with which you started.

Here, the objects to be remembered formed their own chain, one of action, with nothing else needed. This method can be applied in many ways, but exaggeration and distortion must be regular factors, as the links depend on a good imagination.

Figure Codes

These represent the most advanced development of artificial memory systems and will be detailed at length in some of the chapters that follow. They are of different types, those for brief memory needs being quite simple, furnishing basic words that serve as hooks or pegs for remembering unrelated things.

Again, action, exaggerations, and distortions are important factors, something that cannot be overstressed. The more ridiculous, contrary to fact, or actually crazy the artificial association may seem, the more useful it can prove to be.

In its most highly developed form, the code introduces the Figure Alphabet, a complete mnemonic method in itself, whereby numerals can be translated into letters from which words can be formed, greatly increasing the scope and range of one's memory.

2. TECHNICAL MEMORY SYSTEMS: LOCALITIES

Simple Topical System

One of the simplest and best topical systems is to picture yourself taking a trip from a railroad or bus terminal, as a method of placing or recalling ten things.

1. Visualize the *entrance* to the terminal.
2. You are at the *ticket office* in the terminal.
3. Imagine yourself buying something at the *newsstand*.
4. Now you are in the *waiting room,* looking about.

5. Next, picture yourself going through the *gate* to the train or bus.

6. Now you are on board the *train* (or *bus*) and finding a seat.

7. You are looking from the *window*, viewing a scene during the trip.

8. You have arrived at a *station* out in the country or in some other town.

9. Picture a *car* (or *cab*) in which you are to ride to your destination.

10. You have reached a *house* (or *hotel*).

This completes the series.

Now for a sample of how the system may be applied. Suppose you are starting to your office and have the following things to do: (1) Buy some camera film. (2) Call a lawyer regarding a contract. (3) Buy a pair of shoes. (4) Look at some sweaters. (5) Meet a friend for lunch. (6) Take some children to the zoo. (7) Stop at the optician's for a new pair of glasses. (8) Sign some checks back at the office. (9) Wait for a long distance phone call. (10) Go to a lecture on Switzerland.

These could be tied in with the topical list by a series of mental pictures in which you would:

1. Imagine yourself starting into the *terminal* with people stopping you so that they can take pictures of you with their cameras, putting in new *films* as fast as they can.

2. At the *ticket office*, the agent is showing you a *contract* and going over its clauses while people wait to buy tickets.

3. At the *newsstand*, all they are selling today is *shoes*, which are all over the counter.

4. In the *waiting room*, college cheer leaders in *sweaters* are calling on the crowd to sing and cheer.

5. At the *gate*, who stops you but your friend with whom you have the date for lunch.

6. In the *train* (or *bus*) you can hardly find a seat because they

14

are all occupied by odd animals, from lions and tigers to monkeys and giraffes.

7. You are looking from the *window,* studying the passing scene through your *glasses,* which show everything very clearly.

8. You have reached the *station* in the country and people are rushing up with *checks* for you to sign.

9. In the *cab* (or *car*) the driver is handing you a *telephone,* saying he has a *call* for you.

10. At the *house* or other destination, people are sliding down the snow-clad roof or lawn, with mountains like *Switzerland* in the background and everyone in Alpine costume.

After utilizing this system with one list, the old images or associations will fade out when you form a new list a day or so later. This is due partly to the fact that the old list is no longer needed and therefore may be subconsciously discarded; and also partly because concentration on the new list obliterates remaining traces of the old.

The train or bus trip has been used as an example because it is familiar to almost everyone; but the reader is by no means limited to that device. He can picture himself driving somewhere in his car, taking a boat trip, or whatever else he chooses. Two or three such "excursions" can be used as supplementary lists, if needed.

Some Other Topical Systems

Various methods have been devised along the plan of the "Simple Topical System" just described. All are useful in remembering objects and, generally speaking, they are a matter of individual choice, though some are adapted to specific purposes. Because of their similarity, they are given in brief.

House System

You picture a house or apartment with which you are familiar and which is large enough to supply ten suitable locations. As an example, consider a modern ranch house which you might go through in the following manner:

You come up to (1) the *front porch,* from which you enter the front door into (2) the *foyer.* There, you turn into (3) a *living room,* which has a door into (4) a little *study* at the back, from which you enter (5) a *bedroom* and go through to (6) a *hallway* that leads into (7) the *dining room* from which you go out through (8) a *kitchen* to (9) a *patio,* which you cross to reach (10) the *garage,* where your "tour" ends.

In each of these ten "rooms" you can place an object or a person, just as in the mental "train trip," and once you have formed the pictures you can recall them by going through the house, room by room. In fact, by ending your "trip" at the "house" you have in mind, you can carry from one sequence right into the other.

"One-Room" System

Here, the memory "places" are confined to a single room with which you should be sufficiently familiar to picture in detail without hesitation. As an example, take a hotel room arranged thus:

At the left as you enter, there is (1) a *large closet.* Just past that is (2) a *luggage stand* with an open suitcase. In the corner is (3) a *writing desk* and beside it is (4) a straight *chair.* The far wall is featured by (5) a *window ledge* and in the corner at the right is (6) an ornamental *bookcase.* Returning along the wall at the right, you come to (7) a *large armchair;* then (8) a *bed* projecting toward the center of the room; next (9) a small *table;* and finally (10) a *bureau* on the wall to the right of the door.

The ten things pictured under the simple "train trip" system could all be handled by this one quite as well. Take them in the same order: (1) film, (2) contract, (3) shoes, (4) sweater, (5) friend, (6) animal, (7) glasses, (8) checks, (9) phone call, (10) lecture on Switzerland. Then tie them in with the "room list."

The zoo animal (6) perched on the bookcase is something of an exaggeration, which is all the better; while the (10) Switzerland link could be a Swiss yodeler sitting on the bureau.

"Pocket" System

Where comparatively small objects are to be remembered, it is easy to picture them in different pockets of a suit. Men's clothes are particularly adaptable to this, the pockets running in numerical order:

(1) Left trouser pocket, (2) left hip pocket, (3) left jacket pocket, (4) left handkerchief pocket, (5) right trouser pocket, (6) right hip pocket, (7) right jacket pocket, (8) right inside jacket pocket, (9) left overcoat pocket, (10) right overcoat pocket.

Large objects can also be "tabbed" by this system, if only because of their incongruity. A giraffe poking its head out of your right hip pocket is something that you wouldn't forget, even if it couldn't happen. To remember people by this method, you can think of carrying a letter from some person in a certain pocket; or an article belonging to that person.

Neighborhood System

In this system, instead of picturing yourself in a single house, you take those in a neighborhood, including stores or any place else where you customarily go. These are arranged in convenient order and thus serve as a topical list, just like the train trip, the rooms of a house, etc. This can be done with things other than houses, such as fields, street corners, the campus of a school or a college, as well as any other locale that may prove to be suitable. In each case, the objects to remember are placed in the individual houses or segments of the scene and pictured there to form the necessary association.

In all of the systems given, a "linkage" of the objects to be remembered will prove to be a definite help. For example: The *first* object, such as a *film* for a camera, could be used to obtain a photograph of the *second* object, which happened to be a *contract.* That *second* object, the *contract,* would involve the purchase of the *third* object, a pair of *shoes.* The *third* object, *shoes,* once bought, would be wrapped in the *fourth* object, a *sweater.* From there on, the linkage could continue, using any chance associations or logical connections.

These links are subordinate and therefore supplementary to the main associations. It is not necessary to spend much time or effort in forming them, except where such links are especially needed. You may look at it from this standpoint: as you remember objects by any of the topical systems, link them as you go along. Then run through the basic list, and, if you find trouble in recalling an item, strengthen its links to those which precede and follow it. This furnishes a reenforcement that may be needed later.

The more tie-ins the better, as they mean stronger—and sometimes quicker—recollections. It is not precisely a case of over-learning, as often these tie-ins come naturally and are implanted immediately, so that later they fairly leap to mind. What the method does do is give assurance, because when such links keep bobbing up, even when not needed, they give the impression that it is really easier to remember than to forget.

Fifty-Word Topical System

This is an adaptation of one of the first "modern" memory systems which was popularized by Feinaigle more than a century and a half ago. It is better now than it was then, as today it can be applied on a larger scale and there are many more odd items that may be pictured and remembered.

Picture yourself standing just inside the door of a large, square-walled room. Directly overhead is a light, which temporarily represents the figure 0. Looking at the floor, you picture it as forming nine smaller squares, which can form a pattern or mosaic, if that helps.

These squares are numbered from 1 to 9 in three cross rows, coming from the far wall toward you; but it is best to number the middle row from right to left, so that they will read as follows:

$$
\begin{array}{ccc}
1 & 2 & 3 \\
6 & 5 & 4 \\
7 & 8 & 9
\end{array}
$$

Now, imagining that you are gazing at a downward angle, you place nine objects in those squares: for example, a stove, a bicycle, a cat, a baseball, an eagle, a stack of money, a race horse, a pool table, a wastebasket—these being the items that you want to remember.

Having done this, you link them: from the *stove* in Square 1 a *bicycle* is rolling into Square 2 and on the handlebars is the *cat* that belongs in Square 3. The cat is pouncing after a *baseball* in Square 4, but the ball is snatched up by the *eagle* in Square 5, which carries it to the stack of *money* in Square 6. The cash is wagered on the *horse* in Square 7, but instead of running in a race, the horse shoots pool on the *pool table* in Square 8. At the right, in Square 9, is a *wastebasket* to catch the pool balls if they jump from the table.

Note that by having Square 3 adjacent to 4, and Square 6 adjacent to 7—thanks to the "reversed" middle row—the squares allow the formation of a continuous chain.

You now step to the center of the room and turn to face the left wall. On the ceiling just above that wall, you picture a *tenth* item, which we will say is a *box of candy*. Here, you may add the accompanying action of taking the box of candy from the *wastebasket* in Square 9 and placing it in the special ceiling Square 10, where the *box of candy* dominates the wall below.

That *left wall* is now pictured in the form of *nine squares,* running from 11 to 19 inclusive, thus:

11	12	13
16	15	14
17	18	19

Assume that the items to be remembered continue: a dictionary, an ashtray, a wrist watch, a coffee pot, a hat, a pack of cigarettes, a monkey wrench, a typewriter, a calendar.

You place these in Squares 11 through 19, linking them as you proceed. The *box of candy* can be spilling from Square 10 into the top row, all over (11) the *dictionary* and into (12) the *ashtray* and around (13) the *wrist watch*—these items also being linked to each other by any convenient images.

(13) The *wrist watch* can be used to time the cooking of coffee in (14) the *coffee pot* from which the coffee is later poured into (15) the *hat* and from the hat is taken (16) the *pack of cigarettes.* You can picture a man lighting a cigarette while working with (17) a *monkey wrench* which is being used to fix (18) a *typewriter* from which are coming the sheets of (19) a *calendar.* But the list does not have to stop there.

You now turn and face the far wall, and on the ceiling just above it you mentally place a *twentieth* item, say a *bracelet.* You could start to hang the *calendar* there, but decide on the *bracelet* instead, the bracelet being a birthday present (a tie-in with calendar). Under this dominating Square 20, you picture nine more, arranged as follows:

21	22	23
26	25	24
27	28	29

These are stocked with further items from your list and you then turn to the right wall, where (30) a ceiling square dominates the next set (31 through 39). Finally, you face the front wall and use (40) a ceiling square to dominate a set from 41 through 49. For Square 50, use the center of the ceiling—which you originally pictured as 0.

The room pictured can be blank-walled or divided into sections, shelf-fashion. Images can be enlarged, when distortion will help the association. For example, the wrist watch in Square 13 could be pictured as large as a clock, high up on the wall.

To continue with 51 to 100, picture yourself in a courtyard, surrounded by four building walls. The paving, like the walls, is divided into the usual nine squares. The paving is 51 through 59; at the top of the left wall is Square 60 and below that, Squares 61 to 69 inclusive. Topping the far wall is Square 70, and so on, until sunlight, coming straight down into the courtyard, represents 100.

Just as the interior room (1 to 50) can be given the size of an auditorium, so the courtyard (51 to 100) can be imagined as having the proportions of a stadium.

Originally, pictures were assigned to the various squares, so that new items could be associated with them. Ordinarily, this is not necessary, but persons familiar with the Figure Alphabet with its 50- and 100-word lists can use it for that purpose if they wish. Thus, there would be two sets of associations from 1 to 50 (or 100) tied in with each item to be remembered.

Examples of this will be given in a later chapter, which describes the word lists formed from the Figure Alphabet.

Number-Picture "Peg" System

Objects resembling numbers provide the "pegs" that are the basis of this time-tested device for aiding the memory. That is, pictures are visualized to look like the actual numerals from 1 to 10, inclusive, and these become the basic list with which other objects are associated.

The following list represents a well-developed form of this principle.

21

CANDLE. Visualize a tall, thin candle, symbolizing the are 1. Shape and appearance form automatic links.

2. SWAN. The conventional image of a swimming swan, with gracefully curved neck, beak pointed to the left, is an excellent representation of the figure 2.

3. PITCHFORK. The three prongs link with the number three, and if the fork is pictured horizontally, its points to the left, it will resemble the figure 3.

4. PENNANT. A short pennant, pointed to the left, waving from a staff, is a close reminder of the figure 4.

5. HAND. A hand spread with thumb and fingers well apart is the primitive symbol for the figure 5.

6. SNAKE. A coiled snake, raising its head to strike, gives a good representation of the figure 6.

7. SEMAPHORE. A railway signal, with its semaphore half-raised and extending to the left (since the post is on the right side of the track) is an excellent figure 7.

8. HOURGLASS. Still a well-known object, this is shaped much like the figure 8, so can be used to represent it.

9. MAILBOX. Of the Rural Delivery type. Extending toward the road from the right, the box and its post are easily visualized as a figure 9.

10. SPOON AND DISH. Side by side, these form the number 10. Take away the spoon and the dish remains as 0.

In memorizing objects, link them with the "pegs" that represent the numbers, taking the list in regular order. For example, in remembering a series of cities like Chicago, New York, Boston, Los Angeles, Cleveland, Detroit, Paris, London, you could form pictures as follows:

(1) Using a lighted candle to find your way around Chicago. (2) Swans swimming in New York's Central Park. (3) Men with pitchforks digging up Boston's famous Common. (4) Los Angeles excited over a winning baseball team, with pennants

flying everywhere. (5) Shaking hands with everyone you meet in Cleveland. (6) Snakes popping up from the sidewalks in Detroit. (7) Approaching Paris in a train, with a signal stopping you. (8) London's House of Parliament with an hourglass replacing the famous clock.

It should be noted that the list given here is doubly arbitrary. Anyone can make up his own, and in fact such a procedure is recommended wherever it may strengthen a peg. The sail of a boat, for example, might seem a better symbol for the figure 4 than the pennant given in the list. Such a change, or any other, is a matter of individual choice.

Also, pegs may be pictured in terms of numbers themselves rather than the actual appearance of the figures. Example: with the figure 3, the pitchfork's prongs represent both the number and the appearance of the figure, though either would do. Thus, a three-legged stool could be substituted and would qualify from the standpoint of *number,* but not *appearance* or *form.*

For the figure 5, the list uses the hand, which represents the *number,* but does not give the *appearance* of the *figure.* The *form* could be approximated, or reproduced as an equivalent, by bending in the first three fingers, so that the extended thumb and the little finger would represent the Roman numeral V for five. But it would still not be the Arabic figure 5.

Preference should be given to pictures that resemble figures, as that is the real basis of this method, and, once pegged, they are less likely to be forgotten than those which depend on number only.

The "A to Z" Code

This is an effective memory code that can be learned rapidly, giving you a list of 26 key words, with which others can be associated and thereby recalled when desired. Each key word begins with a different letter of the alphabet, running from A to Z, so they do not have to be remembered by number, but merely in alphabetical order.

In preparation, each word should involve a simple object so that it can be readily pictured. In that way, other words can be linked to the list by broadening the picture to include them. Thus, the first "key" could be APPLES (beginning with A) the next "key" could be BREAD (beginning with B), and the next COAT (beginning with C), and so on through to Z.

The weakness is that if these are purely arbitrary or taken at random, the chain itself may develop weak links. You may forget the "key" beginning with D, or H, or some other letter. Fortunately, you can always think up another to replace it, but that means hesitancy or worry, often at the moment when you need to have the system working at its best; namely, when you are forming an associated series of words or ideas.

To avoid that difficulty, the "key" list should be formed into a *connected* chain, with each successive word picture linking to the next. Here is a suggested list. Starting with "A" you have an

ARROW which is being shot at a
BIRD, which is flying away from a
CAT, which in turn is running from a
DOG, that is in danger of being trampled by an
ELEPHANT, which is trumpeting a salute to a
FLAG, which is flying above a
GATE, beyond which there is a
HOUSE, where an attack is being made by an
INDIAN, who is waving for others, while he raises a
JUG, which causes him to look up toward a
KITE, flying high in the sky, from which falls a
LEMON, which is deftly caught by a
MONKEY, who uses it to pound a
NAIL firmly and solidly into an

24

ORANGE, which attracts the attention of a
PARROT, which flies squawking to a
QUARRY, where it picks up a loose
ROCK and drops it upon a surprised
SQUIRREL, which is high up in a
TREE, above which is a large
UMBRELLA, that serves as a protection against a
VOLCANO, which erupts and sends a
WALRUS flying through the air, where it plays a
XYLOPHONE, which lands clanging on a
YACHT, where the skipper is a
ZOUAVE, in uniform of tight jacket & baggy pantaloons.

The items in a shopping list can be remembered by hooking them to the key pictures in alphabetical order. Suppose you intend to stop at the hardware store to buy a can of varnish and a flashlight battery; then at the drugstore for some shaving cream and a newspaper; next at the grocery for baking powder, bread, and tomatoes; after that, at the service station to gas up the car.

You could then form such pictures as:

An ARROW puncturing a can from which VARNISH pours out.

A BIRD sitting on a FLASHLIGHT BATTERY, trying to hatch it.

A CAT with its whiskers lathered with SHAVING CREAM.

A DOG reading a NEWSPAPER.

An ELEPHANT shaking a can of BAKING POWDER with its trunk.

A FLAG wrapped around a LOAF OF BREAD.

A GATE overgrown with TOMATO vines.

A HOUSE where servants are hauling a long hose out to the gasoline tank of a car.

This, of course, could be continued to the full extent of the 26-word key list, if there were that many items to be remembered.

Another use for the A to Z Code, for which it is peculiarly suited, is in the memorization of numbers. Where some other systems utilize numbers as part of their "key," this code is alphabetical only, and therefore free from any confusion where figures are concerned.

To remember a number of up to 26 figures, you have only to visualize your "key" words (Arrow, Bird, Cat, etc.) each in group formations, as follows:

1, a unit; 2, a pair; 3, a triangle; 4, a square; 5, a V-formation or 5 units; 6, two groups of three; 7, a cluster; 8, a double square; 9, a multitude; 0, a blank or an object going from sight.

Example: To remember the number 352608527497305317. .

Picture three ARROWS being shot in triangular formation. BIRDS flying away in V-formation. Two CATS sitting side by side. Two packs of three DOGS barking at each other. An ELEPHANT disappearing into the brush. A FLAG draped over two square picture frames. Five GATES in a wall shaped like a pentagon. A pair of HOUSES within the enclosure. A cluster of INDIANS. Four JUGS set in a square. Overhead, a sky filled with a multitude of KITES. A cluster of LEMONS. Three wise MONKEYS looking at one another. An empty box labeled NAILS. Four ORANGES with an odd one on top, making a pyramid of five. Three PARROTS in a triangle. A single QUARRY. A cluster of ROCKS.

This picturization could also be carried through a series of 26 items, all figures; and it is possible to continue further by beginning a new alphabetical list as a follow-up to the original.

For example: Continue from ZOUAVE to an

ANCHOR, which is dropped overboard, bringing up a
BOWLING BALL, which is rolled against a large

CLOCK, which floats down a stream and over a
DAM, where there is a long
EEL, swimming in the water and coiling about a
FIRECRACKER with a sizzling fuse.

This carries the list to 32 units, which is better than stopping it abruptly at 26. The additional items from A to F will not conflict with those in the original list, as they are not brought to mind until the finish and are then recalled in their own sequence.

3. TECHNICAL MEMORY SYSTEMS: PHONETIC FIGURE SYSTEMS

The Figure Alphabet or Phonetic Numeral Code

This is among the best of memory devices as it translates numbers into words and vice versa by a simple, logical phonetical system. The idea is old but has undergone many changes and improvements, resulting in the use of certain consonant sounds as figures, with vowels filling in to form words helpful to the memorization process.

The most practical and generally used code is the following:

1 is the letter T (also D or TH).
Remembered by the single downstroke in T.
2 is the letter N.
Remembered by the two downstrokes in N.
3 is the letter M.
Remembered by the three downstrokes in M.
4 is the letter R.
Remembered by the fact that R is the fourth and last letter in the word "FOUR."
5 is the letter L.
Remembered because L is the Roman numeral for 50, of which 5 forms the first part.

27

6 is soft G, or J (also CH, SH and similar sounds).

The G looks like the figure 6, as does J when it is reversed as in a mirror.

7 is hard C, or K (also hard G and Q).

The figure 7 looks like a crude KEY and also a CrooKed stiCK, representing the sound of its key letters.

8 is the letter F (also PH or V).

In script, an F has two loops like the figure 8.

9 is the letter P, or B.

The P looks like 9 when reversed as in a mirror.

0 is the letter Z, or S (also soft C).

Remembered by the word ZerO which begins with Z and ends with O. (Also by the hissing sound of a revolving wheel.)

It should be noted that these phonetic equivalents are usable in languages other than English, the "R" for "4" being used because that letter appears in the word for "four" in various European languages. That also explains why "L" was chosen for "5" rather than "V"; the L represents a common pronunciation. In the Figure Alphabet, V plays a subordinate part as a substitute for F or PH.

The alphabet itself can be remembered by a key sentence, such as:

ToNy	May	ReLiSH	CoFFee	PieS
1 2	3	4 5 6	7 8	9 0

The letters that may be used as fillers in making up key words are A, E, H, I, O, U, W, Y (i.e., A, E, I, O, U and WHY).

Since the system is based strictly on phonetics, any arbitrary letters or combinations should be decided upon beforehand. Double letters (as LL) are simply treated as single letters, so that "dollar" becomes DoLaR phonetically, with the figure values of 1-5-4. Words like "tough" and "rough" are pronounced like "tuff" and "ruff" or TuF and RuF, so that they become easy too.

When two letters are pronounced practically together yet still retain their individual sounds, they are considered separately and the sounds themselves can be accentuated. Thus P–L as in "please" becomes "Puh–LeeZe" and T–R as in "try" can be pronounced mentally "Tee–Rye."

Similarly, the single letter X can be broken into K and S when so pronounced, as in "exit," which becomes "ecK–SiT." This gives X the values of 7 and 0 for K and S. In a word like "xylophone" the X is pronounced as Z, and so would be simply 0.

Various other special cases will suggest themselves as they occur; and individual judgment can be used in such instances. Perhaps the commonest of the lot is the ending "ing" as in the word "sing" or "singing." Although the last two letters can be treated as N and G, the usual procedure is to class them as hard G, so that "sing" becomes SinG, or 0–7; and "singing" becomes SinGinG, or 0–7–7. Similarly, "sink" can be treated as though its last two letters were N and K, but the simple K (7) is preferable.

Remembering Dates and Numbers

The Figure Code, once learned, is instantly applicable to remembering historic dates, telephone numbers, street addresses, and the like. For example: Columbus decided to DROP IN on America. The phonetic figures in DRoP iN give the year when he began his voyage, 1492.

A telephone number like 2–4625 can be remembered by the phrase No RiCH NaiL, while many of the lengthy long distance numbers can be worked into sentences, as: "MuST you MaKe CoFFee Now, JiM?" which becomes 301–377–8263.

Some of these codes can be repeated or visualized until they become permanent reminders but, for the most part, they serve as temporary devices for remembering numbers until they can be written down or, in time, are more naturally impressed on the mind.

Remembering Objects

For remembering a list of ten objects, you first form your own key list in terms of the figure alphabet. Thus a TOE would represent 1 (T); an INN would stand for 2 (N); the month of MAY would do for 3 (M); and so on. Anyone can make up an individual list; but the question is, how well can it be remembered unless the objects themselves are linked or related?

One way of doing this is to begin all the words with a neutral letter, like H, or to incorporate that letter into your word so that the links become natural and almost automatic. Here is a recommended list:

1—HAT	4—HAIR	7—HOOK
2—HEN	5—HILL	8—HOOF
3—HAM	6—SHOE	9—HOOP

0—HOSE   DICE—10

Each of the words through "Hoop" starts with the neutral letter H and ends with the code letter for the proper figure, with the lone exception of SHOE, in which the H is joined with S (instead of using J or soft G) so that the link is natural, anyway. The word HOSE is also a logical choice for the figure 0.

The word DICE may be used to represent 10, the D standing for 1 and the C for 0. It introduces the TEN series, which will be explained in a later chapter.

With a list of up to ten items to remember, such as sugar, thread, needles, gloves, electric bulbs, coffee pot, pencil, etc., the following pictures could be formed, connecting each item with a key word:

1. A HAT containing a bag of SUGAR.
2. A HEN pecking at a spool of THREAD.
3. A HAM bristling with large NEEDLES.
4. HAIR growing from a pair of GLOVES.

5. A HILL lighted with large ELECTRIC BULBS.
6. A SHOE being used as a COFFEE POT.
7. A HOOK with a dangling PENCIL.

Other items can be added.

When a new list is being formed, the old one erases itself, as with the simpler Homophonic "Hook" and Number-Picture "Peg" Systems. This gives you one more method that can be alternated with the others since the procedure is essentially the same: New objects are linked with those that are old and well-established, thus forming composite pictures which may be instantaneously recalled to mind.

The extra effort required in first learning the Figure Alphabet, and then the key pictures to go with it, is well worth while, for it can be developed into much more elaborate applications, which will be detailed in later chapters. The Figure Alphabet forms the nucleus of many seemingly masterful feats of memory.

The Homophonic "Hook" or "Peg" Method

This is the simplest and perhaps the most natural of figure codes, inasmuch as it is based on the actual sounds of the numbers from 1 to 10 inclusive, each of which is converted into a suitable picture. It can be learned in a few minutes and checked at any time by simply pronouncing the numbers slowly, "One," "Two," "Three," and so on, thus naming each "hook" automatically.

Ten suitable words and their pictures are:

1. WON. Sound: exactly like "One."
Picture a runner crossing the finish line. He has come in first and he has *won* the race.

2. TUBE. Sound: similar to "Two."
Picture a tube of any size or length. Emphasize the beginning of the syllable ("two") and think of the tube as having *two* ends.

31

3. TREE. Sound: similar to "Three."
Picture a tree, particularly the trunk and lower branches, which can diverge into *three,* as many trees do.

4. FORT. Sound: similar to "Four."
Picture a fort with *four* walls shaped like a square. Here, again, emphasize the beginning of the syllable, as "for" or "four."

5. FIFE. Sound: a sharp pronunciation of "Five."
Picture a fife with a man playing it. He has *five* fingers, including the thumb. The pronunciation "fife" is often used for "five" over the telephone, so that it will not be mistaken for nine. This stresses the "peg" all the more.

6. SIKHS. Sound: exactly like "Six."
Picture a group of Sikhs, bearded Indians wearing turbans. There can be *six* in the group.

7. HEAVEN. Sound: similar to "Seven."
Picture a scene of clouds, stars, or angels. There is a phrase, the "Seventh Heaven," meaning the highest of all. This hooks "heaven" with "seven."

8. WEIGHT. Sound: similar to "Eight."
Picture a metal weight, marked "8 lbs.," and bear in mind that the word *eight* is part of the word w*eight.*

9. DINE. Sound: similar to "Nine."
Picture a table set for dinner with a large clock registering the hour of 9 o'clock. The phrase, *"Dine* at *nine,"* will keep this pegged.

10. TENT. Sound: similar to "Ten."
Picture a group of tents, numbering *ten* in all, as the number comes naturally. Emphasize the beginning of the syllable ("ten") in the word *tent.*

The word "tent" is an apt choice for 10 because the 10 is sometimes used as 0. In that case, simply think of the tent (or tents) being folded or dismantled into nothing.

Despite its limitations, this list is very good because its "hooks" catch things quickly and hang on to them tenaciously. With it, you can remember a list of appointments, or things to do, by simply hanging them on the pegs in regular order.

For example, if you intend to stop at the post office to buy stamps, then pick up some theater tickets, go to the barber's for a haircut, have lunch with an old friend, spend an hour or so in the reading room of the public library, attend a committee meeting late in the afternoon, and start home immediately afterward, your picturization might run thus:

(1) You are winning a race to the post office. (Won) (2) You are looking through a spy glass (Tube) or pair of opera glasses at a stage, so, obviously, you must have tickets. (3) What a peculiar tree we have here. Its trunk is painted with stripes and your barber is sitting up in the branches, inviting you into his new outdoor shop. (Tree) (4) Somebody is waiting for you at the fort, and who else but your old friend? (Fort) (5) High pitched music disturbs you (Fife) and where could it be more out of place than at the library where you are going next? (6) Here are some bearded men (Sikhs) seated about a table. As you enter, they remove their beards and turbans and you are at the committee meeting. (7) Something pleasant now arises (Heaven) and what could be more pleasant than heading home after such a day?

This list can be used as an auxiliary with other and more elaborate lists because its homophonic "pegs" will not conflict with the mental pictures on which other systems depend.

Section B · *Faces and Figures*

1. HOW TO REMEMBER PEOPLE

For practical purposes, the ability to remember people often outweighs all other forms or phases of memory. It is important in both social and business life, often going far toward establishing an individual's popularity and paving the way to financial success.

You can't afford to ignore people if you want them to like you and to value your friendship. Yet forgetting them is the equivalent of ignoring them, and often one leads to the other. Most persons of average memory find it a problem to remember names and faces, with embarrassment the only alternative. Through proper application of accepted memory methods, such embarrassment can be avoided.

Names and Faces

It is the very duality of that phrase that often raises the stumbling block. Separately, they might be remembered; the problem is to link them. Often, when we hear some name mentioned or discussed, it stays in mind, like any topic of conversation, and can be recalled later; there are times, too, when we see a face among a crowd and remember it, or when we recognize someone whom we are sure we have seen before.

But the combining of a name, which is a verbal expression,

with a face, which is a visual impression, is a problem in itself, except when they have something strikingly in common. If you meet a man named Mr. Baer who is as powerful as a grizzly bear, or a roly-poly gentleman named Mr. Ball who looks rotund enough to bounce, it is easy to link the name and the person. But you can't count on things like that too often.

There are contrasts, like Mr. Light, who may be decidedly on the heavy side, or Mr. Little, who may be very big. But those are comparatively rare, too. Not only that, but if you jump from one type of comparison to another, there is the danger of getting them mixed. In remembering people, such pegs may not only prove inconsistent but may be insufficient.

Such simple associations work well with lists of objects that are to be remembered in a group or for a specific period and then eradicated. But, with people, you may need to remember names and faces at almost any time and often on different occasions. Any confusion or even hesitation may then create the very embarrassment that you are anxious to avoid.

The real key to remembering people is found in the primary purpose behind this type of memory. That purpose is to make people like you, or at least to have them recognize your interest in them to the degree that they are willing to return it, which amounts to the same thing. Now, in doing this, the mere ability to look a man in the eye and repeat his name parrot fashion is not enough.

You should also be able to recite facts concerning him, where you met him, where he hails from, something about his family, his business, or a trip he may have taken since you saw him last. All these factors, instead of making it harder, make it easier. They give you that many more associations and a much fuller picture. Far from being forced or artificial, such pegs are geared to the subject at hand, the person himself.

As proof of this we may cite the fact that persons noted for their ability to remember hundreds of people, can usually call their hosts of friends by their first names, or even their nick-names, and drop in mention of personal facts as well. So it is obvious that their methods must follow the pattern just mentioned.

Now to break down that pattern into workable components, these conform to the following general course of action:

1. *Preparation.* The preliminary study of names and faces.

2. *Observation.* Gaining impressions of persons to be remembered.

3. *Association.* Measures and devices for linking names and faces.

4. *Repetition.* Firmly implanting and reviewing the impressions gained.

These various factors will be subdivided and described individually as we proceed, but it should be stressed that they are all part of a continuous pattern. Early preparations can be put into rapid practice, which in turn can move into more advanced stages. Meanwhile, the preparatory measures can be strengthened further, so that the results become cyclic as well as cumulative, often exceeding original expectations.

Preparation

It is recognized that intensive concentration upon the preliminaries about to be described can in itself enable a person to become expert in remembering names and faces. But for practical purposes, such preliminaries may be regarded as study methods, as very few persons will have the time or patience to carry them through to an extreme. Nevertheless, the work will be found fascinating as it proceeds.

The Study of Names

This, applied both to first and last names, can be done in the same fashion as increasing an individual vocabulary through the

study of a dictionary. With names, however, it is m.
and more rapid than with words in general.

For first names, dictionaries themselves provide lists, fron
Aaron to Zephaniah and Abigail to Zoe, together with their
meanings. When you become familiar with such lists, you will
often recognize unusual names when you first hear them. This
forms an immediate link between the person and the name.

The same applies to last names, but here the best reference
volume is the telephone book. In it, you will find a remarkable
array of names, some with definite meanings in various languages.
Tracing these is a study in itself, and variations in spelling provide a particularly fruitful field. Where you find references to
the same name under different spellings, all should be checked to
note those which are most—or least—used.

Almanacs provide many names, including those of famous personages of the past which are still current today because of children who were named in their honor. Names in the news and
in advertisements, frequently strike a familiar note. In short, to
remember names, you should become name conscious, just as a
student of languages becomes word conscious.

It is an excellent plan to form a special list of first names—
and in some cases last ones—with which you can list words that
sound like them, thus forming a permanent table. As examples:
"Hairy" with Harry; "Tom Thumb" with Tom; "Miniature"
with Minnie; "Helen of Troy" with Helen; "Davey Crockett"
with David; "Useless" with Eustace; "Contrary" with Mary.

These are not meant to be flattering, so they should not be
made public but saved simply as "memory links" to be explained
in later associations. They are much safer than any links coined
on the spur of the moment, as they are definitive where your
own memory procedure is concerned. Similarly, it is best for each
person to make up his own list so that the equivalents or associated "word names" will be natural.

endently of the Name Study but with the
amiliarize yourself with people's faces, both
s types. These observations can be made on the
or busses, among crowds, or simply by looking
at ᵖ   magazines or on television programs.

In add   n to studying features in both full face and profile,
facial expressions should be noted. Smiles, nervous glances, any
other mannerisms are all keys to identification and therefore useful in remembering faces. In addition, voices, gaits, build, cloth-
ing, are all valuable tabs.

There are several ways of carrying this type of study further,
namely:

Through books on physiognomy, which divide full faces into
such simple but easily definable groups as Triangular, Oval, and
Square. These same texts refer to profiles as Convex, Straight,
and Concave. Though faces seldom show such exaggerated forms,
they often bear marked traces of those features and others, such
as bushy brows, lantern jaws, slitted eyes, and other descriptions
long used by fiction writers. In short, there are many salient
points to go by.

Police descriptions treat many features verbally, listing persons
as Slim, Medium and Stout; with shoulders Straight, Round,
Stooped; plus color of eyes and hair; appearance of nose and ears;
color and type of mustache, if any; manner of speech, from fast
to slow; and a gruff to soft voice. Charts of this type are therefore
worth close study by anyone seeking to remember people by
their faces or general appearance.

The study of art is an invaluable adjunct in transcribing faces
to memory. How far anyone may want to follow such an endeavor depends upon his individual aptitude or inclination, but
it is a certainty that the process will sharpen his memory for
faces. Many persons with highly retentive minds are unable to

sketch things that they remember quite vividly. This is particularly true with faces because, without art training, it is difficult even to begin, let alone put features in their proper proportions and perspective.

Artists develop their natural skill in visualizing faces and drawing them from memory. Sketching from photographs is a good form of practice, enabling a person to note many details that he might otherwise overlook. Memory sketches can be checked by photos or by later observation of the subjects themselves.

Photographers, too, gain a memory for faces, because they must study them or catch them at the best angles. The phrase, "as pretty as a picture," is usually a tribute to a photographer's skill. Anyone who has given any serious attention to photography will appreciate this. When we speak of a "photographic memory," we mean the ability to recall a scene exactly as it was, as though the human mind had gained a camera-like impression.

While this is by no means an exact comparison, it serves as a guide. Liken what you have to do to the taking of a sound movie, with proper registration of film and an eye to angles, and the results will be that much better. Memory of people is largely accomplished at the outset by concentration upon the name and the face. When a name is lacking, it is helpful to coin one to tie in with the face. This is similar to forming a mental picture of a person whose name you have heard but whom you have never actually seen.

Instead of causing confusion, such a process provides a future peg. The temporary name will link with the real name when you hear it. In the same way, an actual face will adjust to an artificial image. In short, the more you think about people and try to picture them, the better you will remember them.

Often, you may hear someone say, "Why, your friend George was so different from what I imagined he would be like!" In all such instances, you can be sure that the mental picture of the real George will supplant the imaginary one, once he has been seen.

A person's build, his mannerisms, his gait, all fit into the mental picture; and in some instances may be the essential feature. Dress and attire provide further tabs. Often, these conform to existing vogues, so a reference to fashion catalogs, current magazines and newspaper ads will be helpful in the establishing of types.

Observation

Adherence to the preparation details so far given will, in itself, require continued observation, thus leading into the next and perhaps the most important phase. All generalized observation can be reduced to the particular, involving people with whom you are familiar or those with whom you are associated.

These include club members, those who attend meetings, conferences, conventions or other gatherings, which may test your skill at remembering the people you meet. The more you know about them to begin with, the better. A study of their photographs, a review of what you already know about them, is helpful in two ways:

It makes it easier for you to concentrate upon new faces or the lesser known ones.

It gives you an objective where those same new personalities are concerned. If you can bring them into the category of those you already know, your aim will be accomplished.

Such an aim presupposes two factors already established through your preliminary endeavors: Interest and Attention.

Interest must be twofold. It must be impelled by adequate motives and it must be genuine. It includes the making and keeping of friends; potential profit; personal success; betterment of position; development of self-confidence.

Such interest, however, must be directed toward the benefit of others as well as yourself. You must wish people well, because in no other way can you hope to understand them; and if you do not understand them, you cannot expect them to understand you. Hence, memorizing people and their ways, whether in social or business life, must be aimed for completeness, yet at the same time must be relaxed and friendly.

Attention is effective only if you are alert and are giving full consideration to the immediate task, which is learning all that you can about people in order to remember them better. This means that you must disregard distractions and self-interest, other than your main goal. Block out everything else and concentrate, so as to miss nothing that will aid your process of memorization. Look a person in the eye and avoid distractions. Above all, do not try to create an impression of your own importance.

Attention must be concentrated from the very start. Sometimes an introduction is at fault; the person making it may slur over a name because he is not too sure of it. Usually, you can rectify this by remarking that you did not quite catch the name and want to be sure of it. If the friend who made the introduction seems uncertain, you can delay this and ask the person himself later on.

All these elements are combined with your powers of observation, which come under the more specific head of:

Perception. This begins with your general impression of the person whom you meet. Two senses are immediately involved: you *see* his face and you *hear* his name. These are separate items which become associated and thereby linked as you proceed.

Your senses are not limited to the conditions just stated. You *hear* a person's voice and from it you gain a further impression of his personality. You can often *see* his name, in the form of a calling card or a signature. Often, you *feel* a person's handshake at the moment of meeting, so that multiple senses are involved.

From among the general impressions, you may frequently obtain a cue that enables you to recall the overall features of the individual. Watch for such a cue, but do not limit yourself to that one tab alone. Add any further links that will help to strengthen

41

the impression, even if they change the mental picture. Or, putting it the other way about, don't rush for any quick cue that may later prove inadequate. Never hurry.

It is important to concentrate upon one person at a time whenever possible. The exceptions are when meeting members of a family, or two or more persons who happen to be close friends or business associates. Since the memory process is aided and even aimed toward learning as much about the individual as feasible, meeting two at once is something of a short cut and at the same time provides contrasts which would have to be noted later if the persons were met singly.

This, however, has its hazards. You must know a subject sufficiently well in order to look for contrasts. An attempt to do this simultaneously, or to use a dual starting point, can lead to confusion rather than clarity. It is like meeting a pair of twins and thinking of them as such, then trying to tell which is which or to identify them separately. It would be better to meet one individually before knowing that the person had a twin; then enough points will be pegged for contrast.

Check back on persons whom you have met together and you will usually find that your recollection of one has dwindled, often at the expense of the other. This means, in just one word, that *contrast* must be borne in mind as a primary factor of observation in such instances.

Married couples are a specialized case, since it is logical as well as easy to remember them together. At the same time, each should be studied individually so that they can be recognized if met separately.

Never curtail your powers of observation by jumping too quickly to associations, valuable though the latter are. This rule is particularly true when meeting people in a group, as the tendency is to remember them in that form and note their individual differences later. But that is putting the association process into reverse and thus having it work against you.

Cues for each individual must be sharp and well-defined, strong enough to stand on their own, with grouping on a secondary, not a primary, basis. This stresses the importance of the preparatory work already outlined. If you have learned to note people regularly, you will have acquired the ability to put it to use.

When meeting people, you will be at ease while observing them. You can be pleasant and conversational while linking their names and faces. You can absorb facts and details in a natural way, as though intending to write out an account later, which, in certain instances, you may find it helpful to do.

In pronouncing a person's name, be sure you have heard it correctly. Also be sure that it is given distinctly and that the syllables are properly enunciated. Allow time for a short conversation and, when opportunity arises, use the person's name again. In some instances, you will find a chance to pass along an introduction from one person to another, emphasizing names all the more.

Summarized, the observational process requires:

1. Getting the name right.
2. Studying the face for details.
3. Gaining personality impressions.
4. Repeating the name aloud and using it.
5. Making special note of forehead, eyes, nose, mouth, chin, ears, cheekbones, teeth, complexion, skin. Also hair and beard or mustache, if any. Any blemishes, peculiarities, or other special features should be noted.
6. Extending your observations to height, weight, gestures, manner of speaking, accent and whatever else may be distinctive. Be careful as to glasses, since they may be removed later.
7. Obtaining as many facts as possible, later discarding or eliminating those that are irrelevant.

In their early stages, the processes just described and listed lead directly into:

Association

Just as Observation picks up from Preparation, so does Association come into play soon after your powers of observation are put to work. Not only that, but if your preliminary studies have been fairly thorough or extensive, you will already have utilized associative processes and will thus be that much farther advanced toward your goal of memorization.

The twin processes of creating and then combining the separate impressions of name and features are well within the range of practical accomplishment. Inasmuch as things *seen* are more easily remembered than those that are *heard,* maximum attention should be given to the name. Once you are aware of the general features of the person, the sound of the name and a visualized picture of it—if you are able to form one—you are ready to coordinate your powers of observation with elements of association.

The occasion of the meeting and the environment are, of course, immediate links. Sometimes later meetings and surroundings will produce more vivid and lasting pictures or associations. These should be implanted as strongly as possible, often serving as a background for sharper memorization.

Coincidence sometimes provides a link between a person's face or personality and his name (as with a smiling man named Smiley). In contrast, there are rare instances wherein rote is the only practical way of remembering a name, fixing it firmly in mind by sheer sight and sound, writing it over and over, and speaking it aloud time after time. (For some, this would be the case with a name like Hohenzollern.)

In order to form a mental picture that will persist with greater certainty than the name itself, providing a potential tie-in with the features, use any of the following devices:

1. Associate the name with that of a well-known person.
2. Associate the name with that of someone already known to you.

44

3. Associate the name with that of an object with the same or similar meaning.

4. Associate the name with words that are similarly spelled or pronounced.

5. Associate the name with a rhyming word or words.

6. If name has a foreign language significance with which you are familiar, use that as a link.

7. Analyze the name itself, as to spelling, syllables, number of letters, initial letter, etc.

8. Convert name to a mnemonic numeral and reconvert that to another word for tie-in.

In any of these procedures, their modifications or combinations, a picture is first visualized relating to the name, altering it as necessary, exaggerating it when so required, allowing for any oddity that may help the process. This becomes the anchor, serving as the name picture.

Meanwhile, in observing the person's facial features, look for highlights or well-defined impressions that can be attached to that same anchor, so that it will tie in with the name. Here, again, alterations are allowable, but they must not be too far-fetched or they will be remembered rather than the anchor.

You need an anchor, not a chain, as your final picture, though it may include various related features. Among these, a cue word is advisable and sometimes necessary in order to conjure up the complete picture, thus recalling the linked name and face.

First and Last Names

First names can often be linked to last names through direct association. You would give a man named "William" his nickname of "Bill" and then think of him paying a bill or collecting one. For instance, if William "Bill" Martin happened to be on the welfare committee of a club, it would be natural to think of him collecting "bills" in the form of promised contributions.

45

Harry, thought of as "Hairy," could apply to a man with a good head of hair; or, in contrast, to a baldish man. Harry Cushman, with bushy hair, would be thought of as a bushman, associating *Cushman—bushman*. Harry Somerville, with short-clipped hair, would like it that way in the summertime, associating *Somer*ville with *summer*.

Many famous first names tie in with personalities. General Winfield Scott can be pictured *win*ning battles in the *field*. By imagining him in Scottish costume, the last name *Scott* is linked. Similar ties may be made with the names of persons whom you meet, even though they may be extremely far-fetched. Sometimes the more incongruous they are, the better.

Last Names and Faces

The last name usually provides the link to remembering a person's face, often through sheer necessity, because you may be introduced to someone simply as "Mr. Buxton" or "Mr. Callahan" or "Miss Webster." First names, of course, may help, but you can go right into facial links with these last names alone.

Assume, as examples, that:

Mr. Buxton has a rather large mouth with conspicuous teeth and that his forehead is very high, rounded, and somewhat baldish.

Taking the name as two words, *buck* and *stone,* you could think of Mr. Buxton having *buck teeth* and a forehead like a *round stone*. Still concentrating on the forehead, you consider it *heavy,* which suggests *ton*.

This produces *buck—stone—ton* which contracts to *Buxton*. Not a flattering picture of Mr. Buxton, but he will be flattered when you remember him immediately the next time you meet him, provided, of course, that you don't tell him how you did it.

Mr. Callahan has a rather narrow forehead but his face widens from the temples downward into rounded cheeks and chin. In contrast, he has small eyes and a sharp nose, with a friendly smile.

From *Calla,* you can think of *calabash,* which resembles a squash, giving the facial form. From *han,* you picture *hen,* fitting Mr. Callahan's small, quick eyes and beakish nose. Reverting to *calabash,* the *bash* suggests *bashful,* which suits the friendly smile.

You should know Mr. Callahan when you see him again.

Miss Webster has these standout features: Her hair is filmy and reminds you of a *web.* Her eyes are large and inclined to *stare.* From *web* and *stare,* you obtain *Webster.* Just to clinch it, you note that Miss Webster's lips are firm and serious and that she is precise in manner. That fits *Webster,* as represented by a *dictionary,* which is also serious and precise.

All names do not link this easily. With some, it is necessary to form wild exaggerations. Ears can be likened to "sails" or eyebrows to "burrs" or lips to "lump" if any of those happen to approach the syllabic pronunciation of a difficult name.

Simple names present a problem because they often have seemingly little to work with, but this can be handled in many cases by forming a series of associated comparisons. As an example, take the simple name, *George Hill.*

Think of "George" as *gorge* and you have a *hill* rising above it. George Hill has thick hair, so you think of *trees* on the *crest.* His eyes are gray and deep-set; you think of *boulders* in *hollows* on the hillside. His nose is broad, so you think of a *slope,* coming toward you. His wide mouth and straight chin constitute the *brink* and *wall* of the *gorge,* so you are back to George.

All these devices must be stressed and worked to extremes if you have to remember the names and faces of a great many people virtually on sight. Politicians, promoters, lecturers, salesmen and others may need such gimmicks as a regular thing, but most persons can manage with a lot less.

In meeting people in a business or social way, you generally have a chance to talk with them and learn something about them. Often, their personalities impress themselves upon you at the time. Later, you may remember such people when you see them but you have forgotten where it was, or who they are, so the simple way is to peg it at the start.

You meet a man named Drucker. You ride with him in a car or cab. You think how odd it would be if the car suddenly turned into a truck, with Mr. Drucker driving it. But it wouldn't be so odd because *Drucker* suggests *Trucker*.

You meet a man named Roland. The name forms *row* and *land*. Think of him *rowing* a boat to *land*. You are *riding* a *bus* home, he is *rowing* a *boat* home. The next time you meet Mr. Roland, you will remember when and where you parted.

You can think of a man named *Schuyler* as a *scholar;* a man named *Eaton* as *eating* dinner; a man named *McLeod* as flying a plane through a *cloud;* a man named *Alward* as *always* going *forward;* a man named *Leventhall* as on the *eleventh hall* of a building; a man named *Gollomb* discussing a newspaper *column*.

These associations can be strengthened with each new meeting. Often, the mention of a name will bring up the action picture and with it the face of the person concerned; so this helps in recalling faces from names as well as names from faces.

Repetition

In remembering people, the factor of repetition is not only important but especially helpful for very definite reasons. You are dealing, not just with a single factor, but with the dual elements of face and name, plus any additional details that may be noted. These may include anything from nicknames to actual titles, moods, facial expressions and other characteristics.

Think back to someone whom you know quite well and ask yourself how well you really know that person. Immediately, odd thoughts will spring to mind. You will probably recall things that so and so said or did which were quite different from what you might have ordinarily expected.

Now, apply that same rule to the person whom you have just met. You know the person by name and you can recognize him—

as of now. But will you remember the name the next time you see him, or will you know him then? Repetition is your way of insuring that, by turning the new acquaintance into an old friend, right now.

In all memorization, it is best to overlearn, or to fix a fact in mind more strongly than seems necessary at the moment and later. Do that with the person whom you want to remember. Repeat his name both mentally and aloud. Use it as much as you can, in conversation both with the person himself and with others who know him.

Look at the person when you think of or speak his name, thus quietly strengthening your own impression and also adding a new impression of the individual each time his spoken name induces a response.

If you find you can not recall the person's name a short time after hearing it, do not be embarrassed about asking the person to repeat it. It is better to do so right then than later; far better to establish it immediately than to go on pretending that you know the name, only to admit ignorance afterward. That latter course is bad, because it often may cause you to avoid a person at the time when you should be giving him your full attention.

Names may be written in a notebook for later reference, or they may be listed on personal cards. Whether or not they are written down, they should be reviewed after the meeting, both that same evening and the next morning. In reviewing names and repeating them aloud, visualize faces as well.

Here you will find that your repeated study of the person himself will stand you in good stead. You are sure to recall both the name and face more clearly than you would have otherwise. So your later review becomes a fuller picture that builds into anticipation of your next meeting with someone whom you have already begun to know quite well.

In meeting groups of people, you must often plan ahead. Learn the names of such persons, study their pictures if available, find out all you can about them. At a meeting, arrive early so that there will be plenty of time for slow introductions. While others are engaged in small talk, concentrate upon them, paying close attention to whatever they say or do.

Before a meeting ends, or soon after it is over, check the names and faces of the persons you met. Often there is time for this review while no one is aware of it. Afterward, check and recheck the names of various persons with others, or with the chairman or committee members who discussed those persons earlier.

You can always ask one person the name of someone else, or broach other questions regarding them. Such interest is usually appreciated and may produce even more details than you anticipated.

2. RAPID CALCULATIONS

Quickness with figures is frequently an adjunct of natural memory, as is evidenced by child prodigies and other so-called lightning calculators. Such ability, even in a modified form, is a definite asset in many walks of life and is a constant help when applied to simpler daily chores.

Memory plays an important part in the cultivation of this "number sense," as it has been aptly termed, because figures must be visualized and sometimes retained as on a mental blackboard, only to be eradicated when the immediate need for them is past.

Addition

Addition is used more frequently than all other arithmetical operations combined. This can be sped by learning to think in figure groups and results, rather than by counting laboriously in single units. Instead of saying or thinking, "2 and 8 are 10 and 4 are 14"—and so on—just name the results: "Ten—fourteen—"

This leads directly into grouping methods, which speed the process that much more. Simplest of these is:

Single Column Grouping

Take, as an example, the column of three-figure numbers given below, with which the usual procedure is to begin by adding the figures in the unit column, naming the totals as already stated, so that the calculation, running from bottom up to top, would consist of a series of totals: 10, 14, 16, 23, 31, 37, 42.

$$
\begin{array}{r}
135 \\
446 \\
468 \\
657 \\
892 \\
364 \\
538 \\
762 \\
\hline
4262
\end{array}
$$

This can be sped by forming totals from successive pairs: Starting with $2 + 8 = 10$, the addition would run: 10, 16, 31, 42. This should prove very easy, because ordinary familiarity with figures enables a person to call off the total of two figures instantly. The mind automatically goes beyond the "figure by figure" process taught in rudimentary arithmetic.

Further speed is gained by grouping figures in threes, which many persons will find quite natural when they practice it. Thus the addition in the unit column would run: 14, 31, 42, constituting two trios and a pair.

Carrying the 4 to the tens column, it would be added to the first group of three (6, 3, 6) making 19. Adding the next pair (9, 5) would bring 33; then the next three figures (6, 4, 3) would put the total at 46.

In such adding, it is preferable to group each set of figures to form a sum above 10 and below 20, so there will be some uniformity in the additions. Hence 9 and 5 group nicely as a pair between two sets of threes, the 9 and 5 being added as 14.

Continuing with the hundreds column, simply carry 4 and add it to the three bottom figures (7, 5, 3) making 19; adding the next three as a group, you have 37; finally, the last pair, making 42.

The columns can be added down instead of up, if preferred. It is simple addition but with figure grouping for speed. In long columns, clusters of figures sometimes occur, as 3, 3, 3, 3 which can be instantly added as 12. When a 9 appears, it may be easier to add 10 and subtract 1 from the group. Thus instead of thinking that 9 and 6 equal 15, call it 16 and subtract 1, making 15.

Still faster results may be obtained with long columns by forming groups that total between 20 and 30, then adding them accordingly; but care must be taken not to sacrifice accuracy for speed. Unless a person takes to these larger groupings naturally, learning this method may be a slow process.

Two-Column Grouping; Left to Right

This method can be applied effectively to a column of two-figure numbers, taking each number in turn. As an example:

$$
\begin{array}{r}
32 \\
64 \\
73 \\
81 \\
99 \\
45 \\
\hline
394
\end{array}
$$

Working downward, the process is to take the first number, 32, and add the tens of the next (60) making 92; and then the unit (4) to form the total 96. This is continued with the next number, so the reading process runs:

32, 92–96; 166–169; 249–250; 340–349; 389–394.

Almost immediately, you will begin to include units along with tens, making the process: 32, 96, 169, 250, 349, 394. With numbers like 99 it becomes easier to add 100 and subtract 1, all in one quick process.

Adding upward, this same series would run: 45, 135–144; 224–225; 295–298; 358–362; 392–394. This, when gradually speeded up, could soon be read as: 45, 144, 225, 298, 362, 394.

Three-Column Grouping

A column of three-figure numbers can be added in similar fashion to the two-figure column just described, but this is a more involved process. While a good exercise toward acquiring facility in addition, many persons will find it impractical for regular use; hence it is recommended only for those who find they have a flair for it, or are prepared to spend considerable time in developing the skill.

Catch Figure Addition

Here is an excellent way of adding rapidly with pencil and paper. Applied to a single column of figures (as shown at the left) it operates as follows:

7	Starting with the figure at the bottom, 3, work upward,
4^5	adding a group that totals between 10 and 20, coming as
3	close to 20 as possible.
8	Thus: $3 + 1 + 6 + 7 = 17$
6^5	Reject the 10 and place a small 7 to the right and just
9	above the top figure of the group (the ^{7}), as shown.
5^1	Now start at the 4 and add the next group upward, as:
2	$4 + 2 + 5 = 11$
4	Reject the 10 and place a small 1 to the right of the top
7^7	figure of the group (the ^{1}) as shown.
6	Next, add $9 + 6 = 15$. Reject the 10 and place a small 5
1	as shown.
3	Next, $8 + 3 + 4 = 15$. Reject the 10 and place a small 5
—	as shown.
65	These small figures are your "catch figures." Add them and the remainder, the 7 at the top of the column:

$$7 + 1 + 5 + 5 + 7 = 25.$$

The unit figure of that total, namely 5, is the unit total of the column. The tens figure, namely 2, is added to the *number* of catch figures (in this case, 4) to obtain ten's column total of 6, which, combined to the unit figure (5), gives the sum: 65.

With Two Columns or More

This is an extension of the process just described, with the total of the units column being used to begin the addition of the tens column on the left. Catch figures are used in the same fashion and put further to the left:

^{627}	Addition of the units column (at the right) gives a
34^5	sum of 65, as in the previous example.
53	The 5 is put down and the 6 is used to start the tens
68	column, adding upward, forming a group in the 10 to 20
$^586^5$	bracket, thus:
79	
$^795^1$	$$6 + 4 + 2 + 6 = 18.$$
42	Reject the 10 and place a small 8 to the left and just
14	above the top figure of the group (the ^{8}) as shown.
37^7	Add successive groups in the same manner, obtaining
^{866}	additional catch figures as indicated.
21	Add these figures, $8 + 7 + 5 + 6 = 26$.
43	The 6 becomes the sum of the tens column. The 2 is
——	added to the *number* of catch figures (on the left) to
665	obtain the sum of the hundreds column, in this case $2 + 4 = 6$, so that the final total is 665.

Long columns of figures can be added in larger groups, so that each totals between 20 and 30, the closer to 30 the better. This reduces the number of catch figures or "integers" as they are also termed. In that case, each catch figure must be counted as 2 instead of 1.

Period Addition

Instead of catch figures, a dot is put beside each figure that represents a total between 10 and 20. The 10 is rejected and the figure representing the remainder becomes the first figure of the next group.

3 In this case, we are starting at the top so that the addi-
1 tion can be followed downward, step by step.
6 Add the figures $3 + 1 + 6 + 7 = 17$, coming as close as
7· possible to 20. Place a dot to the right of the last figure
4 (7) in the group.
2 Reject 10 and add the remainder (7) to the next fig-
5· ures, $7 + 4 + 2 + 5 = 18$. Place a dot beside the last
9· figure (5) in the group.
6· Reject 10 and add the remainder (8) to the next figure,
8 $8 + 9 = 17$. Place a dot beside the last figure (9).
3 Reject 10 and add the remainder (7) to the next figure,
4· $7 + 6 = 13$. Place a dot beside the last figure (6).
7· Reject 10 and add the remainder (3) to the next figures,
— $3 + 8 + 3 + 4 = 18$. Place a dot at the right of the last
65 figure (4).

Reject 10 and add the remainder (8) to the next figure, $8 + 7$. Put a dot beside the last figure (7). Reject 10 and place the 5 at the bottom of the column, representing the units sum. Count the dots to obtain the tens sum, which comes to 6, making the total 65.

Sight Addition

Here is a rapid way of adding pairs of two-figure numbers, such as the following:

Type A: 42
         37
         —

Type B: 65
         57
         —

Visualize the columns as though separated by dots. Type **A** represents a number in which each column totals less than 10. Type **B** consists of two columns in which the units add up to more than 10, thus:

```
(A)   4 · 2          (B)   6 · 5
      3 · 7                5 · 7
      ─────                ─────
      7   9                  1 2
                           1 1
           •               ─────
                           1 2 2
```

With **A**, the addition of the separate columns becomes immediately obvious and gives the total, 79.

With **B**, when you notice that the unit column adds up to more than 10, fix on the dots and retain the unit of the sum (2) as the final unit, adding the 1 to the sum of the tens column (11) to arrive at the total, 122.

Subtraction

The first step toward speedy subtraction is to practice subtracting up as well as down, without having to put the higher number over the lower. This avoids an extra step in calculations and gives greater facility with figures.

Sight Subtraction

This can be performed swiftly with pairs of two-figure numbers, much in the manner of addition.

```
Type A:  63          Type B:  72
         21                   36
         ──                   ──
```

As with addition, the columns are visualized as though separated by dots. Type **A** has one number in which both figures are correspondingly larger than the figures of the lesser number. In

Type **B,** the units column of the lesser number is higher than that of the larger number.

$$\begin{array}{ll}
\text{(A)} & \begin{array}{r} 6 \cdot 3 \\ 2 \cdot 1 \\ \hline 4 \cdot 2 \\ 42 \end{array}
\qquad\qquad
\text{(B)} & \begin{array}{r} 7 \cdot 2 \\ 3 \cdot 6 \\ \hline -1 \\ 4 \quad \cdot \; 6 \\ \hline 3 \cdot 6 \\ 36 \end{array}
\end{array}$$

With **A,** the subtraction of the individual columns is obvious and automatic: $6 - 2 = 4$; $3 - 1 = 2$. Answer, 42.

With **B,** it is necessary to borrow 10 from the left column to subtract 6 from 12. Hence when the tens column is considered, the difference between 7 and 3 is 4, from which the borrowed 1 must be subtracted to obtain the result of 3, making the answer 36.

Quick Subtraction

In problems like Type **B,** a quick method of subtraction is to add enough units to the smaller number to reach the nearest multiple of 10; then add the same amount to the larger number and subtract.

As an example: Subtract 27 from 63
Process: Add 3 to 27 making 30
    Also add 3 to 63 making 66
    Subtract: $66 - 30 = 36$ (The same as $63 - 27 = 36$)

Subtraction in Couples

This is a way of handling the subtraction of larger numbers. First, break them into groups, with dot separations, thus:

```
8742  is broken into  87 · 42
−4963                  49 · 63

Add 1 to each  88 · 49  Add 7 to each
in left pair   50 · 70  in right pair
```

This raises each pair of the smaller number to the nearest multiple of 10. Then, from 88 borrow 1 to go in front of 49:

```
 87 ·  149      The same as:   8742
−50 ·  −70                    −4963

 37 ·   79                     3779
3779
```

Algebraic Subtraction Method

This also involves the decimalization principle just described and serves as a rapid way of subtracting with two-figure numbers. First subtract the tens and then add the algebraic sum of the unit differences, thus:

$$94 - 27 \text{ becomes } 90 - 20 = 70 + 4 - 7 = 67$$

Multiplication

Many people who consider themselves poor calculators already have that ability in their grasp and are demonstrating it day by day. They would be quite amazed if told what their great secret is. It happens to be their deep-rooted knowledge of the common multiplication table, which too often finds its limit with $12 \times 12 = 144$.

Learning the multiplication table by rote has long been an established custom. To frown upon "rote learning" is also a general practice but it does not apply entirely with anything so basic. The fact remains that $9 \times 7 = 63$ is something that should spring to a person's mind as quickly as that C–A–T spells Cat.

It would be sad, indeed, to limit a vocabulary to 144 words, or 1,400 words, or even 14,400 words that could be recognized on sight. But $12 \times 12 = 144$ was once regarded as the limit of arithmetical capacity.

More and more, modern adult life requires calculations in higher multiples. To know the multiplication table to 20×20 would be a great advantage; and to 25×25 still more. It is important, therefore, that it be learned; and the earlier in life, the better. Frequency of use produces greater facility.

A chart of the 25×25 table accompanies this text. In visualizing it, think of lines blocking the 12×12 section, the 20×20 group and the 25×25 table, as shown. With the table well-learned, even within lesser limits, many short cuts in multiplication become available.

Ordinary Multiplication Simplified

Here is a method of "cross-multiplication" of two numbers of two figures each, such as 63×47.

Conventionally, these numbers would be multiplied thus

$$
\begin{array}{r}
63 \\
\times 47 \\
\hline
441 \\
252 \\
\hline
2961
\end{array}
$$

In cross-multiplication, the procedure is as follows:

First, separate the figures mentally and think of them as connected by cross-lines, thus:

$$
\begin{smallmatrix} 6 \\ 4 \end{smallmatrix} \bowtie \begin{smallmatrix} 3 \\ 7 \end{smallmatrix}
$$

a. Multiply the two figures on the right, $3 \times 7 = 21$.
   Put down the unit figure, 1. Carry the other, 2.
b. Now cross-multiply top left with lower right: $6 \times 7 = 42$
   And cross-multiply top right with lower left: $3 \times 4 = 12$
   Add these along with the carried figure 2
                                                                    ___
                                                                     56

MULTIPLICATION TABLE

×	1	2	3	4	5	6	7	8	9	10	11	12	13	14	15	16	17	18	19	20	21	22	23	24	25
1	1	2	3	4	5	6	7	8	9	10	11	12	13	14	15	16	17	18	19	20	21	22	23	24	25
2	2	4	6	8	10	12	14	16	18	20	22	24	26	28	30	32	34	36	38	40	42	44	46	48	50
3	3	6	9	12	15	18	21	24	27	30	33	36	39	42	45	48	51	54	57	60	63	66	69	72	75
4	4	8	12	16	20	24	28	32	36	40	44	48	52	56	60	64	68	72	76	80	84	88	92	96	100
5	5	10	15	20	25	30	35	40	45	50	55	60	65	70	75	80	85	90	95	100	105	110	115	120	125
6	6	12	18	24	30	36	42	48	54	60	66	72	78	84	90	96	102	108	114	120	126	132	138	144	150
7	7	14	21	28	35	42	49	56	63	70	77	84	91	98	105	112	119	126	133	140	147	154	161	168	175
8	8	16	24	32	40	48	56	64	72	80	88	96	104	112	120	128	136	144	152	160	168	176	184	192	200
9	9	18	27	36	45	54	63	72	81	90	99	108	117	126	135	144	153	162	171	180	189	198	207	216	225
10	10	20	30	40	50	60	70	80	90	100	110	120	130	140	150	160	170	180	190	200	210	220	230	240	250
11	11	22	33	44	55	66	77	88	99	110	121	132	143	154	165	176	187	198	209	220	231	242	253	264	275
12	12	24	36	48	60	72	84	96	108	120	132	144	156	168	180	192	204	216	228	240	252	264	276	288	300
13	13	26	39	52	65	78	91	104	117	130	143	156	169	182	195	208	221	234	247	260	273	286	299	312	325
14	14	28	42	56	70	84	98	112	126	140	154	168	182	196	210	224	238	252	266	280	294	308	322	336	350
15	15	30	45	60	75	90	105	120	135	150	165	180	195	210	225	240	255	270	285	300	315	330	345	360	375
16	16	32	48	64	80	96	112	128	144	160	176	192	208	224	240	256	272	288	304	320	336	352	368	384	400
17	17	34	51	68	85	102	119	136	153	170	187	204	221	238	255	272	289	306	323	340	357	374	391	408	425
18	18	36	54	72	90	108	126	144	162	180	198	216	234	252	270	288	306	324	342	360	378	396	414	432	450
19	19	38	57	76	95	114	133	152	171	190	209	228	247	266	285	304	323	342	361	380	399	418	437	456	475
20	20	40	60	80	100	120	140	160	180	200	220	240	260	280	300	320	340	360	380	400	420	440	460	480	500
21	21	42	63	84	105	126	147	168	189	210	231	252	273	294	315	336	357	378	399	420	441	462	483	504	525
22	22	44	66	88	110	132	154	176	198	220	242	264	286	308	330	352	374	396	418	440	462	484	506	528	550
23	23	46	69	92	115	138	161	184	207	230	253	276	299	322	345	368	391	414	437	460	483	506	529	552	575
24	24	48	72	96	120	144	168	192	216	240	264	288	312	336	360	384	408	432	456	480	504	528	552	576	600
25	25	50	75	100	125	150	175	200	225	250	275	300	325	350	375	400	425	450	475	500	525	550	575	600	625

Put down the right-hand figure, 6, giving you 61.

Carry the other figure, 5.

c. Multiply the two figures on the left, $6 \times 4 = 24$

To these add the carried figure .... $\underline{5}$

29

These become the left-hand figures of the result: 2961.

Summarized: The first multiplication (a) produces a unit that becomes your unit figure. The second process (b) produces a unit that becomes your tens figure. The third multiplication (c) produces the hundreds and thousands figures.

Quick Multiplication of Two-Figure Numbers

Often numbers of two figures lend themselves to rapid multiplication by a very simple process. The multiplication of 23×32 affords an excellent example.

First, multiply 23 (the multiplicand) by the nearest 10 of 32 (the multiplier), which in this case is 30.

Next, multiply 23 (the multiplicand) by the remainder, 2, and add the totals.

Here is the result:

Multiplication by nearest 10 .... $23 \times 30 = 690$

Multiplication by remainder .... $23 \times 2 = \underline{46}$

Total 736

This could be done the other way about: $32 \times 20 = 640$; $32 \times 3 = 96$; $640 + 96 = 736$.

In cases where one number is composed of high figures (as 87) and the other of lower figures (as 42) it is generally preferable to use the smaller figured number as the multiplier.

Mental Multiplication of Longer Numbers by Two-Figure Numbers

This is a more difficult process, but it shows how capacity for mental arithmetic can be developed. The longer number (as

7365) is taken as the multiplicand; while the shorter, two-figure number (as 32) serves as the multiplier.

Starting from the right, multiply the first figure of the multiplicand by the entire multiplier. Put down the unit of the number thus obtained. Carry the other figures.

Multiply the next figure of the multiplicand by the entire multiplier and add the carried number to the result. Put down the final figure and carry the rest.

Continue thus, as illustrated in this multiplication of 7365 × 32:

$5 \times 32 = 160$ Put down 0   Carry 16
$6 \times 32 = 192 + 16 = 208$ Put down 8   Carry 20
$3 \times 32 = 96 + 20 = 116$ Put down 6   Carry 11
$7 \times 32 = 224 + 11 = 235$ Put down 235

The final answer is 235680

Aliquot Parts of 10	Aliquot Parts of 100	Aliquot Parts of 1000
$\frac{1}{9} = 1\frac{1}{9}$	$\frac{1}{16} = 6\frac{1}{2}$	$\frac{1}{16} = 62\frac{1}{2}$
$\frac{1}{8} = 1\frac{1}{4}$	$\frac{1}{12} = 8\frac{1}{3}$	$\frac{1}{12} = 83\frac{1}{3}$
$\frac{1}{7} = 1\frac{3}{7}$	$\frac{1}{8} = 12\frac{1}{2}$	$\frac{1}{8} = 125$
$\frac{1}{6} = 1\frac{2}{3}$	$\frac{1}{7} = 14\frac{2}{7}$	$\frac{1}{6} = 166\frac{2}{3}$
$\frac{1}{4} = 2\frac{1}{2}$	$\frac{1}{6} = 16\frac{2}{3}$	$\frac{1}{4} = 250$
$\frac{1}{3} = 3\frac{1}{3}$	$\frac{3}{16} = 18\frac{3}{4}$	$\frac{1}{3} = 333\frac{1}{3}$
$\frac{1}{2} = 5$	$\frac{1}{4} = 25$	$\frac{3}{8} = 375$
$\frac{3}{4} = 7\frac{1}{2}$	$\frac{5}{16} = 31\frac{1}{2}$	$\frac{1}{2} = 500$
	$\frac{1}{3} = 33\frac{1}{3}$	$\frac{5}{8} = 625$
	$\frac{3}{8} = 37\frac{1}{2}$	$\frac{3}{4} = 750$
	$\frac{1}{2} = 50$	$\frac{5}{6} = 833\frac{1}{3}$
	$\frac{5}{8} = 62\frac{1}{2}$	$\frac{7}{8} = 875$
	$\frac{3}{4} = 75$	
	$\frac{7}{8} = 87\frac{1}{2}$	

Aliquot Parts

An aliquot part of a number represents a number that can be divided into the larger number, without leaving any remainder. Knowledge and recognition of aliquot parts of commonly used numbers is a great time-saver in many calculations. Aliquot parts of numbers like 10, 100 and 1000 should therefore be learned, much in the manner of the multiplication table.

Above are some examples.

Division

Familiarity with the multiplication table is essential with division. The fact remains that $9 \times 7 = 63$ is just as vital when dividing 63 by 7 or 9 as it is when multiplying 9×7. Hence the memorization of the multiplication beyond 12×12 increases a person's ability at division in due proportion.

To bring higher numbers within the range of the simple process of "short division," it is frequently possible to use:

Factor Reduction

This works when the divisor is a two- or three-figure number that can be reduced to small factors. For example: You are to divide 9936 by 48. The divisor, 48, can be reduced to the factors 6 and 8.

Divide 9936 by 6, obtaining 1656 as the quotient; and divide that number by the other factor, 8. This brings the final quotient, 207, which is the same as $9936 \div 48$.

Divisors composed of three-figure numbers can sometimes be reduced to manageable small factors. As an example: $6048 \div 336$. The divisor, 336, can be reduced to factors of 6, 7, and 8. Successive divisions by those numbers bring the answer, 18.

Contractions

This involves the use of aliquots, as listed under "Multiplication." By being on the alert for these, many short cuts may be realized where division is concerned.

To divide by 25, simply note that this number represents $\frac{1}{4}$ of 100, so that if you multiply by 4 and divide by 100, you have the answer. The division by 100 is almost automatic as it merely means pointing off two decimal places.

$$\text{Example: } 137 \div 25$$
$$137 \times 4 = 548 \div 100 = 5.48$$

To divide by 125, note that it represents $\frac{1}{8}$ of 1000, so that if you multiply by 8 and divide by 1000, pointing off three places, you will have your answer.

$$\text{Example: } 2736 \div 125$$
$$2736 \times 8 = 21888 \div 1000 = 21.888$$

Useful Divisibility Devices

To determine a number's divisibility, which is particularly useful when its factors are required, the following rules should be studied and applied:

A number is exactly divisible—

by 2, if its last unit is an even number.
by 3, if the sum of its digits is divisible by 3.
by 4, if the last two digits are divisible by 4.
by 5, if the last digit is 0 or 5.
by 6, if the number is divisible by both 2 and 3.
by 8, if the last three digits are divisible by 8.
by 9, if the sum of the digits is divisible by 9.
by 10, if the last digit is 0.

by 11, if the sum of the digits in the even places equals those in the odd (as 198 in which $1 + 8 = 9$). Or, when the difference between the odd and even placed digits is divisible by 11 (as 209 where $2 + 9 = 11$).

by 12, if the number is divisible by both 3 and 4.

Rules for determining a number's divisibility by 7 are too complicated for practical use. This was stressed many years ago by William Stokes in the following verse, which incorporates the rules just listed and finishes with a challenge that has not yet been satisfactorily answered:

DIVISIBILITY OF NUMBERS

Mnemonic Rhyme

Here are Memory Methods by which to decide,
By glancing at Numbers, the way they'll divide.
When the *Unit is even,* you quickly will see,
The whole of the Number by two cut can be.
When the unit is either a *naught* or a *five,*
A slash with a *five* you throughout can contrive.
Any figures whatever you'll easily trace
By 2 and 5 cut, when beyond unit's place.
If the *last two* by four are divisible, see,
The whole line by four will divisible be.
When you find the *last three* can be cut by an 8,
8 will cut through them all, you may fearlessly state.
Cut the *sum of the Digits* by 9 or by 3,
And in similar manner the Number will be.
A number that's *even,* and by *threes* divides,
Can always by six be divided besides.
When a number will cut up by 4 and 3, note,
It divides too by 12, you for certain may quote.

Whenever you digits alternately take,
And the sum of one series from other will make,
Eleven or *Naught* as remainder, decide
You can by 11 that number divide.
It is only when 0 is the last figure seen,
That the series by ten could divided have been.
For dividing by 7 no rule will apply,
If you doubt the assertion, to find a rule try!

Part II • Advanced and Variety

Section A • Everything Printed and Spoken

1. HOW TO REMEMBER 100 OBJECTS: THE "100-WORD CODE" AND ITS USES

Among the simpler types of memory "hooks" already described is the "Figure Alphabet" with its "phonetic numeral code." As a method for remembering both numbers and objects, this rates among the best, but its great merit lies in the fact that, once acquired, it can be extended, giving a person a list of 50 to 100 key words, according to how far he wants to carry it. These, in turn, can also be used as separate lists of 10 items each, in the memorization of small numbers of objects on different occasions.

The regular phonetic code is taken as our basis, the figures having the following values in terms of letters:

1: T (D or TH)   6: Soft G or J (CH or SH)
2: N (NG, NK optional)   7: Hard C or K (Hard G or Q)
3: M   8: F (PH or V)
4: R   9: P or B
5: L   0: Z or S (Soft C)

From these, a list of 10 mental pictures has already been given; namely: 1—HAT; 2—HEN; 3—HAM; 4—HAIR; 5—HILL; 6—SHOE; 7—HOOK; 8—HOOF; 9—HOOP; 10—DICE.

Since these words are composed of the simple figure values in terms of their respective letters, with the neutral "H" incorporated in each (up to DICE with "D" for 1 and "C" for 0) they are easy enough to remember. But by linking them, they can be solidly locked in mind and reeled off as readily as counting from 1 to 10. For instance:

Think of a HAT from which a HEN is flying and landing on a HAM from which HAIR is growing and forming a HILL topped by a giant SHOE which is being pulled away by a HOOK attached to the HOOF of an animal jumping through a HOOP and landing on a pair of DICE.

Since these associations serve as links only, they will not interfere with other mental pictures wherein lists of objects are tied in with the figure code. You can still remember a bag of "sugar" in the "hat," a spool of "thread" which the "hen" is pecking, "needles" bristling from the "ham," and so on.

In short, the "linked list" is simply your basic numerical code in a more permanent form, so it is preferable to form your own links as you go along, not only with the key words representing 1 to 10, but with the additional "keys" composing the 1 to 100 list shown in the accompanying text.

There, numbers from 10 to 20 are represented by the letter "D" for 1, followed by units of the Figure Alphabet, so that DEED signifies 11 (D and D); DOWN stands for 12 (D and N); DAM for 13 (D and M) and so on up to NEWS for 20 (N and S).

For 21, we have KNOT, with the K silent, forming 21 from N and T. Numbers in the thirties begin with the letter M as the basis of each word picture; and this plan continues with each new set of ten, until the list is completed with DOSES for 100, formed by the letters D–S–S.

It is not necessary to learn the whole list up to 100. Many people find that a list up to 50 is enough for practical use. Nor does the whole list have to be learned at one time, even when abbreviated.

1	HAT	21	KNOT	41	ROAD	61	JET	81	FOOT
2	HEN	22	NUN	42	RAIN	62	GIN	82	FAN
3	HAM	23	NAME	43	RAM	63	JAM	83	FOAM
4	HAIR	24	NEAR	44	ROAR	64	JAR	84	FIRE
5	HILL	25	NAIL	45	RAIL	65	JAIL	85	FILE
6	SHOE	26	NICHE	46	RICH	66	JUDGE	86	FISH
7	HOOK	27	NECK	47	ROCK	67	JACK	87	FIG
8	HOOF	28	KNIFE	48	ROOF	68	JOVE	88	FIFE
9	HOOP	29	KNOB	49	ROPE	69	JAP	89	FOB
10	DICE	30	MOUSE	50	LACE	70	GOOSE	90	PIZZA
11	DEED	31	MAT	51	LADY	71	GATE	91	POT
12	DOWN	32	MOON	52	LAWN	72	GUN	92	PEN
13	DAM	33	MOM	53	LOOM	73	GUM	93	POEM
14	DEER	34	MARE	54	LYRE	74	GEAR	94	PEAR
15	DOLL	35	MAIL	55	LILY	75	GALE	95	PAIL
16	DISH	36	MATCH	56	LASH	76	GASH	96	PATCH
17	DECK	37	MUG	57	LOCK	77	GIG	97	PICK
18	DOVE	38	MUFF	58	LEAF	78	GOOF	98	PUFF
19	DOPE	39	MAP	59	LIP	79	GOB	99	PIPE
20	NEWS	40	RICE	60	JUICE	80	FEZ	100	DOSES

A convenient way is to take each set singly, first learning the pictures from 1 to 10, then from 11 to 20, and so on, getting each series of ten properly pegged and linked before going on with the next.

After a new set has been learned, it should be utilized. For instance, if you have a shopping list of half a dozen items to remember, try starting with 31 (MAT) instead of going back to 1 (HAT) every time. This will keep the various code words well activated.

If the list has been learned up to 100, a neat plan is to use the days of the week as starting numbers when remembering small groups of objects. On Sundays, use those starting with 11 (DEED) as your first number. On a Monday, start with 21 (KNOT); and so on, with 71 (GATE) as your starting point on Saturdays. Sunday and Monday may also serve for starting with 81 or 91, respectively.

In using the key words, it is preferable to think of them as actual things, using nouns wherever possible rather than other parts of speech. Take the word DOWN (12) as an example. It can mean "down" in the form of a bird's fluffy feathers, or "down" as a meadow. It can also be used adverbially, referring to something going "down," which is the way many persons will want to use it.

Here, too, there is a chance for individual choice. For DOWN, you could take the fixed picture of an elevator or a cellar stairway, the more familiar the better, provided of course that the key word, DOWN, remains predominant. That, however, is not difficult. The number itself identifies the word, thus keeping it properly pegged.

The word NEAR (24) can be similarly pictured in terms of anything close by, or of an approaching object. A key word like ROAR (44) can be the roar of a lion or of an airplane passing overhead. The final word DOSES (100) can be pictured as spoonfuls of medicine or pills being measured from a bottle.

It is not necessary to use the exact key words given in the accompanying list, as many others are possible in certain instances. For 69, instead of JAP, such words as CHIP, JEEP, SHABBY, SHIP or GIBE could be used. This is a matter of individual choice, but the words in the list have a certain uniformity and therefore are recommended.

A practical policy would be to use the listed words until you strike one that doesn't seem to fit as well as the rest, and in that case supply your own. Often, this may give it a more natural touch.

Although short lists of under 50 words are handy and rapidly acquired, it is still a good plan to aim for the 100 mark, as the higher numbers come in useful. More key words can be acquired and firmly fixed through practicing with the lists in the following ways:

Take the names of a dozen friends and associate them with HAT, HEN, HAM, HAIR, and so on. Later, you will be able to call off the names with assurance by simply running through the key list.

Go through the ads in a newspaper or magazine, associating them with key list words in order. Later, check back on the list and call them off.

Plan things to do, tying them in with words from the key list, beginning with a specific number. Then go over them, working from the pictures that you have formed.

Form mental files of more important items, things that you want to remember more permanently, using the same key list to visualize your associations.

A significant difference between *temporary* and *permanent* associations is partly in the type of things remembered and partly in a repetition of the association process.

A shopping list, a group of friends, the day's news, are of a temporary or momentary nature and can be fixed rapidly in mind without the need of more than a brief review to make sure that you have them. The next day, a new list of that type may be formed and it can automatically obliterate any traces of the earlier one.

In a sense, what happens is that the old list has faded to such degree that concentration on the new list wipes out the conflicting associations, especially since they are no longer needed. This is interesting indeed, as it helps to show how forgetting can become an essential part of the memorizing process itself. It also stresses the importance of utilizing this system frequently in order to obtain the best results.

Soon you will find just how quickly you can implant a new series of pictures in mind, as well as how strongly you must concentrate upon it to obliterate all traces of the older series. In short, "practice makes perfect" in this as well as other types of

71

endeavor while, at the same time, it furnishes a twofold exercise in memory training.

Twofold because, along with acquiring the knack, you also learn to think in such terms. You will find yourself putting many ideas into appropriate pictures instead of trying to remember them in less secure ways. New uses for the "word code" will crop up in everyday life. Not only that, but you will not be restricted to temporary memorization, as of shopping lists or daily appointments; it may be turned into what will prove to be a more permanent process as well.

Forming Permanency Associations

The first step toward the more permanent process is to recognize that you are planning such a list, as, for example, remembering important addresses and telephone numbers or the names of the states or the presidents.

Care should then be taken to form a sharp, strong mental picture rather than the quickest thing that comes to mind. With the key word as a nucleus, it should expand into the name or object to be remembered, which in turn can be bolstered by any appropriate associations to give a full and vivid picture.

This renders it unique, so that such a list becomes a fixture. Since it will never be supplanted by another set, it will not be subjected to an overriding obliteration, as with the temporary types. You may form similar lists from the same key words— for example, after picturing states of the United States, you may do the same with nations of the Americas—but each will be individualistic enough to hold its own.

A real danger lies in such lists dimming through disuse, but this can be offset in two ways:

With phone numbers and addresses that are used frequently, the mental pictures are automatically kept fresh and further strengthened.

With historical lists and others used only occasionally, the simple act of repeating them at given intervals will accomplish results similar to regular use.

Methods of using the "Figure Alphabet" and the "100-Word Code" in more permanent or special forms of memorization are given in some of the following pages.

2. MEMORIZING THE STATES OF THE UNITED STATES, WITH THEIR CAPITAL CITIES

Here the first 50 words of the "100-Word Code" are linked to the names of the states composing the United States of America. These are taken in alphabetical order and the name of each capital city is associated with the mental picture of the state, in some cases strengthening it considerably.

1. ALABAMA. *Capital*, MONTGOMERY. *Key-word*, HAT.

There is a saying, "Stars fell on Alabama." Think of stars pouring out of a big HAT all over ALABAMA. The *hat*, when empty, drops on a *mountain* peak and sticks there as though *gummed*, representing MONTGOMERY.

2. ALASKA. *Capital*, JUNEAU. *Key-word*, HEN.

Think of a HEN cackling, "Kluck-kluck-kluck-Al-aska—ALASKA." Picture yourself about to visit Alaska, once the winter is over, with someone saying, "In *June, you* can go to Alaska," giving JUNEAU.

3. ARIZONA. *Capital*, PHOENIX. *Key-word*, HAM.

Picture a HAM hanging over a fire from which smoke *arises*, suggesting the name ARIZONA. The smoked *ham* becomes a big bird that flies away, this being the PHOENIX, the fabled bird that rises from its own ashes.

4. ARKANSAS. *Capital*, LITTLE ROCK. *Key-word*, HAIR.

Think of Noah and his sons, all with big beards and long shaggy HAIR, looking from the *Ark*, which is the abbreviation of ARKANSAS, as it bumps a mountain top projecting from the flood like a LITTLE ROCK.

5. CALIFORNIA. *Capital,* SACRAMENTO. *Key-word,* HILL.

Picture a HILL sloped like the eastern boundary of CALIFORNIA. Up the *hill,* a man (such as a Mexican) is carrying a *sack,* which is filled with *mementos,* the two words suggesting SACRAMENTO.

6. COLORADO. *Capital,* DENVER. *Key-word,* SHOE.

Think of footprints, representing a SHOE, on a mountainside where the snow is *colored* red by the sunset, suggesting COLORADO. The tracks lead to a *den where* a bear is trapped, producing DENVER.

7. CONNECTICUT. *Capital,* HARTFORD. *Key-word,* HOOK.

A HOOK is used to *connect* things. Often a *hook* must be *cut* loose, as with a fish-hook. These words (connect-cut) suggest CONNECTICUT. If you were fishing near the *heart* of Connecticut at a *ford* across the Connecticut River, you would be close to HARTFORD.

8. DELAWARE. *Capital,* DOVER. *Key-word,* HOOF.

HOOF suggests a cow belonging to a farmer, which in turn suggests the song, "The Farmer in the Dell." From *Dell* comes *Del,* the abbreviation of *Delaware.* The cow is eating clover, suggesting the words of another old song, "Through the fields of clover, we will ride to Dover," giving DOVER.

9. FLORIDA. *Capital,* TALLAHASSEE. *Key-word,* HOOP.

Visualize a HOOP composed of colorful *flowers* representing FLORIDA. Circus animals are jumping through the hoop which is held high by a *tall lass,* representing TALLAHASSEE.

10. GEORGIA. *Capital,* ATLANTA. *Key-word,* DICE.

Picture a pair of mammoth DICE rolling in from the ocean onto a wide beach. They were rolled by England's King George, whose name *George* represents GEORGIA; and since the ocean they came across was the *Atlantic,* the *dice* keep rolling inland until they reach ATLANTA.

74

11. HAWAII. *Capital,* HONOLULU. *Key-word,* DEED.

The word DEED suggests a gift; and HAWAII was practically given or deeded to the United States. Though *Hawaii* is the largest island of the group, the capital is on the island of *Oahu;* and these two names (Hawaii-Oahu) roughly suggest HONOLULU.

12. IDAHO. *Capital,* BOISE. *Key-word,* DOWN.

Here a visualization of the state helps. Its eastern boundary is like a giant slide coming DOWN from snowy Canada. Picture a girl named *Ida* calling *"Ho!"* as she slides *down* and the result is IDAHO. At the bottom are a lot of *noisy boys,* which produces BOISE (pronounced "boy-see").

13. ILLINOIS. *Capital,* SPRINGFIELD. *Key-word,* DAM.

Like a huge DAM, the state of ILLINOIS holds back the waters of Lake Michigan. If the *dam* gave way, it would be *ill* for everyone and there would be a great *noise.* The *spring* flood would go all over the *fields,* suggesting SPRINGFIELD.

. 14. INDIANA. *Capital,* INDIANAPOLIS. *Key-word,* DEER.

Simply a DEER being stalked by INDIANS. The *deer* walks in among some wigwams which form an *Indian city* or *metropolis,* namely, INDIANAPOLIS.

15. IOWA. *Capital,* DES MOINES. *Key-word,* DOLL.

Picture a DOLL in a store window. Imagine that you promised it to a child, thus coining the mental phrase, *"I owe a doll,"* tying in IOWA with DOLL. To buy the *doll,* you must have *the money,* which roughly suggests DES MOINES.

16. KANSAS. *Capital,* TOPEKA. *Key-word,* DISH.

A DISH is flat and so is much of KANSAS. For a DISH of corn (a Kansas product) you open a *can,* suggesting KAN, an abbreviation for KANSAS. In opening the *can,* you remove the *top* with a *key,* suggesting TOPEKA.

17. KENTUCKY. *Capital,* FRANKFORT. *Key-word,* DECK.

Visualize a large DECK above the pillars of a Colonial mansion, representing the "old KENTUCKY home." It is thronged with people watching a horse race (tying in the Kentucky Derby) and they are buying and eating hot dogs (frankfurters) signifying FRANKFORT.

18. LOUISIANA. *Capital,* BATON ROUGE. *Key-word,* DOVE.

A tame DOVE flying back and forth between two drum majorettes, one with a sweater bearing the letter L, the other a letter A. These stand for *Louise* and *Anna,* and the letters L–A are the abbreviation LA., for LOUISIANA. The girls have *batons* on which the dove alights; and these are painted *red,* signifying BATON ROUGE.

19. MAINE. *Capital,* AUGUSTA. *Key-word,* DOPE.

A man selling packages containing DOPE on a *main* street (which can be indicated by sign MAIN ST. overhead). This links DOPE and MAINE. The packages are suddenly blown away by *a gust of* wind, thus adding AUGUSTA.

20. MARYLAND. *Capital,* ANNAPOLIS. *Key-word,* NEWS.

Here, history and geography can be linked with the word NEWS, which represents the points of the compass and fits MARYLAND perfectly. Though a Southern state (S) Maryland stayed with the North (N) during the Civil War. Maryland has a section called the Eastern Shore (E) and another portion of the state is termed Western Maryland (W). Think of a girl named *Mary* reaching to the branch of a tree to pluck *an apple* and *polish* it, which signifies ANNAPOLIS. It's easy to remember the apple, because "An apple a day keeps the doctor away" and there you have the abbreviation MD. for MARYLAND.

21. MASSACHUSETTS. *Capital,* BOSTON. *Key-word,* KNOT.

The word KNOT ties in perfectly with MASSACHUSETTS, long known as the "Codfish State," as well as the "Bay State." Picture fishermen on board a schooner, tying knots in ropes and fishing lines. Then think of them as sailors, being ordered to the rigging by the boatswain, or *bosun,* which suggests BOSTON

22. MICHIGAN. *Capital,* LANSING. *Key-word,* NUN.

The word NUN is easily associated with MICHIGAN, as the lower peninsula of that state resembles the robed figure of a woman. Michigan is divided by the Straits of Mackinac, which can be pictured as *lancing* their way between the two peninsulas, thus suggesting the name of the capital, LANSING.

23. MINNESOTA. *Capital,* ST. PAUL. *Key-word,* NAME.

The NAME of MINNESOTA means "water that is clouded" which can be interpreted as a muddy river, or the clear lakes that reflect every detail of the sky. Thus, the Indian NAME is associated with MINNESOTA while, in contrast, the *name* of an early settlement was adopted for the capital, ST. PAUL.

24. MISSISSIPPI. *Capital,* JACKSON. *Key-word,* NEAR.

Think of coming NEAR the mouth of a river, which becomes larger and larger until it can only be the MISSISSIPPI. Children are playing *jacks on* a wharf as you draw *near,* producing JACKSON.

25. MISSOURI. *Capital,* JEFFERSON CITY. *Key-word,* NAIL.

A man is driving a NAIL and he must be careful not to *miss* as he will be *sorry* if he hits his thumb. This gives MISSOURI. The man is putting up a placard which proves to be the Declaration of Independence, which was written by Thomas *Jefferson*. People gather about to read it until the whole *city* is there, forming JEFFERSON CITY.

26. MONTANA. *Capital,* HELENA. *Key-word,* NICHE.

Picture a great NICHE like a cleft in a *mountain,* suggesting MONTANA. Near the mountain is a smaller *niche* in a *hill,* which suggests HELENA.

27. NEBRASKA. *Capital,* LINCOLN. *Key-word,* NECK.

Consider the word NECK in terms of someone "risking his neck," thus coining the phrase, *"neck risk a,"* which by modified repetition can be converted into NEBRASKA. During the Civil War, Nebraskans "risked their, necks" by siding with the North and proposing that Nebraska be made a state. *Lincoln* was then president; hence the name of the capital, LINCOLN.

28. NEVADA. *Capital,* CARSON CITY. *Key-word,* KNIFE.

Compare the key-word KNIFE with the shape of NEVADA, which tapers to a *point* like a KNIFE. In Nevada, there are many *cars* but few *cities.* From *"cars and cities"* form CARSON CITY.

29. NEW HAMPSHIRE. *Capital,* CONCORD. *Key-word,* KNOB.

Think of great towering KNOBS of rock, which feature NEW HAMPSHIRE, known as the "Granite State." Its highest *knobs* or summits have been *conquered* by mountain climbers, giving CONCORD.

30. NEW JERSEY. *Capital,* TRENTON. *Key-word,* MOUSE.

Picture a MOUSE gnawing its way through a fancy sweater, or NEW JERSEY. On the jersey is the letter T and the mouse has chewed a *rent on* it, forming TRENTON.

31. NEW MEXICO. *Capital,* SANTA FE. *Key-word,* MAT.

Visualize a new MAT brought from MEXICO and you have NEW MEXICO. Picture the *mat* as a Christmas present brought by *Santa,* who charged no *fee.* Result: SANTA FE.

32. NEW YORK. *Capital,* ALBANY. *Key-word,* MOON.

Think of a MOON shining on the skyscrapers of Manhattan, the island metropolis of NEW YORK. It is also shining on the Hudson River and it is a half-moon, which was the name of the ship in which Hendrik Hudson sailed "all the way" up the river to "Al–ban–ay" or at least to the site of that capital city, ALBANY.

33. NORTH CAROLINA. *Capital,* RALEIGH. *Key-word,* MOM.

Historically, the term MOM is appropriate for NORTH CAROLINA, as it was the "mother colony" of the English settlements on the Atlantic Coast. Sir Walter Raleigh established the first colony and also popularized tobacco, today one of the state's chief products. This links with the name of the capital, RALEIGH.

34. NORTH DAKOTA. *Capital,* BISMARCK. *Key-word,* MARE.

Visualize a MARE heading *north* all *day* and wearing a *coat* against the cold. From *"North-Day-Coat"* you have NORTH DAKOTA. If you picture the *mare* being ridden by *Bismarck,* the famed Prussian statesman, leading a charge against the Dakota Indians, you will have a good link to the capital, BISMARCK.

35. OHIO. *Capital,* COLUMBUS. *Key-word,* MAIL.

The MAIL is being carried down the OHIO River on a ship commanded by COLUMBUS.

36. OKLAHOMA. *Capital,* OKLAHOMA CITY. *Key-word,* MATCH.

Keep a MATCH away from those oil wells and all will be *O.K.* at *home* in OKLAHOMA. From the *match,* picture burning oil wells lighting up a whole city, giving OKLAHOMA CITY.

37. OREGON. *Capital,* SALEM. *Key-word,* MUG.

Picture a MUG shaped like the state of OREGON, brimming over at the mouth of the Columbia River. Think of *salmon* going up the river toward SALEM.

38. PENNSYLVANIA. *Capital,* HARRISBURG. *Key-word,* MUFF.

Start with an old-fashioned MUFF and imagine a PENCIL being brought from it, to be used as the VANE or pointer of a weather-vane. From *pencil* and *vane,* you form PENNSYLVANIA. Memorizing the name of the capital is largely a matter of rote but it will help to note that it was founded by a man named *Harris* and that it is one *burg* that begins with an H instead of ending with an H, namely, HARRISBURG.

39. RHODE ISLAND. *Capital,* PROVIDENCE. *Key-word,* MAP.

Picture a MAP showing a dotted line indicating a route where people are *rowed* by boat to an *island*, also on the map. This gives RHODE ISLAND. The boat *provides* a way to reach the island which is dense with trees, producing PROVIDENCE.

40. SOUTH CAROLINA. *Capital,* COLUMBIA. *Key-word,* RICE.

As RICE was once the great product of SOUTH CAROLINA, it automatically suggests the state. Picture a great shower of RICE falling over a statue of COLUMBIA.

41. SOUTH DAKOTA. *Capital,* PIERRE. *Key-word,* ROAD.

If driving along a ROAD going *South,* you may *take a coat off* because the weather gets warmer. Hence: SOUTH DAKOTA. Picture the *road* ending in a long *pier* for PIERRE.

42. TENNESSEE. *Capital,* NASHVILLE. *Key-word,* RAIN.

Picture a heavy RAIN flooding a *tennis* court and turning it into a regular *sea,* forming TENNESSEE. Around are disappointed players who *gnash* their teeth like a *villain,* suggesting NASHVILLE.

43. TEXAS. *Capital,* AUSTIN. *Key-word,* RAM.

Visualize a RAM with horns as large as a TEXAS longhorn's, the bigger the better since this is a big state, TEXAS. So big you can get *lost in* it, suggesting AUSTIN.

44. UTAH. *Capital,* SALT LAKE CITY. *Key-word,* ROAR.

Imagine the ROAR of rocks pushed down from the mountainsides by UTE Indians, the original mountain dwellers of this area, now UTAH. The rocks tumble into a *lake,* where they dissolve like *salt,* suggesting SALT LAKE CITY.

45. VERMONT. *Capital,* MONTPELIER. *Key-word,* RAIL.

Picture a RAIL like a ski-lift going to the top of a *very* high *mountain,* suggesting the name VERMONT. The last syllable of the state name, VerMONT, is the same as the first syllable of MONTpelier, thus suggesting the capital, MONTPELIER:

46. VIRGINIA. *Capital,* RICHMOND. *Key-word,* RICH.

The key-word RICH symbolizes VIRGINIA, which is *rich in*

tradition and *rich* in resources, in short a *rich world* in itself, as indicated by the name of the capital, RICHMOND.

47. WASHINGTON. *Capital,* OLYMPIA. *Key-word,* ROCK.

Think of a ROCK with *washing* spread all over it and held down by *tons* of stones, thus suggesting WASHINGTON. Imagine the *rock* growing in size until it becomes as large as the famous *Mt. Olympus,* from which is derived the name OLYMPIA.

48. WEST VIRGINIA. *Capital,* CHARLESTON. *Key-word,* ROOF.

Above a ROOF of a cabin, the sun is setting in a gap in the mountains. This represents WEST, while the gap appears as a V and the cabin roof as an A, the letters VA completing the name of WEST VIRGINIA. In the foreground, villagers are holding a Square Dance and are dancing the CHARLESTON.

49. WISCONSIN. *Capital,* MADISON. *Key-word,* ROPE.

A man is holding a ROPE and giving it a *twist.* The T's are eliminated, leaving WIS, an abbreviation of WISCONSIN. Picture the man using the rope to hold back a *mad* bull which is trying to gore *his son,* suggesting MADISON.

50. WYOMING. *Capital,* CHEYENNE. *Key-word,* LACE.

Think of LACE in the form of clouds above a fertile valley shaped like a "Y" where cattle are *roaming,* thus coining the word WYOMING. Then picture the *lace* as the fringe of a fan, with a *shy* girl named *Anne* peering above it, forming CHEYENNE.

This list has been given in its entirety, to show how some of the more difficult picturizations can be handled. Anyone who has learned the 50 code words from HAT to LACE can readily associate them as suggested, making any changes or modifications that are desirable.

Forming one's own individual associations is usually the best policy, but some are apt to prove difficult or awkward in a list

81

as exacting as this, hence many persons may prefer to use those given here and spend the extra effort in fixing the images in mind.

3. MEMORIZING THE PRESIDENTS

The "100-Word Code" can be applied toward memorizing the names of the Presidents of the United States from George Washington on. For example, you could picture:

1. WASHINGTON, raising his HAT (1) to receive the plaudits of the crowd.

2. ADAMS, something of a fuss-budget, fluttering about like a HEN (2) and speaking in a cackly tone.

3. JEFFERSON, a *bon vivant* from Virginia, feasting on a HAM (3), which is a prime product of his native state.

4. MADISON going "mad" and tearing his HAIR (4) during the British invasion in the War of 1812.

5. MONROE ascending the famous HILL (5) to the Capitol in order to read the Monroe Doctrine.

6. JOHN Q. ADAMS trying to fill his father's shoes—from SHOE (6)—as president.

7. JACKSON using a big HOOK (7) to yank members of rival factions out of office after he took over.

This list can be continued with individual associations along the same line. It should be noted that personality, politics and historical incidents are included in these "presidential portraits," which is helpful but only to a limited degree.

Beyond that, the question arises as to whether the "word code" is required in memorizing presidents. If a person's knowledge of American history is fairly thorough and continuous, the names of the presidents will link with the events occurring in their terms.

In that case, you may be able to name most of them in order without a "key list" and any blank periods can be "filled in" with chance associations or the acquisition of further historical facts.

Memorizing Lists of Other Historical Names

In memorizing lists of other names, such as those of vice-presidents, generals, or other historical personages, the key list can be utilized in the same fashion. Here, however, it may be applied more directly, as you are apt to be dealing with names more than facts pertaining to the persons involved. But, again, you will have to call upon facts to pin down those names that do not readily associate themselves with the key words. In addition you may need strained or freakish associations, but as a rule these are all the better, as they can be recalled by their peculiarities.

The vice-presidents, for example, run in the following order:

1. ADAMS Think of the popular brand of headgear known as Adams Hats. This links ADAMS with HAT.

2. JEFFERSON Think of "Jeffer's, then HEN."

3. BURR A famous duel was fought between BURR and HAMilton.

These are all quick and natural links to the key list.

4. CLINTON Historical associations are needed as a link for Clinton. He had long been governor of New York, so you can think of CLINTON wearing a big wig, which ties in with HAIR.

5. GERRY When governor of Massachusetts, Gerry created the "Gerrymander" or odd shaped political district. So you can think of Gerry "meandering" his way around a HILL.

The technique is the same as with the presidential list, but in this case facts are largely supplementary to names. Occasional names can be remembered almost by rote, without benefit of any close associations, but this should be avoided as much as possible rather than have too many weak links in the chain.

Lists of names of kings and queens and other leaders can all be linked by this system. The fuller the facts and the more varied the possibilities for association, the more effective the system.

4. REMEMBERING ADDRESSES AND TELEPHONE NUMBERS

If a New Yorker happened to be driving an ox cart up Fifth Avenue and found himself halted by traffic outside the Public Library at Forty-second Street, he would probably remember it.

Not that New Yorkers drive ox carts; in fact very few do. But most of them know the Public Library when they see it and, since the library receives many phone calls a day, it needs a number easy to remember. So it took OXford 5-4200.

There is your OX cart; there is FIFTH Avenue; there is FORTY-SECOND Street, all rolled into one, linking the address and the phone number. If you don't fancy driving an ox cart, you can picture yourself entering the Public Library to consult the OXFORD Dictionary. Either way—or both ways!—it makes the mental tie-in.

If all addresses and phone numbers linked that neatly, it would be very easy to remember them. Or would it? More probably it would work in reverse, since everything would become so obvious that mental links or hooks would become confused with one another. In short, individual effort in the formation of a pictured link helps toward its retention.

Since obvious links are fairly rare, it is good policy to use them when they do occur. These come under the general head of "dodges," which are described in another chapter, but you can form occasional links of your own if you keep watching for opportunities. Anything so coined generally becomes a sure memory jog.

One man had trouble remembering the address 111 East 56th Street. He could recall the "One Eleven" but kept forgetting which of the Fifties it was in, until he made mental note that 5 and 6 added up to 11, which became his cue for 56th Street.

A combination like 1449 can be fixed in mind by the fact that it is composed of 7 plus 7 (14) and 7 times 7 (49). The same applies to 1664 (8 plus 8 and 8 times 8).

Lacking such obvious jogs or any that you find you can keep in mind without straining them too far, you must resort to memory systems to peg addresses and phone numbers. Earlier, we mentioned how the Figure Alphabet can be used in this connection, by forming a word or phrase containing consonants of the correct phonetic values in their proper order, as:

No	RiCH	NaiL
2	4 6	2 5

This works well with some phone numbers where you are familiar with the exchange, and for modern long distance codes when you are able to form fairly meaningful sentences. But you cannot afford to carry in mind too many phrases that are otherwise unrelated. So where it is necessary to remember a fairly long list of telephone numbers that are used at rather infrequent intervals, the "100-Word Code" may be brought into play.

First, link the person or place you are calling to the telephone exchange. This is usually quite simple but the process may be variable, as in large cities the first two letters of the exchange are often followed by a purely arbitrary figure. In New York City, for instance, there is a Circle 5 (CI–5), a Circle 6 (CI–6) and a Circle 7 (CI–7), which alone makes sense because the third letter "R" is at the same position as the figure "7" on the dial.

For CI–5, you could think of a CIRCLE on a HILL (5); for CI–6, a CIRCLE around a SHOE (6); for CI–7, a CIRCLE hanging on a HOOK (7). Many other exchanges, however, are much easier to remember, particularly in smaller cities where a person may remember a few dozen numbers all on one exchange.

Fortunately, too, some exchanges are so unsuitably named that they are easy to remember once you become aware of them. In New York City there is an exchange called "Oregon" and another named "Rhinelander" (which people are apt to dial "RI" instead of "RH"). Odd names help, and often you can coin your own nickname for an exchange, along with its figure.

That leaves the four figures of the number itself. These are simply broken into pairs and remembered by means of the "100-Word Code" which appears in this section.

This is best illustrated by an example:

Your friend George's home phone number is MItchell 8-3932.

If you are familiar with the exchange, you can take it as is; if not, think of being annoyed or "miffed" at having to call George. That gives you MI as the first two letters, with the figure 8 represented by F. (MI–FF–ed or MI–8)

The number 3932 breaks into 39 (MAP) and 32 (MOON). So you picture George beside the telephone, looking at a *map* which represents the surface of the *moon*.

Now consider another number:

Louise's phone number is ORegon 7-1793. If you have to "peg" the exchange, think of giving Louise an "orchid" which she would doubtless appreciate. You then have OR as the first two letters, with the figure 7 represented by CH. (OR–CH–id or OR–7)

The number 1793 is composed of 17 (DECK) and 93 (POEM). So you picture Louise standing on the *deck* of a cruise ship, reading a *poem* that she has written.

With both these examples, the question arises: What if you should get the second number ahead of the first? Or, in other words, after you have formed the double picture, how can you tell which is which?

Simply enough. Your word images are personalized, which enables you to recall them in sequence as *action* pictures instead of a still composite. This "sequence system" takes care of itself step by step.

You saw George looking at a map and finding the moon, which definitely spelled out 39–32. You couldn't make a mistake and call it 32–39 because, in that case, you would have thought of George being on the moon and pulling a map out of his space suit to find his way back to earth.

You saw Louise standing on the deck, where she began to read a poem and that signified 17–93. It couldn't be 93–17 because then Louise would have been reading the poem when the phone rang and the poem would have been "The Boy Stood on the Burning Deck."

You will find in practice that it works out perfectly if the sequence is clearly thought out. When calling hotels, business offices, shops, or stores, you can remember the numbers in the same way, adding the personalized touch by thinking in terms of the clerk, switchboard operator, manager, or whoever else is likely to be on the other end.

Thus a call to a flower shop at PLaza 2–9586 would first of all be "planned" (PLa–NN–ed or PL-2) and you would think of carrying a PAIL (95) and pouring its contents, not on the flowers but on a FISH (86) lying on the floor of the shop.

While special key words can be used in forming these pictures (as PILL instead of PAIL) it is preferable to adhere to your regular list, as these personalized sequences will not interfere with other memory exercises involving the "100-Word Code." Instead, they will help toward acquiring it more strongly.

5. MEMORIZING DATES

Remembering dates is a problem for many people and the process was truly painful in the old days when schoolmasters were as rigid as the sticks with which they drilled home historical facts. Fortunately, today's methods are not so exacting and many minor dates are no longer regarded as necessary to an education; but major dates will always retain a definite importance.

Also, in modern life, such dates as birthdays of family and

friends, anniversaries, reunions, sporting and various other events, have taken on new social significance. So, in all, the need to remember dates is strong but the trend has gone from ancient history to current events.

The major psychologic influences favoring the process of memorization, Attention, Observation and Association, are also fundamental in remembering dates. There is often a tendency to slur over a date as something inconsequential and to be avoided, so that the first factor, Attention, hardly begins to register. But even when noted, a date may soon slip the attention unless the factor of Interest has been applied.

The Battle of Gettysburg, for example, was fought on the first three days of July, 1863, with both armies appropriately taking July 4th as a holiday. That night, a heavy rain set in, aiding the withdrawal of the Confederate forces. That could have given rise to a popular notion that persisted for many years, to the effect that rain invariably occurred on July 5th, due to the powder from fireworks set off during the annual Independence Day celebration.

In this example, with *attention* focussed sufficiently on the three day battle, its aftermath contributed to the *interest; observation* was in the reading; *association* included organization of the data, understanding the meaning and picturing events in relation to material already stored in the mind. Ordinarily, such a process becomes increasingly automatic. Persons will tend to recall that the Battle of Gettysburg was fought on July 1st, 2nd, and 3rd, 1863, because that year was the mid-point of the Civil War and that battle the high-water mark of Southern hopes. Thus considered, it becomes harder to forget than to remember.

Picturing Dates

Of primary importance in remembering a date, then, is to include it with the scene, building it into the actual picture if it is

88

possible or convenient to do so. This is often quite easily done with the dates of years only; or with the days of the month in the case of holidays.

Many people can quickly tell you that the Norman Conquest of England took place in 1066; that Columbus discovered America in 1492; that the Pilgrims landed in Massachusetts in 1620; and that World War I began in 1914.

Similarly, they can reel off the dates of certain holidays, as Washington's Birthday, on February 22; Memorial Day, on May 30; or Columbus Day, on October 12. These seem so natural to some people that they feel they must have always known them.

Actually, such dates become fixed in mind largely through rote or repetition. People don't forget them because they keep cropping up regularly and are often mentioned in between times, or have been drilled home one way or another.

A good procedure is to take the year of a date that you feel is important to remember and to visualize it written in large or heavy pictures. Repeat it aloud as well, gaining both a visual and aural impression. Actually write it out with pencil if you find that such will help.

Compare the date with others of the same period, as they may not only prove mutually helpful but may add purpose to the project. Too frequently, historical facts are learned by individual countries, in "vertical" succession so to speak, rather than in relation to events elsewhere, in "horizontal" fashion.

As an example of strong picturization using artificial memory aids, take Henry Hudson discovering Manhattan Island in his ship the *Half Moon* in the year 1609. Here the 0 gives the shape of a moon; by dividing it in half, there is a 6 to the left and a 9 to the right, as reversed halves. This helps the *visual* impression of the date.

Rhymes and Jingles

With the picturization of dates (as just detailed) mention was made of aural impressions gained by speaking dates aloud. This is frequently helped by rhymes or jingles, such as:

> In fourteen hundred ninety-two,
> Columbus sailed the ocean blue.

Far from being mere word plays on historical events, such rhymes have been designed purposely to assist the learning process. More examples of jingles are given further on page 99 and it is possible to compose others to suit certain dates, all adding to the effectiveness of aural repetition.

Actually, this is stronger than the picturization process in those instances where it is well applied. But the fact remains that both procedures are time takers and are limited in scope. That has brought about the more systematic device of:

Phonetic Numerals

Applied in cases of years as dates to be remembered, this is simply a use of the Figure Alphabet given previously.

In full form, the year should consist of a word (or words) containing all four figures of the date in their proper order. As an example:

THE EUROPEAN who discovered America was Columbus.

The "key" is THe euRoPeaN, in which the letters of the Figure Alphabet are: TH (1)—R (4)—P (9)—N (2), which gives the date: 1492.

For practical purposes, the first figure (1) can be eliminated, so that the simple word EUROPEAN with R–P–N signifying 492 will be sufficient to denote the Discovery of America.

Because we know that it took place after the year 1000, the last three figures are sufficient. With later dates in which the exact century is known, only the last two figures are needed and, in some cases, merely the final figure.

For example, the year of Washington's birth is aptly expressed by the word: MAN. Since we know that he was born in the 1700s, the key letters MaN add the figures 3–2 making the date 1732.

With Lincoln, we need only his nickname: ABE.

Since Abraham Lincoln was born in the 1800s, the key-letter in aBe, which signifies 9, is sufficient for the date 1809.

For Thomas Edison, born in 1847, the key-word is ARC.

This ties in with the electric arc and the key-letters in aRC give the last two figures of his birth year.

Benjamin Franklin was recognized as a SAGE.

He was born in 1706 and the key-letters SaGe give the last two figures of that year.

Phonetic Numeral Words in Sentences

The phonetic examples so far given are very apt ones but, unfortunately, they are not too easy to prepare. When available, they should be used; otherwise some other device must be used. One way is to stretch or modify the meaning of a key-word, but it cannot be overstrained or it will lose its true significance.

For example: Queen Victoria was born in 1819. If we think of her as a debutante, or "deb," we have the key-letters D–B for 1–9. This would be a fairly good analogy, as she was only seventeen when she became Queen.

However, by putting the statement into sentence form and stressing certain appropriate words, we can drop the term "DEB" entirely and simply declare:

"Princess Victoria, England's Queen TO BE, was born in the year 1819."

You can't miss, because those two "key-words" To Be— with the key-letters "T" and "B"—automatically give you the date 1819.

Many readable sentences can be formed, stating the case clearly and ending in appropriate key-words which give the date. In that case, the key-words are immediately identified and can be rather odd ones.

Here are some examples from ancient history:

The Destruction of Troy was completed by the raging flames of a HOT WOOD FIRE. (T–D–F–R or 1184 B.C.)

Rome was founded, according to historians, by a felonious COLONY. (C–L–N or 752 B.C.)

The tragic deaths of Antony and Cleopatra have inspired many a poetical MUSE. (M–S or 30 B.C.)

In modern times, we have the following:

Halley's Comet last appeared as stealthily as though on TIP-TOES. (T–P–T–S or 1910)

When it next appears, it will glide in as smoothly as a FISH. (F–SH or 86, making 1986)

Manhattan Island was purchased from the Indians as the result of a DUTCH HUNCH. (D–TCH–N–CH or 1626)

At Waterloo, Napoleon's hopes proved TOO FUTILE. (T–F–T–L or 1815) Here, "FUTILE" would suffice, giving "815."

The discovery of gold in California was a rumor that everyone wanted the government TO VERIFY. (T–V–R–F or 1848)

First Letter Sentences

Another memory device is to phrase a sentence containing the exact number of *words* as the date, with the first letter of each word representing a figure. This allows much more choice of words, hence is helpful when there is difficulty in forming a single key word.

The "first letter" of a word signifies the first one that conforms to a symbol of the Figure Alphabet. These are given in *italics* in the following examples of American history:

*D*ISCOVERED A*R*EAS *P*REVIOUSLY U*N*KNOWN
   (D–R–P–N) 1492
America discovered by Columbus

DONS LANDED SHOCK LEGIONS (D–L–SH–L) 1565
Spanish establishment of fort and settlement at St. Augustine, Florida

(*THE*) *LOST·VIRGINIA COLONY* (TH–L–V–K) 1587
Lost English settlement at Roanoke Island.

(*THEN*) *JAMESTOWN WAS COLONIZED* (TH–J–S–K) 1607
First permanent settlement in Virginia.

THEIR SHIP NEVER SANK (TH–SH–N–S) 1620
Landing of Pilgrims from the "Mayflower" in Massachusetts.

DUTCHMEN CHOSE NEW AMSTERDAM JOYFULLY (D–CH–N–J) 1628
Settlement of New Amsterdam (later New York).

THEY SHARED MARYLAND'S REFUGE (TH–SH–M–R) 1634
First colony in Maryland.

(*THE*) *CHARLESTON COLONY ESTABLISHED* (TH–CH–K–S) 1670
First Carolina settlement at Charleston.

DESTINY SHAPED PENN'S NATION (D–SH–P–N) 1682
Founding of Pennsylvania.

(*THERE*) *OGLETHORPE MANAGED MEN* (TH–G–M–M) 1733
Establishment of a refugee colony in Georgia.

DECLARATION GAVE GREAT CHEER (D–G–G–CH) 1776
Declaration of American Independence.

The words in parentheses are not needed, because the sense of the statements are the same without them and they merely represent the figure 1, which is understood in each case. But it is preferable to keep them, as then any statement with exactly four words, each with a key-letter, can be recognized as a "date."

Other slogans covering Colonial and later periods of American history can be fitted into the above list. Memorizing them is much easier than trying to fix dry, meaningless dates in mind. The slogans are descriptive and give the dates as well.

Other Date Devices Using Figure Alphabet

The nickname "Abe" (aBe) has been mentioned as a device for pegging the date of Lincoln's birth as 1809. Similarly, the name E. A. Poe, has the lone figure 9 (for the letter P) thus establishing 1809 as the birth year of Edgar Allen Poe, as well as of Abraham Lincoln.

Robert E. Peary (P or 9) reached the Pole (P or 9) in 1909.

President Martin Van Buren was born in 1782 and if we take his nickname "Van," its key letters V–N (8–2) fit the date perfectly.

Carrying this idea further, the first two "consonant" letters of a name may sometimes be keyed to a date of definite significance to the person involved. As examples:

Andrew Jackson (*JACK*SON) produces J–K (6–7), giving 1767 as Jackson's birth year.

William Henry Harrison (*HARR*ISON) produces R–S (4–0) giving 1840 as the year of his election to the presidency.

Philip Sheridan (SHeR or 6–4) made a famous ride in 1864.

John Glenn (JohN or 6–2) orbited the Earth in 1962.

These are direct examples of partial use of "key" figures, which depend upon accidental links, as with jingles and other dodges. But special words can be coined, utilizing the first two key letters only, to pin down important events. Here are some:

The first Atlantic cable failed and was *LIFTED*. 1858 (58)
It succeeded later through better *JUDG*MENT. 1866 (66)
Lincoln was assassinated by *J. WILKES* Booth. 1865 (65)
Stanley found Livingstone near a *CATARACT*. 1871 (71)
The Brooklyn Bridge immediately became *FAMOUS*. 1883 (83)

94

Survivors of the Great Blizzard died of *FEVER*. 1888   (88)

The Boer War surprised the British *POPULACE*. 1899   (99)

Mt. Pelée blasted Martinique and has not erupted *SINCE*. 1902   (02)

The San Francisco earthquake came as a great *SHOCK*. 1906   (6)

The outbreak of World War I brought home many *TOURISTS*. 1914   (14)

Instead of peace, the armistice brought *DEFIANCE*. 1918   (18)

Again, the nations of the world were *MOBILIZED*. 1939   (39)

At last, another peace was partly *REALIZED*. 1945   (45)

Many other key-words could be introduced to suit any required events that there is special reason to remember. No great amount of ingenuity is necessary, as there are many words to choose from, but the stronger the association the better. Since the final word is the key in every case, there is no confusion. A single figure, as 6, is obviously 1906, as it could not be in the 1960s.

Combined Biographical Data

By using ingenious final phrases, biographical dates can be combined, as in these examples:

Benjamin Franklin was the first man to obtain from lightning a harmless, YET *COPIOUS FIRE*. (T K–P–S) (F–R)

These key-letters give 1790 as the year of Franklin's death, with 84 as his age. Subtracting, the year of his birth was 1706.

George Washington, as a wealthy planter, could afford TO *KEEP A PAY CHECK*. (T K–P P) (CH–CK)

The key-letters give 1799 as the year of Washington's death, with 67 as his age. Subtracting, his birth year was 1732.

Napoleon has been described as a *DIVINE ITALIAN*. (D–V–N–T) (L–N)

The key-letters give 1821 as the year of Napoleon's death, with 52 as his age. Subtracting, his birth year was 1769.

With persons who died before reaching the birthday in their final year, omit the 1 at the start of the year. This means that one extra year must be subtracted to determine the year of birth.

Queen Victoria's famous Diamond Jubilee was recognized as England's *BEST FETE.* (B–S–T) (F–T)

The key-letters give 1901 (901) as the year of Victoria's death, with 81 as her age. Subtracting 81 plus 1, we have 1819 as her birth year.

Woodrow Wilson took peace as the great goal he was intent *UPON REACHING.* (P–N–R) (CH–NG or G)

The key-letters give 1924 (924) as the year of Wilson's death, with 67 as his age. Subtracting 67 plus 1, his birth year was 1856.

Various phrases may be coined to suit other cases, though some may prove rather difficult. An interesting variation or extension of this system is the use of "Homophonic Analogies" in which the memory of a name is reenforced by tying the "date word" into a sentence containing a word—or words—similar in sound to the name or fact which is to be remembered.

Examples:

COLUMBUS (Christopher) died in 1506, age about 71.

A *column or bust* (sounding like Columbus) may be clothed with a *LOOSE JACKET.* (L–S J for 506 or 1506.) (CK–T for 71)

TAYLOR (Zachary), U.S. President, died in 1850, age 66.

A *tailor* (like Taylor) is more competent to judge the fit of a coat than a *FALSE JUDGE.* (D–L–S for 1850) (J–DG for 66)

(In this instance, the age is taken according to the birthday in the final year, so the subtraction gives the birth year as 1784. This is usual with the Homophonic Analogy method.)

Memorizing Exact Dates

Here, the Figure Alphabet is used to fix in mind a specific day, such as a birthday or an anniversary. This includes the day and the *month;* and the method can be extended to give the *year,* as well. It will be considered first in simple form.

Start with the number of the month: January, 1; February, 2; and so on, as if you were writing the date in simple numerical form. Then take the figures of the date and form an appropriate key-word from the entire group.

Suppose you have a friend whose birthday falls on January 26 and you are anxious to remember it. Put the figures 1–2–6 into key letters as D–N–SH, forming DANISH. Think of your friend in Danish costume, eating Danish pastry and you will have the date pegged.

Another example: May 4. Turn 5–0–4 into L–S–R and your friend becomes a LoSeR. It is disappointing to be a "loser" on one's birthday, but that makes it easier to remember. Note that the 4th day of the month is treated as "04." Similarly, the 5th would be "05," the 6th "06" and so on.

For a date like September 12, you would obtain 9–1–2 or B–N–T, which naturally forms BoNNeT. Here you would think of the person wearing a bonnet as a birthday present.

There is no problem with dates in October (10), November (11) or December (12) because they automatically run the key-word into letters representing four figures.

Thus, October 15 would be 1–0–1–5 which could be TH–S–T–L or THISTLE. There could be no confusion between January 26, or 1–2–6, as given earlier, and December 6, which would be 1–2–0–6 because of the included zero. This could be formed into two descriptive words like THiN SaSH, so you would think of the person wearing a thin or flimsy sash.

Phonetic Values for Months

An alternate system for pegging exact dates is to give a two figure value derived from the first two consonants in the month's name. A few slight variations are necessary: May has only one

97

consonant, so this is arbitrarily repeated, giving May the value of 3–3 to represent M–M.

Since June, with its key letters J–N, would be the same as January, the "N" of June is replaced by "M"—which follows N in phonetic numeral sequence. Two different digits are thus obtained for each month; and, for consistency, the days are also used as two digit combinations, 1 to 9 being represented by 01 to 09.

The monthly values thus appear:

JaNuary	6–2	May-M	3–3	SePtember	0–9
FeBruary	8–9	JuN(M)e	6–3	OCTober	7–1
MaRch	3–4	JuLy	6–5	NoVember	2–8
APRil	9–4	AuGuSt	7–0	DeCember	1–0

Note that the key letters must occasionally be used exactly as they are, the word MoRe being formed from the "M" and "R" in March, as an example. Similarly, PooR can be formed from the "P" and "R" in April but, in this case, BoRe could be used instead, as "P" and "B" both fit the figure 9. So it is important to remember that you are dealing with *phonetic values,* even though you may often make a direct jump, like changing FeB (for February) into FiB.

With this list, plus ordinary date figures for the day and year, separate words or phrases can be coined to establish an exact date. Begin with the *day,* then the *month* and, finally, the *year.*

As a classic example:

Benjamin Franklin, born on 17th of January, 1706.
(Day: 17   Month: 62   Year: 1706)

At his birth, Franklin had not yet attained the THICK CHIN of an ATTIC SAGE. (TH–CK 1–7) (CH–N 62) (T–C S–J 1706)

Historical Jingles

Various historical dates have been incorporated into jingles and songs, some for the purpose of recalling them, others because the date simply fitted the theme. Either way, the rhyme and the date are thereby linked as a memory tab.

Simplest and perhaps the most widely known is the couplet that gives the year of America's discovery:

> In fourteen hundred ninety-two,
> Columbus sailed the ocean blue.

More detailed in its historical significance is this first stanza from a poem by Longfellow:

> Listen, my children, and you shall hear
> Of the midnight ride of Paul Revere,
> On the eighteenth of April, in Seventy-five;
> Hardly a man is now alive
> Who remembers that famous day and year.

The alarm spread by Revere and others roused the Massachusetts countryside and resulted in the first armed conflict of the American Revolution at Concord and Lexington, on the next day, April 19, 1775. In Massachusetts and Maine, which was originally part of Massachusetts, April 19th is celebrated annually as "Patriot's Day" and that holiday can be remembered from the poem.

English history provides some catchy "date jingles." As an example:

> William the Fourth, he went to Heaven
> In eighteen hundred and thirty-seven.

That couplet is a good tab, as the death of William IV marked the accession of Queen Victoria, first monarch of the present ruling house of Windsor.

An old familiar song includes the lines:

. . . Lived a miner, Forty-niner,
And his daughter, Clementine.

That pegs the year of the famous California Gold Rush, 1849, when miners swarmed all over the state and became known as "Forty-niners."

The opening lines of another song of the period run as follows:

'Twas in Fifty-five on a winter's night,
Cheerily, my lads, yo-ho!

This refers to 1855, the principal year of the Crimean War, which began in 1854 and ended in 1856. It sets the date of that conflict.

Many other jingles or catch phrases can be made up as "date pegs" along these patterns, often serving to remember difficult or isolated events.

Calendar Memory

A remarkable stunt performed by lightning calculators is that of naming the day of the week of any modern date from 1753* to the year 2000 or beyond. For example, if asked, "What day of the week was February 12, 1809?" a calculator will quickly answer, "Sunday." A checkup will prove this to be correct.

Far from being a mere trick, this has its practical uses. Someone may want to know the day of the week on which he was born; or people may be interested in learning on what day a certain holiday may fall a few years hence. In many forms of research, it is often necessary to check the weekdays of back years.

So-called "perpetual calendars" have been devised for this purpose, but some are cumbersome and few are available when required. So it would prove helpful indeed if you could be your

* Actually from September 14, 1752, when the Gregorian calendar became official in England and America.

own lightning calculator where dates are concerned. This you can be, thanks to the greatly simplified system about to be described.

First, the days of the week are numbered in a simple rotation: Sunday, 1; Monday, 2; Tuesday, 3; Wednesday, 4; Thursday, 5; Friday, 6; Saturday, 0.

Next, the months are given special values, which can be called to mind immediately by a simple application of the Figure Alphabet, which furnishes special key words forming easily remembered sentences, as follows:

Month:	January	February	March	April
Value:	3	6	6	2
Key Words:	My	CHimp	CHews	Nuts

Month:	May	June	July	August
Value:	4	0	2	5
Key Words:	Ripe	Seeds	Need	Land

Month:	September	October	November	December
Value:	1	3	6	1
Key Words:	Try	My	Juicy	Tobacco

Note that the capital letters of the key words represent the month values: M for 3, CH for 6, N for 2, and so on according to the Figure Alphabet.

When a date is given, take the last two figures of the year as your basic number. Divide that by 4 and drop any remainder. Add the result to your basic number.

The month comes next. Go through your key sentences and add the month value to your total. Then add the day of the month. Divide the grand total by 7.

This time, it is the remainder that counts. If the date is in the 19th century (the 1800s) that remainder gives you the day of the week: 1 for Sunday, 2 for Monday, and so on.

If the date is the 20th century (the 1900s) you must subtract 2 from the remainder to get the day of the week. If the date is in

101

the 18th century (from 1753) you must add 2 to the remainder.*
Here is an example:

Date: July 15, 1922

Take the last two figures of the year................ 22
Divide by 4 (discarding remainder) to add......... 5
Add value of month (July—Need)................. 2
Add day of month................................ 15
                                                   ——
    Total 44
Divide by 7 (goes into 42) and keep remainder.... 2
Subtract 2 for 20th century......................... 0
The final figure gives Saturday (0) as the day of the
week on which the 15th of July fell in 1922.

(Note: Since the days of the week run in rotation, if the
remainder should be 1, a subtraction of 2 would result in 6. With
a remainder of 0, a subtraction of 2 would give a final figure
of 5.)

Leap Year

In dividing the last two figures of the year by 4 at the start,
an even result (with no remainder) indicates a Leap Year. This
means that you must subtract 1 from the key value of January
(which then becomes 2) or February (which then becomes 5).
Other months are not affected.

As an example:

Date: February 12, 1896

Take the last two figures of the year............... 96
Divide by 4 (no remainder) to add................ 24
Add value of month (6) less 1 for Leap Year...... 5
Add day of month................................ 12
                                                   ——
    Total 137

* For 21st century, add 4 to the remainder. For 22nd century add 2 to
the remainder.

Divide by 7 (goes into 133) and keep remainder.... 4
The final figure gives Wednesday (4) as the day of the
week on which the 12th of February fell in 1896.

(Note: The years 1800 and 1900 were *not* Leap Years, as any
century year must be divisible by 400 to become a Leap Year.
In these calendar calculations, 1800 is treated as any ordinary year
beginning with the two figures 18; while 1900 similarly is treated
as one of the 1900s.)

Example:

Date: August 5, 1900
Take the last two figures of the year.............. 00
Too small to be divisible by 4...................... 0
Value of month (August—Land).................. 5
Add day of month................................ 5

Total 10
Divide by 7 (goes into 7) and keep remainder...... 3
Subtract 2 for 20th century (beginning with 19).... 1
The final figure gives Sunday (1) as the day of the week
on which the 5th of August fell in 1900.

(Note: If final figure in any calculation is more than 6, subtract
7 from it to obtain day of week.)

6. DODGES

One of the most interesting as well as entertaining forms of
artificial memory methods is the use of specially coined devices
that help recall specific facts. Some of these are actual memory
methods; others are mere oddities or chance discoveries.

All have one factor in common; they stimulate other "dodges"
along similar lines. Thus the reader may be able to invent a
better device than one of those listed here; or one possibly better
suited to his own needs.

There is little logic involved in these devices. Their merit lies chiefly in their efficacy. If they really help someone to recall a fact that he would otherwise have forgotten, their purpose has been served. If not, they should be forgotten, perhaps, along with the thing itself.

Since many of these devices are quite isolated, even in their relation to others of similar pattern, they have been grouped in general categories. Through casual perusal, the reader can determine their value; or, better still, decide if it is worth while to adapt their patterns to devices of his own.

Accidental Dodges

These are strictly oddities of association in which names, dates, or other facts can be recalled through some peculiar similarity to others that are actually unrelated.

Biblical Question. Where are the Ten Commandments found?

Answer: In the book of Exodus, Chapter XX.

Key: Exodus incorporates "X" for "10" and the word "duo" or twice. Twice 10 (the number of Commandments) gives the Chapter 20.

Calendar Device

To remember months with 31 days, as opposed to those with less: set both fists downward on the table and start counting knuckles of fingers from left to right, as well as the hollows between them; thumbs are not included. Knuckles represent 31 day months; hollows, less.

Jan.	Mar.	May	July	Aug.	Oct.	Dec.
Feb.	Apr.	June		Sept.	Nov.	

Descriptive Letter Words

E Z = Easy   M T = Empty   QT = Quiet or Sub rosa

I N X I N X I N = Ink sinks in

104

Food

Catch phrase relating to oyster production:

"Oysters R in season during months containing R."

This excludes the months of May, June, July, August, during which the lack of adequate refrigeration formerly made it difficult to keep oysters from spoiling.

Geographical Spellings

The spelling of *Mississippi* can be remembered by:

M—I *double* S,
I *double* S,
I *double* P,
I

The spelling of *Cincinnati* can be remembered by thinking of prepositions set regularly between key letters:

C *in* C *in* N *at* I

The spelling of *Tallahassee,* capital of Florida, can be recalled by thinking of $\underset{c}{A}$, representing a "tall" A holding an ordinary letter c. From this comes the phrase:

Tall A has See = Tallahassee

Phonetic spelling of *Ohio* is remembered by:

o O = O—High-O = Ohio

History

Sidelight on the American Revolution:

"The new nation went from one George to another."

George III, as king, was supplanted by George Washington as president.

Presidential Succession. The first name of the first president, George Washington, begins with "G" pronounced as "J." Following Washington, the next six presidents had "J" in their names: John Adams, Thomas Jefferson, James Madison, James Monroe, John Q. Adams, Andrew Jackson.

It was during Jackson's administration that King George IV died, so that the coincidence of the "G and J" succession ended with the four Georges.

Coincidence with *Abraham Lincoln's* name: The last three letters of the first name, coupled with the first three of the last name, give the name of Lincoln's running mate and vice president during his first term:

Abra*ham Lin*coln = *Hamlin* (Hannibal Hamlin)

Mathematics

There are many oddities with figures that are closely akin to memory "dodges." Here are a few samples:

Reversed Multiplication:

Multiply $12 \times 12 = 144$
Reverse $21 \times 21 = 441$
Reversed numbers produce reversed result.

Freakish Figures:

$$0 \times 9 + 1 = 1$$
$$1 \times 9 + 2 = 11$$
$$12 \times 9 + 3 = 111$$
$$123 \times 9 + 4 = 1111$$
$$1234 \times 9 + 5 = 11111$$
$$12345 \times 9 + 6 = 111111$$
$$123456 \times 9 + 7 = 1111111$$
$$1234567 \times 9 + 8 = 11111111$$
$$12345678 \times 9 + 9 = 111111111$$
$$123456789 \times 9 + 10 = 1111111111$$

Ophthalmology

To remember the inventor of bifocals: The letters B and F, as in *bi*focals, are found in the name of the inventor: *B*enjamin *F*ranklin.

Spelling

Many words commonly misspelled can be recalled in their correct form by easily linked associations, in some of which coincidence is the only key.

Here are some examples:

Francis, the man's name, can be distinguished from *Frances,* the woman's name, because Franc*is* ends in "is" like h*is*. *Francis* is therefore *his* name.

In the word *repetition,* you *repeat* the "e," spelling "r*e*petition" (not repitition).

A *battalion* fights in a *battle* and therefore should be spelled similarly. (With a double T, not a double L)

In the word *desert,* you find only one S, as in *sand,* which is not good to eat. Therefore do not confuse it with *dessert,* the last course of a meal.

Wireless Telegraphy

In the early days of radio, the initial letters C Q D were used to call all stations within range. Hence they summoned aid to the sinking steamship *Republic* in 1909, the first time wireless figured in a sea rescue. From that event:

The call letters *C Q D* were turned into the popular catchphrase: *Come Quick, Danger*.

When the call letters S O S supplanted C Q D, new phrases were formed. From then on:

S O S was interpreted as *Save Our Ship*. And also as *Suspend Other Service*.

Acronyms

Among modern memory devices is the use of Acronyms, or words coined from initials or abbreviations of parts of successive words making up a compound term. Although the word acronym is comparatively new, derived from Greek words meaning tip and name, the device is of ancient origin.

Simple abbreviations have long been in common use, as "A A A" or "Triple A" for American Automobile Association; "A M A" for American Medical Association; "F D R" for Franklin Delano Roosevelt. A stronger type is a word like "T V," which takes both its letters from one word, "television," and could be spelled out like a word, in the form "teevee."

Still better examples are initials containing combinations of consonants and vowels that enable them to be pronounced as they are spelled; and still others which incorporate syllables from the words which signify their full meaning.

Once noted and defined, the words in the list are easily remembered; and the same applies to others that are similarly derived. Letters given in the form of a word are pronounced as the spelling indicates. Those with separated letters are pronounced letter by letter.

List of Representative Acronyms

A B C . . . American Broadcasting Company

A Bomb . . . Atom Bomb

ACTH . . . Adrenocorticotropin

ACTION . . . American Council to Improve Our Neighborhoods

A M . . . Ante Meridian (forenoon)

AMOCO . . . American Oil Company

A'S . . . Athletics (baseball team)

ASCAP . . . American Society of Composers, Authors and Publishers

AWOL (or AWOL) . . . Absent Without Official Leave (military)

BOSOX . . . Boston Red Sox (baseball team)

BRUNCH . . . Breakfast and lunch combined

CARE . . . Cooperative for American Remittances for Europe

CHISOX . . . Chicago White Sox (baseball team)

CPA . . . Certified Public Accountant

DEW Line . . . Distant Early Warning Line

EMSEE (MC) . . . Master of Ceremonies

ESSO . . . Standard Oil

EST . . . Eastern Standard Time

GARD . . . Gamma Atomic Radiation Detector

GI . . . General Issue (military)
. . . Enlisted Man (military)

H-Bomb . . . Hydrogen Bomb

HQ . . . Headquarters (military)

KAYO (KO) . . . Knockout

KC . . . Kansas City

KP . . . Kitchen Police (military)

LA . . . Los Angeles

MD . . . Doctor of Medicine
. . . Medical Department (military)

MOTEL . . . Hotel for Motorists

MS . . . Manuscript
. . . Master of Science

NABISCO . . . National Biscuit Company

NADAR . . . North American Data Airborne Recorder

NASA . . . National Aeronautics and Space Administration

NATO . . . North Atlantic Treaty Organization

NBC . . . National Broadcasting Company

PAL . . . Police Athletic League

PM . . . Post Meridian (afternoon)

PS . . . Postscript

PTA . . . Parent-Teachers Association

PX . . . Post Exchange (army)

RADAR . . . Radar Detection And Ranging

SHAPE . . . Supreme Headquarters Allied Powers Europe

SMOG . . . Smoke and Fog

SNAFU . . . Situation Normal, All Fouled Up (military slang)

SOHIO . . . Standard Oil Company of Ohio

SPARS . . . Coast Guard Women's Reserve (Semper Paratus-Always Ready, USCG Motto)

STRAF . . . Strategic Army Force

SUNOCO . . . Sun Oil Company

TEL & TEL . . . American Telephone and Telegraph Company (A T & T)

T V . . . Television

UNESCO . . . United Nations Educational, Scientific and Cultural Organization

UNIVAC . . . Universal Automatic Computer

U S . . . United States

U S O . . . United Service Organizations

VEEP . . . Vice President (V P)

V I P . . . Very Important Person (military)
. . . Very Important Passenger (Air Force)

WAC . . . Women's Army Corps

WATS . . . Wide Area Telephone Service

WAVES . . . Women Accepted for Volunteer Emergency Service (United States Navy Women's Reserve)

WHO . . . World Health Organization

Acrostics

An acrostic, in its simple form, is a group of words so arranged that the initial letters of each word in sequence form a name, word, or phrase. From this developed the acrostic verse, in which the first letters of the lines—or sometimes other letters—spell out the desired word or words.

Two excellent examples of the standard acrostic verse, both composed by Robert Blackwell, are the following:

Composed of vapors shining bright,
Of wondrous size, yet harmless light,
Men view thee as a burning ball
Expecting soon to see thee fall
To this low world, and kill us all.

The capital letters spell the word COMET which is described in the verse. As the second example, we have:

Boundless source of information,
Information for the blind,
Bringing words of consolation
Life and peace to soothe the mind,
Exposed to grief of every kind.

Here, BIBLE is the subject of the verse.

Though excellent in themselves, the verses just given have little value as memory devices, due to the length of the poems. A much simpler example of a prose acrostic was this playbill of the 1920s:

Many a girl
Answers
Right out loud when
You call, "Mary!"

Every one who saw that remembered the show "Mary," which went on to have a long run and record receipts. But for the simplest of acrostics, in most pointed terms, here is a gem:

Under
Steady
Steaming

Our
Run

East
Gained
Our
Name

This referred to the U.S.S. OREGON, as spelled by the column of initial letters, which in 1898 made the fastest trip then on record around Cape Horn to join the American fleet at the Battle of Santiago. Those nine words, once remembered, will always bring up the name of the ship.

In still simpler form, the acrostic uses any suitable words that provide the needed vertical or initial letters to spell a desired word. In such form, it can be adapted to the memorization of speeches. As an example:

A speech is to be given to a sales group. In it, the speaker must emphasize these points: (1) *Sales:* That is, the important purpose. (2) *Product:* That is, what the salesmen have to sell. (3) *Excellence:* The product has it. (4) *Extras:* Those are furnished, too. (5) *Customers:* They are always satisfied. (6) *Humor:* The message has been delivered, so this is the closing note.

These six words are set down in acrostic fashion:

Sales
Product
Excellence
Extras
Customers
Humor

Vertically, they spell the word "Speech." Horizontally, they list the subjects. During the speech, the speaker pauses at the end of each brief discussion and refers to the next letter in his key word "S-P-E-E-C-H" to pick up the next theme.

Code Devices

Among code devices, many of which are too intricate for memorization, a few are specially designed for immediate recognition, due to some mnemonic aid. Simplest of these are the secret price codes used by merchants.

These are remembered by simple key words, or a key name, composed of ten different letters, each representing a figure from 1 to 0. Merchandise is marked with these letters and a person knowing the code has only to count through them to identify each figure.

Example:

```
1 2 3 4 5   6 7 8 9 0
B L A C K   H O R S E
```

Here, with the words "Black Horse" as a code, a clerk would identify an article marked A O K as priced at $3.75.

Others:

```
1 2 3 4 5   6 7 8 9 0
C L E A N   S H I R T
```

```
1 2 3 4   5   6 7 8 9 0
M A R Y   B   J O N E S
```

In any of these codes, an odd letter (as Z) can be used for repeated letters. Thus, in the "Mary B. Jones" code, B Z S could represent $5.50.

Some merchants use a special letter (as X) as an alternate for zero (0) only, as it occurs so often. Thus M S X would be $1.00 and if desired could be varied as M X S.

113

Coined Sentences

Initials of words in coined sentences or "sentence hooks" give the clue to the initials of words in a group which has to be remembered.

Anatomy

To remember the Cranial Nerves, use the following rhyme:

> On Old Olympia's Towering Top
> A Finn And German Vault And Hop.

The capital letters give the names of the nerves in the following order: Olfactory, Optic, Oculomotor, Trochlear, Trigeminal, Abducens, Facial, Auditory, Glosspharyngeal, Vagus, Accessory, Hypoglossal.

Epochs and Eras

These can be remembered by a key phrase:

Key phrase:	Careful	Men	Pay	Easily
Epochs:	Cenozoic	Mesozoic	Paleozoic	Eozoic

Music

A popular memory hook for musicians who start with the lines of the treble, the letters of which are E–G–B–D–F, is

> *E*very *G*ood *B*oy *D*eserves *F*avors.

The keys with sharps can be remembered by *GooD AlE* and *BeeF*. For keys in flats the reverse order must be taken.

Another sentence that signifies the same letters of the keys is *Go Down And Eat Blue Fish*. (G–D–A–E–B–F)

Mythology

The names of the nine muses can be remembered by the phrase "See, See, My Puttee," using phonetics for the first three letters, then all the letters in the final word, thus: C C M PUTTEE, each letter signifying the subsequent names: Calliope, Clio, Melpomene, Polyhymnia, Urania, Thalia, Terpsichore, Erato, Euterpe.

Planets of Solar Systems

These can be remembered in order, starting from the Sun and continuing outward, by the initial letters of words in a statement which match the initial letters in the names of the planets, as follows:

Men	....	Mercury
Very	....	Venus
Easily	....	Earth
Make	....	Mars
All	....	Asteroids
		(Minor Planets)
Jobs	....	Jupiter
Serve	....	Saturn
Useful	....	Uranus
Needs	....	Neptune
Promptly	....	Pluto

Prophets

The names of the Minor Prophets of the Bible can be remembered in the order of their Books, by the following key sentence:

How	Just	And	Obedient	Jonah	Made	Nineveh
Hosea	Joel	Amos	Obadiah	Jonah	Micah	Nahum

Rainbow

The names of the colors of the rainbow conform with the initial letters of words in the following key sentence:

Real Old Yokels Gorge Beef In Volumes
Red, Orange, Yellow, Green, Blue, Indigo, Violet

Coined Words

These resemble Acronyms and Acrostics in that they are formed from the capital letters of certain associated words. The chief difference is that the coined words considered here are simply memory tabs for individual groups of disordered facts. Often, too, they resemble or form existing words that have no direct bearing on the components, though sometimes they are singularly appropriate.

AID . . . Aeolic, Ionic, Doric.
                  Ancient Greek tribes.

AIDCA . . . Attention, Interest, Desire, Conviction, Action.
                  Elements of good advertising.

CABAL . . . Clifford, Ashley, Buckingham, Arlington, Lauderdale.
                  List of five ministers in reign of Charles II.

COGS . . . Class, Order, Genus, Species.
                  Zoology.

HOMES . . . Huron, Ontario, Michigan, Erie, Superior.
                  Great Lakes.

FACE . . . F–A–C–E, Musical Notes.
                  Names of spaces in treble clef.

F.BEAD . . . F–B–E–A–D, Musical Notes.
                  Names of keys with flats in them.

MACEY . . . Marie, Annette, Cecille, Emile, Yvonne.
                  Dionne quintuplets.

NEWS . . . North, East, West, South.
                  Geography, Points of the compass.

PAD . . . Pia, Arachnoid, Dura.

Anatomy. Membranes of the brain, from surface out.

PLAN . . . Pressure, Length, Area, Number of revolutions. Horsepower.

ROY G. BIV . . . Red, Orange, Yellow, Green, Blue, Indigo, Violet.

Colors of the spectrum: Name of imaginary man.

SLIDE . . . Sacral, Lumbar, Iliogastric, Dorsal, External cutaneous.

Anatomy. Nerves crossing iliac crest.

STAB . . . Soprano, Tenor, Alto, Bass.

Music. Quartette.

Letter Counts

These are accidental dodges or coined phrases in which the letters in certain words are counted, thereby obtaining an appropriate number. Hence the words, themselves, serve as memory devices.

Books of the Bible

The number of books in the Old and New Testament can be determined by a neat application of the number of letters in the word OLD (or NEW) and in TESTAMENT as follows:

Key words: OLD (or NEW) TESTAMENT
Letters: 3 *with* 9 = 39 Books in Old Testament
            3 × 9 = 27 Books in New Testament

Presidential Coincidence

This type of numerical coincidence is quite rare, so whenever one is encountered or noted, it should be pegged as a mental reminder.

Franklin Pierce was elected 14th President of the United States of America.

His name, FRANKLIN PIERCE, has 14 letters.

He was born at HILLSBOROUGH, N.H., which contains 14 letters.

He became PRESIDENT OF U.S.A., which is composed of 14 letters.

To Remember Numbers

Use the Letter Count device by coining a key sentence with each word containing a number of letters identical with each successive figure of the number to be remembered.

Mathematical Example:

To remember *Pi* to eight decimal places: 3.14159265

MAY I HAVE A LARGE CONTAINER

3 1 4 1 5   9

OF COFFEE CHEAP

2   6   5

Historical Dates:

Discovery of America: 1492

A SHIP DISCOVERS US

1   4   9   2

Declaration of Independence: 1776

A COUNTRY CREATES ITSELF

1   7   7   6

Lindbergh's flight from New York to Paris: 1927

A CHALLENGE TO COURAGE

1   9   2   7

Population Figures:

Washington, D. C., by 1960 census: 763,956

This system may be used as a substitute for the Figure Code or other mnemonic methods.

Personalized Memory Tokens

Various mementos or memory tokens have been used as personal reminders from antiquity on. While some of these at first may seem effective in recalling special events, duties, or chores, they dwindle in value when applied to different purposes, day by day.

Bells in miniature form have been attached at times to hats, so their jingle would annoy the wearer until he completed some set task for that day. Tiny bells also have been worn in lapels for the same purpose. These enjoyed a wave of popularity in a different way during the Gay Nineties, when they were manufactured by thousands in Connecticut as "chestnut bells" which party-goers wore and jingled mockingly whenever anyone told an old joke or "chestnut."

Colored Threads. These, too, were tied to lapels and represented things to do during the day. The colors were not hard to remember since they followed a regular order, as red, white and blue. The problem was to remember the things they signified, particularly when the color scheme was used over and over. The same applies to

Finger Strings. Some people still rely on this hackneyed device, tying a string around one finger, another string around the next, and so on. In this case, no colors are needed, as each finger represents a different item to be remembered. But the problem is the same. You look at your fingers and wonder what the strings around them mean. That applies even to a single string if the device is used too often. You are apt to remember yesterday's errand tomorrow, as there is no "tie-in" except that of the string itself.

119

Knot in Handkerchief. The expedient here is simply to tie a knot in the center or corner of a handkerchief as a reminder of something important. The handkerchief is then placed in a pocket or in some other convenient spot. Generally, the device is quite unreliable even if you don't forget the handkerchief itself. Sometimes you may come across two or three of them, all too late. Scarves have been used similarly.

Ring Turned Inward. This is perhaps the most famous of the lot, turning a finger ring, so that the stone or signet is toward the palm of the hand. It can be varied by changing the ring to another finger. It may serve as a brief reminder of some immediate duty; but like the other devices, it is very apt to be overlooked or its purpose may be forgotten if used too often.

Rhymes with Reason

Many rhymes and jingles serve as memory aids and the mere fact that they are chiefly learned by rote does not count appreciably against them. Often, they have proven their worth by test.

Among the most famous is

The Calendar Rhyme:

> Thirty days has September,
> April, June and November.
> All the rest have thirty-one
> Except February alone
> Which has twenty-eight in fine
> 'Til Leap Year gives it twenty-nine.

And as an added reminder:

> A year that will by four divide
> To be a Leap Year we decide.

Historical dates are sometimes versified, as:

> In fourteen hundred ninety-two
> Columbus sailed the ocean blue.

120

Number Rhyme and Rhythm. Large numbers, broken into small, can sometimes be remembered by a rhythmic jingle as:

> 369743869 broken into 369—743—869
> "Three-six-nine! Seven-four-three! Eight-six-nine!"

Musical Aid. In tuning a ukulele, this catch phrase can be sung:

> "My dog has fleas——"

Sing and Spell. Words of popular songs have occasionally incorporated the spelling of states or cities and thereby serve as memory jogs. Examples:

MISSISSIPPI: M—I—S——S—I—S——S—I—P—P—I!
CONSTANTINOPLE: Con—stan—tin—ople!
  or C—O—N—S——T—A—N—T——I—N—O—P——L—E!

Street Names. Jingles for memorizing street names are aptly covered by this gem from Philadelphia, which lists the streets going north and south by "hundred" blocks:

> Market, Arch, Race and Vine,
> Chestnut, Walnut, Spruce and Pine.

Weather Prognostications. These are well known and frequently quoted, as:

> Red in the morning, sailors take warning;
> Red at night, sailors delight.

> Evening red, morning gray,
> Sends the traveler on his way;
> Evening gray, morning red,
> Brings down rain upon his head.

> Mackerel sky and mare's-tails
> Make tall ships carry small sails.

> Ring around the moon
> Brings a storm soon.

121

Thunder in the forenoon
Showers in the afternoon.

Word Exaggerations

To remember the spelling of the word "Expense," think of it as spelled with the dollar sign:

EXPEN$E

This is a key to the use of "S" instead of "C."
Popular Definition. "Cash is necessary for *Success.*" Spell both as dollars and cents:

¢A$H = $U¢¢E$$

Most famous of insurance organizations: LLOYDS
Spelled *Lloyds* because they deal in pounds (L), pence (d) and shillings (s).
Key to word pronunciation. GHOTI spells FISH.
Among the oddities of the English language we find that:

The word ROU*GH* is pronounced as RU*FF*.	So GH = F
The word W*O*MEN is pronounced as W*I*MMEN.	So O = I
The word INI*TI*AL is pronounced INI*SH*AL.	So TI = SH
Added up, the letters *prove* that	GHOTI = FISH.

PRINCIPAL and PRINCIPLE. The *principal* thing to remember about spelling is that it often depends on simple *principles.* (This sentence illustrates the uses of the italicized words.)

7. READING

Reading is the best of all ways to acquire a wide range of knowledge; and it is the greatest of memory builders as well. In order to read at all, a person must first have memorized a fair

122

assortment of words and have them at instant call. From the reading process itself, new words are learned and impressions of them strengthened and mentally stored away for futue use. In short, memory constantly begets memory where reading is concerned.

There is a reason for this. New words form new associations; they create new pictures and stimulate imagery. The older, simpler words—and often some of the more complicated ones— become so familiar that they are absorbed as rapidly as punctuation marks. As a person learns to read faster and faster, he begins to reject some of the inconsequential and retain the more important material. Literally, "Weed while you read," becomes his motto.

There was once a common misconception that slow, painstaking readers learned more than rapid readers, who were often rebuked for their speed. Modern findings show that the opposite is the case. The plodding reader is so wrapped in his "word by word" process that he fails to catch the complete ideas that the fast reader grasps almost on sight.

Strongly suggestive proof that Americans have become fast readers is found in the vast number of books now printed and sold annually in this country. There seems to be almost no limit to their production, nor the eagerness of readers who devour them. America was a highly literate country when this modern surge began; and book consumption has increased despite the distractions of sports, travel and television. So it is very likely that rapid reading is here to stay.

To keep in pace, many people must speed their reading processes; and to move ahead, they should remember the essential things they read. If anything, this becomes easier as they proceed, because with proper rapid reading, absorption and memorization go hand in hand. The main reason is that rapid reading demands more concentration than the slow style. The fast reader delves deeply but more selectively, applies more concentration, and summons more of his own recollective processes to aid him in his task, leaving the plodder that much farther behind.

Preparatory Reading Techniques

Since you read to understand, you should aim for speed with comprehension. With newspaper reading and lighter forms of magazine and book reading, you can try forcing yourself to speed. Read phrases or whole sentences at a time, thus reducing the number of pauses per line. Develop a rhythm in moving the eyes quickly across the page and down to the next line.

Newspapers are printed in narrow columns especially to speed this process. Along with "spilling the beans" by giving the gist of the story in the lead paragraph, they follow through with concentrated comments and statements in the body of the story, often supplying catchwords that prove further aids to holding reader interest or allowing him to reject the remainder.

Magazines have adopted the narrow column as a help toward quick reading; and it is even found in some books. As you gain speed in reading such material, you will find that your eye runs down the column as well as across it, so that you practically zigzag your way from top to bottom. Practice thus gained helps to speed your reading of more serious material where longer lines are encountered.

Learn to spot a key or action word in a sentence; then to grasp two or three words in a group; and finally to read phrases or whole sentences at a time. In concentrating on this, look for significance or meaning, which may tie in with what follows. Thus you can retain the salient points of what you read; you do not just glimpse and forget.

Develop word recognition, by shape, sound and meaning. Analyze words, sentences and paragraphs. But do not let this hinder your aim toward faster reading. It is often better to check unfamiliar words and look up their meaning afterward, rather than waste time at the moment. The same applies to obscure or unwieldy sentences and overlong paragraphs. Come back to them later if need be.

Speed in reading can be developed *systematically* by applying the following processes, each of which begins with the letter "S" as a suitable reminder:

Selecting material to read, by sampling it to see if it is sufficiently new or useful to continue reading that book.

Skipping through a book or article to find wanted material or information, in order to concentrate on such.

Skimming a book for main ideas, examining and considering it as a whole, but without close reading.

Scanning to pick up main ideas, then giving close attention to their details to gain adequate understanding.

Some persons are already versed in certain of these methods, but often they do not use them to a full degree. Therefore, it is a good plan to practice them all, but often with special emphasis on the final pair (Skimming and Scanning) which have been more neglected than the others.

Added advice on *Speed Reading* includes the application of frequent or constant effort toward the following:

Reduction of eye pauses, which are regressions.

Moving of eyes only in reading, not the head.

Eliminating lip movements and speaking words aloud.

Guessing at meaning of unfamiliar words, at the same time tabbing them mentally for later reference.

Endeavoring to pick up thoughts quickly, even instantly as you proceed.

Avoiding use of pointers—such as pencil or finger tip—which slows the reading except when a visual problem exists.

Improve and expand your vocabulary as you read. This involves natural memorization along with special devices and is an absolute "must" where better and faster reading is concerned. Vocabulary development is treated as an individual subject in another chapter.

Experts have estimated that the average reader may run between 25 to 50 per cent below the speed of which he is capable. This is frequently due to the fact that the person does not read enough to develop proficiency and, in turn, is discouraged because he doesn't get enough out of it. An important step toward increased efficiency, therefore, is to read more, allowing additional time for it.

As with anything else, this will prove a time saver, as it means picking up the process faster, covering more ground through longer reading periods and thereby acquiring the reading habit. The reader should look for the main ideas in a story or article, subordinating lesser points.

This is done for the reader regularly in magazines of the "digest" type and the individual will find that he, too, can "edit" much of what he reads as he proceeds. This aids retention, because the emphasis is on related facts rather than side issues. It also improves the reader's ability at comprehension as, with each new book, he can increase his scope.

The reader can then place time limits on the assignments that he sets himself, gradually speeding the reading of new books without missing their more important context. There is, of course, a limit to such speed and this, in turn, can be determined by short tests, or work-outs. After getting a little way into a book, to acquire a sense of familiarity with it, the reader should speed up to his limit for a short, intensive period.

From this, he can estimate his potential where wordage is concerned and gauge his speed of comprehension accordingly. That becomes his pace for that type of reading, until he finds— through further tests—that he can get the same results still more rapidly. In any case, he turns a short-range trial into a long-range goal. Such purpose, together with its fulfillment, is an aid to deeper and more consistent concentration, which in its turn improves and strengthens all the contributing factors so far mentioned.

The basic principles of memory apply directly to reading. These principles are: Incentive, Attention, Observation, Association and Review. For reading efficiency, you may utilize all memory aids and mnemonic devices to help as needed.

Incentive includes the determination to read faster, along with a desire to remember and the intent to learn. You want to *know* and *remember* as a means toward achievement or advancement. In reading, make mastery of the substance your main goal.

Attention can be properly retained only when you are in the best of health. For reading, especially, have your eyes checked periodically by a physician and wear your correcting lenses as required. Have adequate light and choose an environment conducive to reading or study. Be comfortable, but not too comfortable, as the purpose is to relax but stay awake. Some persons study or read while walking around; others get up and exercise periodically to keep alert.

Concentration is a key to successful study and it demands attention to the exclusion of everything else. If your mind wanders, stop and begin your reading or study again. To avoid fatigue, it is advisable to space these periods, 60 to 90 minutes being the maximum for effectiveness.

Observation is held at peak through such procedure. It is also sharpened by considering small amounts of material at a time, so that the subject can be broken into reasonable lengths. By studying a variety of subjects in sequence periods, any lag of interest is avoided and danger of fatigue is lessened.

Association aims to link together the chain of principal ideas, as in the creation of a motion picture. The substance forming the basis of each of these ideas must first be analyzed, understood and tied in with facts already known to you, a process helped by forming vivid impressions throughout. Further help is sought in charts and illustrations. Where possible, free play is given to the emotions. Chronological arrangements are associated with facts. Definitions may require learning. For a series of unconnected dates, facts, or for any topics or ideas which must be recalled in that manner, you may resort to memory aiding devices as described in other sections of this book.

Review enables you to grasp and weigh the relationship of each part to the whole, thus strengthening the entire structure. Along with short, concentrated reading sessions, there should be equally frequent reviews. The most important thing is to finish the job; and review invariably encourages a renewal of that task.

This leads directly into the purpose of reading, as well as the classes of material involved. These include:

Reading for Pleasure

This affords excellent opportunity for experiment and improvement where rapid reading and retention are concerned. Fiction is frequently the type of reading chosen for relaxation and entertainment, which makes it all the easier.

Some novels, particularly the modern type, open with an intriguing scene that fairly carries the reader along, enabling him to speed his reading from the very start. Others must be taken more slowly in the early stages, to help establish locale as well as characters. This is often true of historical novels or others introducing places unfamiliar to the reader.

With important fiction, it is good to read a review, if available, thus learning enough about the book to plunge into it rapidly. Some books carry brief reviews or other comments on the jacket, thus pointing up the story. It is also a good plan to scan the first chapter or so of a book, noting names of characters and even jotting them down for reference, rather than have to "read back" in the story.

This is like the list of characters at the beginning of a play; and in recent years, such lists have been included at the front of many mystery stories, so the reader can follow them with the same absorbing interest. Simply tabbing the characters is usually sufficient, as they are frequently developed and given further delineation as the story progresses.

Though this type of reading is primarily for fun, it can be developed along lines of higher appreciation through the choice of finer fiction. In any case, smooth, fast reading often catches the tempo of the story, wherein the reader abandons himself to his emotions. Afterward, in review, it is easy to note how much of the story has been implanted in the memory.

In reading plays, the characters should be visualized, as in fiction; this enables the reader to supply actions that are not described but are understood. The lines should be considered in "breath groups," the number of words uttered in a single exhalation. Dialect should be read with "eyes and ears," transcribing the printed word into imaginary sound.

This applies to poetry, in which rhythm and meter should be noted, often as though the words were being recited, and with suggestions of sounds as well. All these are aids to later recollection.

Cultural Reading

With non-fiction books, covering travel, world affairs, history, biography, art, music, anything short of a technical or instructional work, the same rapid reading process may be applied but in a more concentrated form.

Here it is advisable to note the contents beforehand and take each chapter on an individual basis, especially when subject changes are involved. A book on travel, for example, may take you from one country to another, in which case, each should be located and surveyed, so to speak, before proceeding with it.

Similarly, each chapter should be summarized and reviewed before proceeding with the next. Later reviews can follow; and the book itself checked for any missing points. Here, special memory devices can be applied to good advantages. This has a two-way advantage: It not only enables you to recall what you have read more quickly; it may help you to decide which memory system is best adapted to your needs or how well a specific system works.

Factual reading of an interesting sort may be interwoven with fiction of a serious type, sometimes with direct results. A biography of George Washington, for example, would form an excellent complement to a historical novel of the American Revolution. In many cases of this sort, reading for pleasure is combined with cultural reading to the benefit of both.

Books and articles dealing with personal problems come into this category and can often be supplemented by fiction devoted to the subjects under consideration. In all such reading, notes should be made of unknown or unfamiliar words and their meaning should be checked in the dictionary at the first convenient opportunity.

Informative Reading

This is a category all its own. It covers current events, as given in newspapers and magazines, but it is found increasingly in the book field as well. The essential method in such reading is to use discrimination judiciously and with attention. A mere glance at the title or the first few paragraphs enables the reader to decide whether to read on.

Newspapers set the pace for this. They use "heads" in big type to catch the eye. They follow with "leads" in the form of paragraphs that tell enough of the story for the reader to continue with the details or skip the account entirely. Various "news" magazines have adopted the same policy; whether for better or for worse is a question of individual viewpoint.

Most certainly, any individual can profit by using the same formula, but applying it to his own personal needs and profiting proportionately. In reading informative material, break it down into the journalistic categories of "Who—Which—What" that refer to a person or thing, and "Where—When—Why—How" covering the place, time, reason or method.

This is epitomized in the story of the schoolteacher who was told never to give her pupils a lead to the answer of an examination question. Shortly before, she had told the class about the siege of ancient Troy, where the Greek champion, Achilles, chased the Trojan hero, Hector, three times around the city's walls.

So, in her examination questions, the teacher included this gem: "Who chased whom how many times around the what of where?"

Self-Improvement

This demands the maximum effort of study and therefore cannot be covered by ordinary speed reading methods. Two techniques that have gained prominence in this field are:

The SQ3R, also known as the SURVEY Q3R formula, which follows these five steps:

SURVEY: Examine headings for core ideas.

QUESTION: Turn headings into questions based on your knowledge of what the author is trying to convey.

The Three R's

Read to find the answer of each question.

Recite each answer, in your own words, after it has been obtained. Check the book, if necessary, and write a brief cue, thus forming an outline while reading.

Review: Examine notes as a whole, reviewing main and subpoints. Recite these and check if correct.

The PQRST Formula

The PQRST Formula follows a similar pattern, designating its five points as: Preview, Question, Read, State, Test.

For an efficient formula of your own, proceed as follows:

Preview the book by studying its essential elements.

Skim through its chapters for headings, summaries or key paragraphs and sentences.

Read systematically at a steady, properly established pace, concentrating on more important facts to be remembered.

Compare the whole, as you have defined it, with the individual parts as you cover them, thus forming the final picture.

Memorize important features but do not clutter them.

Associate ideas as you absorb them, taking advantage of the natural memory, so that a chain of ideas is linked in succession.

Review material, linking chapter by chapter.

8. VOCABULARY

The development of a good vocabulary is of great importance; and in this endeavor, memory plays the key part. Command of language, which depends so much upon the knowledge of words, directly involves the application of memory. Words are the symbols of ideas that they transmit, like the picture writing of the ancients. Hence words should be visualized, as pictures of their own, or in terms of the ideas they express.

The two major types of vocabulary are the *Vocal* and the *Reading*. The Vocal is also known as the *Use Vocabulary,* as it serves for every day expression in speech; while the Reading Vocabulary is called the *Recognition Vocabulary* because, through it, we learn to recognize words, whether or not they form part of the vocal vocabulary.

The Reading Vocabulary is more extensive than the Vocal; sometimes too much so. Instead of using words they already know, many people devote their time to learning new ones through reading. Thus their improvement in conversation fails to keep pace with their increasing knowledge.

Words may be learned through hearing as well as reading, which is why listening to lectures and attending dramatic presentations has a very broadening influence. Hearing words you already know but seldom use is a stimulus toward including them in your own vocal vocabulary. It is also a help toward pronunciation, a stumbling block with people who recognize words that they read but do not know how to say them.

In subconscious speech and rapid writing, the Reading Vocabulary is often used. This accounts for the way an orator goes into impressive or sometimes flowery phrases and how authors develop a literary style. The fact that Basic English requires only 850 words for the expression of ideas, whereas the unabridged dictionary contains some 500,000 terms, allows considerable leeway between the spoken and the written language.

As preliminary to increasing your own vocabulary, it is a good plan to estimate its size. Take a large abridged dictionary, say of about 150,000 words, and turn to a typical page representing each letter, excluding X. Avoid pages where the words have the same beginnings, as "anti" or "re."

Count the number of words you recognize on each of those 25 pages. Add them up and divide by 25 to strike an average. Multiply that by the total number of vocabulary pages in the dictionary. The result will be your approximate vocabulary. Don't worry if you miss the exact mark. Estimates of Shakespeare's vocabulary run from 15,000 to 24,000 words, which is a lot of leeway. By modern standards, of course, it might have run a great deal higher, due to the tremendous increase in words since Shakespeare's time.

Sources for new words include the speech of people whom you know or meet, daily newspapers and weekly news magazines; various types of informative reading; and finally dictionaries and other lexicons.

Dictionaries serve a double purpose: That of checking new words that you have heard or read, and also finding new words on your own. In the first instance, do not delay or you will pile up a backlog of words that may be forgotten before you look them up. In studying new words, some people read two pages of a dictionary daily, considering each word even if it is already known. Another plan is to look for words related to those that you have just learned.

Here lists of synonyms, or words expressing the same idea, and antonyms, or words with opposite meanings, prove themselves worthy of study. Special lexicons have been composed of these; and a thesaurus, or dictionary of related words and ideas, is also highly helpful.

Words are fixed in the mind by the processes of *Observation, Association,* and *Repetition,* three functions which play such an important part in all memory work. In vocabulary building, observation is chiefly a prelude to what follows. You hear or see a word and, immediately upon learning its meaning, you go into the next process, association, which is of prime importance.

Association demands the immediate linking of a new word with an old, familiar word whenever possible. A knowledge of word roots—Latin, Greek, French, German, Spanish and other languages—is very helpful here. Often, however, you can find other word sources of a political, historical, colloquial, or scientific nature. You can also work from derivatives themselves.

For example, the word "automobile." Some people feel that the automobile never should have been invented, and most definitely, that it should not have been given that name. Literally, it means "self-moving" but the "auto" comes from the Greek and the "mobile" from the Latin, a combination that must have shocked conservative scholars of the early 1900s more than the sight of a snorting automobile itself.

Remember that and, whenever you encounter a word like auto-suggestion or automation, you will know that the "auto" refers to self while anything containing "mobile," such as the mobilization of troops or a mobile home, means that it is movable. Many words may thus be learned without studying the language from which they originally came.

Many words link automatically, as "fence" and "defence"; and, with these as patterns, you can often form associations that are logically correct, even though their sources vary; for example, "dens" in a "dense" jungle. All this involves ideas where words are concerned; and since words must be regarded as ideas, it becomes all the more helpful.

Mark Twain once remarked that the first man who ever saw a hippopotamus must have taken just one look and said: "Ah! That is a hippopotamus." The reason, so Mark Twain avowed, was that you can't think of a hippopotamus as anything else. From the visualization standpoint, he was right. The word is as clumsy as the beast itself, even though its correct definition, from the Greek, is "river horse."

Words like "splash" and "puff" suggest meanings by their sounds. So do "bang," "ping," "roar," and "boom." From "boom" there is a direct link to "bomb," a device which explodes with a loud sound. From "bomb" there is an associated link to "bombast" which refers to loud, boastful talk.

From "jingle," which expresses a ringing sound, you can imagine temple bells in a "jungle," thus gaining an image of the latter. A man in a *dudgeon,* or state of rage, should be put in a *dungeon* or cell, going from "high dudgeon" into a "deep dungeon" as the terms are commonly applied.

This brings us to words which are frequently confused with each other, as *stalactite* and *stalagmite.* The "tite" suggests "teeth" in sound and thereby identifies "stalactite" as the long, sharper formation hanging like an icicle from the ceiling. Another way is to picture the *stalactite* as *tight* to the ceiling; the stalag*mite,* a mere *mite* on the cavern floor.

Words that are pronounced alike but spelled differently cause even more difficulties, but there are many ways of handling these, often by use of certain catch phrases involving one or both of the words.

Here are some examples:

Waist——waste

Think of the phrase "*Haste* makes *waste*" in which the spelling is the same.

Stationery——stationary

You write (with an E) on stationery (with an E).
Whatever stands (with an A) is stationary (with an A).

It's——its

It is consists of two words, which, when contracted, require an apostrophe, becoming *it's*. Just as *he is* becomes *he's*.

Its means "belonging to it" just as *his* means "belonging to him." No one writes *hi's* for *his*. So *don't* write *it's* for *its*.

Peace—piece

When wars *cease,* we have *peace* (similar spelling).
When we have *pie,* I'd like a *piece* (similar spelling).
This link of "pie" and "piece" is also important as the exception to the following rule covering words spelled with "ei" and "ie." The rule runs:

> Put I's before E's
> Excepting with C's
> Or when sounded like A
> As in "neighbor" or "weigh."

Thus words like *believe, relieve, grief, thief, chief* (in which "ch" is an individual sound), *liege* and *frieze,* all have "I" before "E."

Words like *deceit, receipt, receive, perceive,* all have "E" before "I" because of the "C." So does the word *seize,* which is pronounced like C's.

That leaves *piece* as an exception; and also *niece*. In both of these, the "I" and "E" are before the "C." That puts them in the "I" before "E" class.

Words like *neigh, sleigh, freight* all sound like "A," so they are "E" before "I." But you must make an exception with *height,* remembering that it is associated with *weight* and therefore should be spelled much the same. Another exception is *weird,* but such a word would never conform to any rule. Naturally not; or rather, unnaturally not.

Many people are bothered by the "I and E" question with the words siege and seize. They can be remembered by the statements that:

> Arm*ie*s are bes*ie*ged in cit*ie*s.   (Repeated "ie")
> V*e*ss*e*ls are s*e*iz*e*d on the s*e*as.   (Repeated e's)

Many words using GHT can be remembered by such "keys" as STRAIGHT, WEIGHT, and NIGHT.

> There was a type of automobile called a *Straight Eight.*
> All *freight* is shipped by *weight.*
> Creatures take *fright* at *night.*
> *Fight* for the *right,* with all your *might.*

Here, words that are spelled similarly are paired, or clustered, forming memory jogs to one another. This prevents confusion between such words as *straight* and *strait, eight* and *ate, weight* and *wait, right* and *rite, might* and *mite.* Those other words can then be studied for their own meanings.

Other interesting words are those beginning with the letters W—R, as *write.* All denote action, mostly with the hands and body, such as *wrench, wrestle, writhe, wring, wrap.* Even such words as *wrist, wreath, wrath* and *wreck* seem logically related. It is a good plan to go through such groups, visualizing, comparing the different words and noting any exceptions, which sometimes stand out all the more.

Give sounds to words and exaggerate their spelling. Take "grate" and think of it as "grr*AAA*tte" with a *grating* sound. You will then have no trouble remembering its meaning and its spelling as pictured; thus it can always be distinguished from "great."

As a final note, when telling "which from which" where words are concerned, don't become careless and spell the word "which" as "wich" or "witch." If you do, you will definitely become be*witch*ed, and don't forget it!

Many more examples could be given, but it is better for each person to proceed with his own study of various words, thus handling any slight difficulties as they are encountered. Try to feel words, to sense some emotional effect as you use them. When thought is given to this, persons frequently find that they are already doing so, perhaps unknowingly.

Verbs, for example, rouse thoughts of action. Words like *run, fight, hurry, look* create a natural response. If they are uttered aloud, under certain circumstances, people who hear them are apt to follow the suggestion automatically. This shows definitely that the mental impulse is already there.

Adjectives produce rounded, developed impressions, adding dimensions to ideas. The word *golden* may bring a glow to the mind; *horrible,* a flash of leering faces; *balmy,* the sensation of a light breeze. These are words that stir emotions; and adjectives add much to poetry. They are easily acquired and therefore valuable to a vocabulary, but care must be taken to avoid trite, overworked expressions.

Nouns, as the names of things, furnish concrete ideas. Speech, through the use of verbs and other nouns, tells what is happening to those things. Nouns should be sought for broadening of your own interests and the acquisition of knowledge. Often it works the other way about; as interests increase, you learn the names of more things. Do not overlook them, as the closer they are to things you already know, the easier they are to remember and the more valuable they may prove to be.

That is because words must be used to retain a place in an individual vocabulary. Words that are noted only passingly, or which are immediately discarded, are not normally needed. For example, there are lists of literally hundreds of words that simply mean the verb "to say"—words such as *stated, spoke, announced, related, parried, predicted, exclaimed,* and so on. In fact, a whole book of such words has been compiled, along with shaded meanings and adverbs that go with them.

Such words are invaluable to writers who want to embellish and enliven the dialogues in their stories. You may have read many of them, time after time but, unless you are a writer, there are few such words that you need recall actively. They are the very sort of words that can be skipped, or noted much like punctuation marks, nothing more. They are used to round out the text but not to be implanted in the reader's memory.

That stresses the final point in vocabulary building:

Repetition, which in this case means use. Many people speak, read, hear or write thousands of words a day; and often these follow a somewhat general pattern. Therefore, familiarity with many words becomes ingrown, a matter of habit, a demonstration of how strongly instantaneous memory may function in our lives.

To attempt to learn new words by mere rote would therefore be futile, since you do not intend to recite them, like a poem. In fact, such efforts at rote would waste valuable time that could be spent in learning usable words that would develop through the repetitive qualities of normal speech.

So the *use* of new words, *repeatedly,* is a sure way to help *remember* them. Often, however, uncommon words need to be remembered. The best way is to keep notes of them and refer to these repeatedly. Also recommended is a persistent study of the dictionary, emphasizing new words that are unfamiliar but which you judge to be currently useful.

Noticeable results can be obtained from this if you make certain to use a few such words in a sentence written or spoken the same day, or before you have forgotten the words. In short, put them to use to strengthen them through the normal process of repetition and also to test their practical value. Your purpose is not to show off your vocabulary by spieling erudite terms that go above the heads of your listeners, but to bring that speaking vocabulary up to the standard of your recognized knowledge and capability.

Once you have acquired the dictionary habit, use it to review doubtful words that you have encountered, in addition to learning those that are unfamiliar. If you can find time and proper company, engage in word games as vocabulary builders. If alone, use that same spare time in working cross-word puzzles and other word challenges in handy newspapers and magazines.

There is no limit to the world of words. Whatever is new in outer space, when man finally discovers it he will find a name for it as well.

9. DICTION

Poetry, Prose, Speeches, Lectures, Dramatic Acting

There is a close relationship between poetry, prose, oratory and drama where memorization is concerned. Some persons, however, are singularly adept at remembering one class of material, even to the point of genius. Any such inclination naturally establishes a *motive* for memorization. Many persons have learned to recite poetry, for example, simply because they showed an early flair for it.

Special motives are frequently responsible. One person may like poetry and therefore want to learn it; another may be called upon to give impromptu talks or make speeches; still another may have ambitions to become an actor and must therefore concentrate upon memorizing lines. Additional motives may include a desire for popularity, self-improvement, or a spirit of competition.

Once a positive motive has been established, attention and concentration must be cultivated. *Observation* and formation of *associations* also play an important role in memorization for purposes of diction, along with a correct understanding of *repetition* as distinguished from mere rote.

Memorization of Poetry

This forms a basic pattern for remembering material *verbatim* because the rhyme, the meter, and each verse or stanza, all carry the mind along its way, providing memory jogs in the process.

Song lyrics have the additional advantage of musical associations to facilitate memorization. Some prose has a poetic quality which allows it to be remembered much as verse would be. While other prose is lacking in this quality, the same basic rules of memorization apply, though the task may be more difficult.

Rote was once used almost exclusively in the memorization of poetry on the theory that if a pair of lines could be committed to memory, singsong fashion, so could the next and the next and so on, until the entire poem was learned. Such a process frequently proved difficult, time consuming and, worst of all, untrustworthy before an audience. Often the slightest hitch can throw a rote-memorized poem completely from its track.

Learning a long recitation by rote is akin to the story of the strong man who found that he could lift a baby elephant. So he kept lifting it day by day on the theory that, by the time the elephant grew up, he would still be lifting it the same way and would be the only man in the world who could lift a full-grown elephant. There can be limits to learning as well as lifting when brute force is the only factor.

In memorizing poetry, form and structure should be noted, along with such mechanical points as rhyme and rhythm, while first reading through the entire poem to gain a full picture of its principal ideas. These should be reviewed in sequence to make sure that they are fully understood. Any obscure or doubtful

141

words and references should then be checked in a dictionary or other suitable source.

Specially accented words should be noted, along with those contracted into single syllables. Alliteration and other repetitions of sounds, words, or thoughts should be given consideration. During such analysis, key words can be sought out for each stanza, effort being made to reduce these to a comparative few.

If this is done methodically and without haste, the result is that the poem is actually being learned in whole, through natural links, without artificial aids.

As a simple example, note the first verse of the classic poem, "The Village Blacksmith."

> Under a *spreading* chestnut tree,
> The village *smithy* stands.
> The smith, a *mighty* man is he,
> With large and *sinewy* hands;
> And the muscles of his *brawny* arms
> Are strong as *iron bands*.

From the key words in the second, third, fourth and fifth lines, we gain an alliterative effect, *smithy, mighty, sinewy, brawny* almost rhyming in their own right, like a verse within a verse. Later, the single word *smithy* will serve as the key word for the complete stanza, linking it to the next.

With *logic* forming the basic structure, *rote* can be utilized to advantage, not just in parrot-like fashion. Rote is useful in committing to memory certain passages that lack strong associations or must be given forced ones. Then rote-learned phrases may come to mind as a carry-over.

One effective method for memorizing material is to read it aloud, *as a whole,* paying strict attention to its meaning. This is repeated immediately, for a total of three times, so that rote helps logic implant the material in mind. After an interval of at least six hours, the entire operation is repeated, again three times over.

142

With short poems or selections, four readings may be done at each sitting, three times a day. But with longer recitations, approaching an hour's duration, only two sessions are possible. In any case, early morning and late evening are the preferred times.

Each reading should be done carefully, keeping in mind the relation of each part to the whole and paying more attention to the weak parts. From 10 to 20 days may be required for memorization, dependent somewhat on the length or difficulty of the material.

The superiority of the "whole" method of learning over the "part" method is accepted by many, despite the fact that tackling a long poem or oration in full may seem hopeless or too formidable to persons who have never tried it. Its great value is that it succeeds better in keeping the material intact and properly placed, so there is little danger of skipping stanzas.

There is a method, however, where that can be accomplished while learning a poem by parts. Learn the first verse; then the second; after that, repeat the first and second together until they are well linked. Next, learn the third; then repeat the second and third together. Next, learn the fourth; repeat the third and fourth together; and so on.

The same process can be used with prose, by learning sentences and paragraphs in interlocking pairs. It can also be applied to dramatic lines. After all the parts have thus been mastered, the whole selection can be recited as a unit and any weak parts stressed and strengthened.

Such "part" learning is advantageous when a person's time is too limited to use the "whole" method. It is also suited to anyone who tends to tire after short periods of concentration, and whose attention and observation will thereby lag if he goes beyond his capacity. In attempting to ease the task, he is apt to resort to rote at the expense of logic. Rote, in itself, may cause the mind to drift or wander.

Much may be gained by a judicious combination of various

methods. If the material proves too long, break it down to smaller portions according to basic thoughts, but read the whole frequently.

Very often, in the first reading of a poem, the overall survey shows that it breaks into logical sections which provide a natural sequence.

As an example, America's national anthem, the *Star Spangled Banner,* has four verses, each with a distinct theme:

1. Is the flag still flying above the fort?
2. The flag is seen flying there.
3. The attacking host has departed, thwarted.
4. The significance of the triumph is discussed.

By fixing these in mind at the outset, each verse can be learned separately, with little danger of omission when reciting the entire poem.

With some poems, it is possible to formulate an appropriate theme, even though it is not actually expressed. Once that has been incorporated as a series of idea pictures, it is easier to decide how to learn the selection most effectively.

In Poe's *Bells,* there are four stanzas, each dealing with a different type of bells and their significance: (1) Silver sleigh bells, (2) golden wedding bells, (3) brazen alarm bells, (4) iron funeral bells.

These can be recalled in order by picturing (1) A happy courtship during the sleigh ride; (2) the marriage of the couple; (3) a fire in their home, years later; (4) the death of one, still later. Each stanza may then be learned singly.

Further assistance in the learning of poetry can be found in artificial aids to memory; and one of the better ones for poetic purposes is a *Topical System.* Its use was aptly described by Professor L. A. Post of Haverford College in *The Classical Weekly* for February 1, 1932. Here is his account of how he helped his nine-year-old son commit a poem to memory:

144

The poem to be learned was Heman's *The Landing of the Pilgrim Fathers,* as given in a school textbook of English. It has ten stanzas of four lines each. The first stanza is as follows:

"The breaking waves dashed high
On a stern and rock-bound coast,
And the woods against a stormy sky
Their giant branches tossed."

The instructions I gave my son for learning follow.

"Put this verse on the porch of 1 College Lane. You know what the porch looks like. Now you see the breaking waves dash high at one side of it. You see them break—then dash—so high that they wet the porch roof. See now just to the right a stern and rock-bound coast. You can remember that it is stern because there is the stern of a wrecked ship showing among the waves. You also see the rocks. Now behind the rocks on the coast you see a mass of green woods and a dark sky with flashes of lightning showing. The woods are leaning to the right against the sky. The woods are tossing their branches. You see them moving furiously up and down, and among the branches you see a giant. Now, repeat the stanza seeing the pictures."

When the first stanza had thus been accurately connected with a series of pictures seen in the frame of 1 College Lane, the second stanza was pictured on the lawn at the side of 2 College Lane. The porch was not chosen this time, because it was not sufficiently different from the porch of 1. The second stanza does not lend itself to vivid picturization. Consequently arbitrary symbols were used for enough words to recall the lines. The stanza runs as follows:

"And the heavy night hung dark
The hills and waters o'er,
When a band of exiles moored their bark
On the wild New England shore."

It would be possible to put a symbol for each word, but that was not found necessary in practice. A vague picture of hills and waters in the nighttime was enough, supplemented by two symbols. To suggest

145

the first word "and" a red hand was planted against the dark sky, and for "heavy" a yellow spring scale, fully stretched, was placed to the right of it. This was enough: the boy actually recalled the first two lines, with no other assistance. The stanza was completed by a single picture for the last two lines with no artificial symbols.

> "Not as the conqueror comes
> They the true-hearted came,
> Not with the roll of the stirring drums
> And the trumpet that sings of fame."

The third stanza was represented at the back of 3 College Lane, which happened to be a familiar playground. Here it was enough to picture a procession in honor of a conqueror; some members of the procession were to wear conspicuous blue hearts on their jackets, some to roll drums on the ground in front of them, others to sing through trumpets. The key word "not" was remembered by stamping mentally a large green representation of a knotted rope of huge size against the background to the left of the pictures.

The other verses were represented in the same way against familiar backgrounds taken in order. It took about five minutes to learn a stanza. Some phrases were recalled with little effort. Those that proved elusive were provided with special symbolic images so that in a very short time the poem was learned accurately, and any stanza could be recited, by number, without confusion. It was still necessary to repeat the poem at intervals to ensure its permanent acquisition.

Memory images fade away rapidly if they are not repeatedly recalled but, once the poem is learned, the fading of the images is an advantage. The verbal memory is still retained, and the same backgrounds may be used for another poem. The pupil soon learns to use his own code adapted to his special needs. As proficiency is attained by practice, less machinery is needed. In any case the machinery of pictorial imagination works with such accuracy and speed that its actual operation is not nearly so clumsy as the attempt to describe it. There can be no doubt that individuals differ greatly in their ability to utilize such a system.

Localized memory methods of this nature were used by Cicero and other ancient orators. This is a reminder that *Topical Systems* are particularly valuable in remembering prose. For example, Memory Rooms can be imagined, each with 10 places for key words; and a "prompter" word can be tied in with each place.

The same can be applied to the stanzas of a poem, with five rooms taking care of 50 stanzas. Blank verse may be treated 6 to 8 lines at a time, each group in the manner of a stanza.

A good device for linking stanzas or prose paragraphs is to tie in the last word of one with the first word of the next. With poetry, this may require the use of linking nouns and, sometimes, ideas as expressed in the respective lines. The same applies to prose, but is often more flexible.

More practical, however, is the device of connecting key words, each representing a stanza or paragraph, according to whether poetry or prose is involved. If the selection itself has been well learned, this should be enough to bring up the next idea in complete form. These can be linked into an unbreakable chain.

The 100-Word Code, described previously, can be applied to the memorization of poetry or prose by associating each key word of the code with a key idea of the selection to be memorized. This can be done line by line, verse by verse; or sentence by sentence, paragraph by paragraph. As each is recalled in turn, the material represented is recreated.

In reviewing memorized material, points of hesitation or error should be worked on further. You may refer to the text at such times. Memorizing, reciting, reviewing are best done before retiring, and should be repeated in the morning. Sessions of 15 to 30 minutes are generally well tolerated. Rereading the original text from time to time is wise, as errors are bound to creep in.

Orations, and other prose selections that must be delivered word for word, follow the memorization rules that apply to poetry.

There is a similarity between poetic expression and the flow of oratory, particularly when both are of a classic type. But other factors apply in the modern delivery of

Speeches and Lectures

Except in cases where a speech or lecture must conform precisely to a text, *verbatim* memorization should be utilized only when specially necessary, as in quoting a passage or repeating a speech of a well-known orator of the past.

The most popular speech of today is the *extemporaneous* type. This requires thorough preparation in advance, though it avoids the constraints of verbatim memorization. It is delivered with or without notes. The speaker must, to borrow a few punch expressions, really "know" his subject and be able to "sell" it.

The *spur of the moment* speech differs from the extemporaneous in that little time is given for its preparation, though it does not have to be entirely unprepared. You generally know in advance the nature of the group you are to meet. You can thus anticipate what you should talk about briefly, if called upon, and this allows opportunity to study up or review facts on the subject. You can also consider the introductory and closing remarks, appropriate anecdotes, and make mental notes or check recent statistics pertinent to your intended possible discourse.

The *extemporaneous speaker* should prepare himself in a general way by learning the fundamentals of public speaking and practicing them as much as possible. Methods of speaking, expression, gestures, all other factors must be developed.

Specific preparation applies to the topic itself. It must be studied and reviewed; it should also be researched. As you become more certain of your facts, you become more certain of your speech. In mastering the topic, your vocabulary on the subject should be built up as well.

Speech making and delivery take advantage of *natural memory* but, while practicing, *artificial aids* may prove of initial

148

value. They can be discarded as soon as the natural memory takes over, after they have assured security and have cut down learning time.

In preparing an *outline,* aim to stay within the time limits of the talk. While 45 to 60 minutes is a practical approach, shorter talks are apt to be more effective. In the outline, the main ideas are arranged as a skeleton to form logical associations, each section having appropriate subheads. The speech should be brisk, informative and well-ordered, with uncommon words properly defined. A *first draft* can be made from this outline.

This is put aside for a day or two, then re-examined and a *second draft* prepared. This should be in complete form, orderly, well-balanced, with the introduction trim and pointed, the finish vigorous and aimed toward creating applause. The second draft can be discussed with interested persons and suggested changes made. A final reading and new outline are then made, with key thoughts listed and studied as links to the text.

More assurance is given to *natural memory* by putting the outline on 3 x 5 inch cards, which are numbered, given large headings and smaller subheads, then arranged in order. These should include opening and closing notes, as well as statistics, and quotations. The cards should be set aside once the speaker is sure of them, with the exception of statistics and quotes. But, if need be, they can all be kept in the pocket for emergency.

The simplest plan is to rehearse with the cards handy for reference, to learn how much they are needed, up to the very time of the speech. One great help in modern speechmaking is the use of a tape recorder, from which you can hear a playback of your own voice and make changes accordingly.

Artificial memory aids for extemporaneous speeches take the form of key words covering each idea, opinion, anecdote, or argument, forming a skeletonized version in itself. These are made into concrete words, being exaggerated as required, and then utilized in one of the following ways:

Topical Method. Each key word is tied in with a series of objects in the lecture hall, or in the room where the speech was rehearsed. Other topical devices may also be used.

Linking Chain. Link the ideas represented by key words in a sequence of combination pictures: Number 1 with 2, 2 with 3, 3 with 4, and so on.

Mnemonic Code Words. Associate each key word with a word of the "mental hook" type, as listed elsewhere. If there are no more than 10 key words, one of the various systems may be used; with more, it is better to use the "100-Word Code List."

Acrostic words may sometimes be formed from the initial letters of each key word in sequence, making a simple, effective list, the equivalent of an alphabetic reference.

In delivering the speech, keep in mind that your audience is interested in *ideas,* not exact *words*. Watch your listeners for their reactions; repeat or add stronger arguments if those seem necessary. If the audience shows signs of tiring, omit further portions of your talk, shortening it proportionately.

When in doubt, don't "clear your throat" or give yourself away by some other slight nervous habit. Make a few "ad lib" remarks while finding a chance to pick up the chain where you left off.

Dramatic Acting

Performing on the stage requires the adept memorization of poetry, prose, oratory, and most of all, conversational portrayal. Verbatim memorization is generally essential, although ad libbing is allowed in some situations and is often used to pick up a lost continuity or fill in a stage wait.

The basic principles of efficient memorization apply to acting: motive, attention, observation, association are all important; and particularly *repetition,* since *verbatim* memorizing is involved.

The element of *emotion* is very significant in an actor's memo-

150

rization process. To impart it, he must feel it, without letting it overwhelm him. He must judge the character to be portrayed, then try to reproduce attitudes and facial expressions. He then abandons himself to the part he plays, fitting his words to imaginary moods, with suitable tones and glances, even visualizing objects about him as actual people.

Strong motive usually dominates an actor's work, stimulating his natural memory. In memorizing parts, he may use this pattern: A *silent reading* of the part, repeated several times for familiarity. A *reading aloud,* also repeated, allowing a projection, which should improve each time. *Memorization* of each portion, as with poetry stanzas or prose paragraphs. A *rehearsed reading* with members of the company or a director.

Short lines may prove harder to memorize because, with long lines, an actor may build many associations, physical as well as mental. With shorter lines, he may need artificial memory aids. This also applies to picking up his own words or action from *cues* provided in the final line or word spoken by another actor. The cue can be linked with the first word of the actor's own line, forming a mental picture as with other types of memory work.

Often, some gesture will help pick up or carry a line. Actual learning of parts should be spread over several days and rehearsals, held as needed, including periods between shows, to keep closer to a uniform performance. Many elements of memory are adjuncts to acting, including motor memory, memory for music, poetry, prose and oratory, so a study of all is helpful.

10. LANGUAGE MEMORY

Memory plays an important part in learning languages, particularly for the adult who must pick up a new vocabulary and retain it as he goes along. With almost everyone, the mere desire to learn a foreign language is reason enough to pursue its study;

but, with the desire, there must be the ability to observe words, concentrate on them and associate them with the ideas they represent, along with customs, manners, and people.

Some persons are natural born linguists and may even learn more than one language in their youth. Others—and this applies to the large majority—must acquire new languages through sheer perseverance and arduous study. However, their aim, especially in this global age, is one and the same. All want to be able to think, talk, read and write in the foreign language.

An ideal way to learn a foreign language is to live in a country where it is spoken exclusively. This requires thinking in the language in order to speak it, as the only means of self-expression. You learn it as the people themselves have learned it and you remember it through a series of natural memory patterns.

This extended stay in a foreign land may not be possible, however, so other equivalents must be utilized. One way is to associate with people who speak the language frequently or constantly; other ways can be through adult education groups and cultural programs.

Since these are not always possible, the best and most modern substitute is the use of records or tapes, such as an audio-visual course which links the spoken word with actual objects. This has the advantage of constant availability, which is not always the case with foreign language movies or foreign radio programs, though those have strong supplementary value, especially in the advanced stages.

But it is the early stages which are the most important. To think and speak a language, you must immerse yourself in it, learning the manner of speaking it, the sounds, intonations, rhythm, even the music of the language, as well as its meaning. The method should be functional, gaining comprehension without translation. In short, you learn the language in itself, avoiding English in the process, or, for that matter, any language except the one you are trying to acquire.

In this natural and efficient method, you combine learning, or the fixing upon an idea, with memory, or the retention of that idea. Through this combination, you can aim for a working vocabulary of 1500 of the most commonly used words, gaining that goal by degrees as a real start toward effective use of the language itself.

The suggested order of learning consists first in speaking, then in reading, and later in writing. This is exemplified by the audio-visual approach, which works as follows:

Spoken words are learned by listening to those most frequently used and at the same time looking at pictures which illustrate the spoken words or phrases. You *hear* the language while you *see* the picture; hence the term audio-visual. Grammatical rules are avoided at this stage.

After having just heard the words and seen the picture, you speak the words themselves in imitation of the native voice. Going over the same words and pictures repeatedly, establishes the details more clearly and leads to accurate acquisition of each spoken word.

Reading is begun after a considerable series of spoken phrases and action pictures have been mastered. Here, again, as part of the logical process, the reading is applied to a special text accompanying the voice and pictures. This combines *reading, viewing* and *hearing,* again without resort to English.

Writing consists of copying what has been read, while listening to the spoken words. This is done picture by picture, referring to the text at first, then learning to put the spoken words directly into writing, as in dictation, checking with the text later. The speed or pace with which these steps are acquired depends upon the individual.

Dialogue forms an important part of audio-visual training, and grammatical study follows along as required. In short, the training simulates the natural learning procedure that builds the comprehension necessary for progress in the language, just as in

153

English. During the primary stages, reference to a dictionary is a last resort.

Close contact with a language and the repeated hearing of its most common words are the positive and obvious ways of learning it, as is emphasized by the fact that in small countries, or along borders, people speak two or three languages. The Swiss are examples of this; and Poland is famous for linguists who can speak six or seven languages.

Many people in India and the Far East speak more than two languages. Children who hear their parents speaking a foreign language at home may not try to speak it until they have been schooled in the language of the country. Then, one day, most unexpectedly, they may speak quite well in the language their parents have been using at home. These are not prodigies; they are natural, average children who have been listening and absorbing while memory did the rest.

It is clearly desirable that children should be encouraged and taught more than one language. They readily learn to think and play in a language other than their native tongue. Youth is going to find a need for these languages and it is during the early years that children should learn to use this potential power. It is a great intellectual stimulant for them to be able to converse with people of other nations in other tongues. Though they may not immediately require these languages, memory will recall the words for them when needed.

In learning a language, observation is an initial consideration, passing into associations. Incentive, intent and confidence are required at the outset. Observation requires attention, which is one reason why spending a few months in a foreign country or associating with study groups can prove so effective.

Attention during self-instruction requires a quiet room, comfort and concentration, particularly when listening to spoken records and viewing accompanying pictures. Observation also includes perception; as hearing spoken words, seeing the pictures, and later perceiving the printed word in conjunction with the others.

Associations occur during the acts of hearing, vision, speaking and writing. In studying the details of a picture or scene, they are tied in with the sounds of the spoken word and the actions involved. All these conform to various methods of memorization and mnemonic aids. Logic enters as meanings are woven into the whole.

As a direct comparison, the hearing of a spoken word in a foreign language, together with the seeing of a picture of the thing it represents, or the object itself, is much like hearing a person's name when you first meet him. The association of the two and their retention fits, in a way, with the memorization of the names and faces of people as described under that chapter.

This, however, is only one of the memory tie-ins where the learning of a language is concerned. Many others will be found applicable as you proceed with language study, particularly where more difficult words or phrases are involved.

Repetition is, of course, one of the strongest measures. This is always true in the simpler or more primitive forms of memorization; and repetition is still more valuable when raised above the level of mere rote. In learning foreign words, you listen, imitate, repeat, and again repeat. But you do not stop there.

You must ask and answer questions, using the words that you have learned. Work them into various sentences, forming the same links and associations, or applying the same usage, that gave you facility in English. You need the same practice in a foreign language, so you should seek it in the ways listed previously at the beginning of this chapter.

The great purpose of repetition is to retain words or facts for duplication without conscious effort. In the study of a foreign language, repetition can be applied to the acquisition and review of a vocabulary, but it does not stop there. As more words are learned, they will produce their own associations, so that the growing vocabulary will become all the stronger. Generally, however, it is best to introduce a limited number of words at a time.

The sooner you learn to speak a language, the faster you will learn it. Try to speak to people as soon as you have acquired enough basic words and you will find that your vocabulary will increase with every chat. After you have gained a good speaking knowledge, turn to reading foreign newspapers and magazines to hasten the association of words with their meanings. In reading, try to learn ten new words a day. After many are learned, it becomes easier to add new ones while reading, as they will be understood from the context.

When you have learned to speak and read the basic foreign language, you can extend your grammatical study through textbooks, as you would with English. Incidentally, knowing your own language well helps in acquiring the new one. Otherwise, declensions, conjugations, rules of syntax may prove difficult because of your own unfamiliarity with the use of such grammatical rules.

It is encouraging to know that there are words in many foreign languages that are already in the English vocabulary. There may be other words that, by comparison, are easily recognizable. They sound, or are constructed, similar to the English equivalent. During the study of reading, each foreign word may be classified with an associated word or words. The tie-ins can be set up as follows.

1. Words that are spelled the same, with the same interpretation but with a different pronunciation.

Examples:

English:	animal hand	hotel	hospital	notable	piano	pianist
Spanish:	animal	hotel	hospital	notable	piano	pianist
French:	animal	hôtel		notable	piano	
German:	hand	hotel				pianist

2. Words with the same interpretation but the spelling and pronunciation differ slightly. These have a variation of letters.

Examples:

English:	blue	circus	rich	rose	occupation	parasol
Spanish:		circo	rico	rosa	ocupación	
French:	bleu	cirque	riche			
German:	blau	cirkus	reich			
Italian:	blu	circo	ricco	rósa	occupazióne	parasóle

3. Words derived from another language, related in meaning. A reminder word can be used as a memory link.

Examples from Latin:

	reminder word	meaning
Mentis (Latin genitive)	mental	mind
Tempora (Latin plural)	temporary	time

4. Closely related words, as to meaning, can be associated by use of a linking word.

Examples:

		link word	English word
Spanish:	vaso	vase	glass
	vender	vend	sell
French:	blé	blade	wheat, corn
German:	leicht	light	easy

5. Words that have been taken from foreign languages that are in common usage in English.

Examples:

Spanish: patio, siesta, rancho, fiesta

French: chauffeur, café, consommé, encore, ensemble, sabotage, salon

German: pumpernickel, wanderlust, kraft

Italian: aria, opera, pianissimo, fresco, ballerina, antipasto

6. Unfamiliar foreign words that are difficult can be associated with a linking word or words that will help convey the meaning. Liberties may be taken in' transforming a foreign word into

one or more familiar ones as in the use of "know, no; two, too; for, four; ant, aunt; fir, fur." These are identical sounds. Analogous words, those that resemble each other in sound, can also be used. Examples of these are "pen, pin, pan; cup, cap; goat, coat; quest, guest." Difficult foreign words of many syllables may be divided for convenient change into a number of short familiar words. If at all possible, the meaning of the linking words should be similar to the meaning of the foreign word. When such words cannot be found, use the first syllable of one or more words to imitate the sound of the foreign word.

Examples:
(*Japanese*) "keng" (sword) : cane
          "mong" (gate) : monger
          "yujin" (friend) : ewe and gin
          "seitong" (fine weather) : sa-ten (*sa*ble and *ten*ant)

Another possible link can be formed with the beginning or ending letters of two or more English words, the beginning letters being more preferable.

Examples:
(*German*) "Gewinnen" (to win) : ge–vin–nen (*ge*t *vin*tage *net*)
(*Russian*) "Nētsuka" (thread) : nee–ts–ka (*nee*dle, frui*ts, ca*rt)

Short sentences can be formed to remember the linkage.

Examples:

(*Japanese*)	*meaning*	*link word*	
"ichi"	(one)	itch	The *itch* is good for *one*.
"kata"	(shoulder)	catarrh	I have *catarrh* in the *shoulder*.
"samusa"	(cold)	some sack	I took *some sa*cks on a *cold* day.

If reading is an object in acquiring a language such as Greek, mnemonic principles may be applied to the learning of the alphabet. Forms of letters are associated with the names of imaginary objects as Δ—the Greek letter "delta"—suggesting the delta of a river. A serious student of literature and languages can form individualistic associations for letters and words that become a secret code, known only to the student as a time-saving memory chart.

Supplement

A comprehensive set of rules for learning a foreign language is the classic one that Professor John Stuart Blackie proposed:

1. If possible always start with a good teacher. He will save you much time by clearing away difficulties that might otherwise discourage you, and by preventing the formation of bad habits of enunciation, which must afterwards be unlearned.

2. Name aloud, in the language to be learned, every object which meets your eye, carefully excluding the intervention of the English. In other words, think and speak of the objects about you in the language you are learning from the very first hour of your teaching; and remember that the language belongs, in the first place, to your ear and to your tongue, not to your book merely and to your brain.

3. Commit to memory the simplest and most normal forms of the declension of nouns.

4. The moment you have learned the nominative and accusative cases of these nouns, take the first person of the present indicative of any common verb and pronounce aloud some short sentence according to the rules of syntax belonging to active verbs.

5. Enlarge this practice by adding some epithet to the substantive, declined according to the same noun.

6. Go on in this manner progressively, committing to memory the whole present indicative, past, and future indicative of simple verbs, always making short sentences with them and some appropriate nouns, and always thinking directly in the foreign language, excluding the intrusion of the English. In this essential element of every

rational system of linguistic training, there is no real, but only an imaginary difficulty to contend with, and, in too many cases, the pertinacity of a perverse practice.

7. When the ear and tongue have acquired a fluent mastery of the simpler forms of nouns, verbs, and sentences, then, but not till then, should the scholar be led, by a graduated process, to the more difficult and complex forms.

8. Let nothing be learned from rules that is not immediately illustrated by practice; or, rather, let the rules be educed from the practice of ear and tongue, and let them be as few and as comprehensive as possible.

9. Irregularities of various kinds are best learned by practice as they occur; but some anomalies, as in the conjugation of a few irregular verbs, are of such frequent occurrence, and are so necessary for progress, that they had better be learned specially by heart as soon as possible. Of this the verb *to be,* in almost all languages, is a familiar example.

10. Let some easy narrative be read, in the first place, or, better, some familiar dialogue, but reading must never be allowed to be practised, as is so generally the case, as a substitute for thinking and speaking. To counteract this tendency, the best way is to take objects of natural history, or representations of interesting objects, and describe their parts aloud in simple sentences, without the intervention of the mother tongue.

11. Let all the exercises of reading and describing be repeated again and again and again. No book fit to be read in the early stages of language-learning should be read only once.

12. Let your reading, if possible, be always in sympathy with your intellectual appetite. Let the matter of the work be interesting and you will make double progress. To know something of the subject beforehand will be an immense help. A translation of the Bible is always one of the best books to use in the acquisition of a foreign tongue.

13. As you read, note carefully the difference between the idioms of the strange language and those of the mother tongue; underscore

these distinctly with pen or pencil, in some thoroughly idiomatic translation, and after a few days translate back into the original tongue what you have before you in the English form.

14. To methodize, and, if necessary, correct your observations, consult some systematic grammar so long as you may find it profitable. But the grammar should, as much as possible, follow the practice, not precede it.

15. Be not content with that mere methodical generalization of the practice which you find in many grammars, but endeavor always to find the principle of the rule, whether belonging to universal or special grammar.

16. Study the theory of language, the organism of speech, and what is called comparative philology or glossology. The principles there revealed will enable you to prosecute with a reasoning intelligence a study which would otherwise be in a great measure a laborious exercise of arbitrary memory.

17. Still, practice is the main thing; language must, in the first place, be familiar; and this familiarity can be attained only by constant reading and constant conversation. Where a man has no person to speak to he may declaim to himself; but the ear and the tongue must be trained, not the eye merely and the understanding. In reading, a man must not confine himself to standard works. He must devour everything greedily that he can lay his hands on. He must not merely get up a book with accurate precision; that is all very well as a special task; but he must learn to live largely in the general element of the language; and minute accuracy in details is not to be sought before a fluent practical command of the general currency of the language has been attained. Shakespeare, for instance, ought to be read twenty times before a man begins to occupy himself with the various readings of the Shakespearian text, or the ingenious conjectures of his critics.

18. Composition, properly so called, is the culmination of the exercises of speaking and reading, translation and re-translation, which we have sketched. In this exercise the essential thing is to write from a model, not from dictionaries or phrasebooks. Choose an author

161

who is a pattern of a particular style, steal his phrases, and do something of the same kind yourself, directly, without the intervention of the English. After you have acquired fluency in this way you may venture to put more of yourself into the style, and learn to write the foreign tongue gracefully. Translation from English classics may also be practiced, but not in the first place; the ear must be tuned by direct imitation of the foreign tongue, before the more difficult art of transference from the mother tongue can be attempted with success.

Section B · Movement and Form

1. MOTOR MEMORY

Motor memory applies to a person's ability to perform certain coordinated muscular movements that he has learned. These movements come under the head of "motor skills" as they include the actions of the muscles, tendons, and joints when directed toward purposes with which they have become familiar.

These movements require some expression of the will, as opposed to mere reflex action. Thus they become part of an active thinking process, either conscious or subconscious. As a result, motor memory is sometimes called "motion memory" and the necessary actions have been defined as "psychomotor skills," but all this nomenclature amounts to the same thing.

You acquire some ability by means of steady practice. This is a known factor, along with the fact that such practice must often be prolonged. Quick results are not to be expected; hence slight but steady improvement gives the needed encouragement. This also becomes an incentive because, the longer it takes to gain the goal, the greater the reward, often because the competition has fallen by the wayside and there are fewer persons on hand to claim it.

Of added significance is the fact that mental intelligence is not necessarily essential to the success of motor skills and may even retard their development. Often, an individual with com-

163

paratively low mentality may become a remarkable acrobat or an excellent horseman or a star athlete. Such abilities may be inherited to a very marked degree. Natural abilities also vary, as teachers and students rapidly discover. Therefore, measures must be taken to aid the processes of a latent motor memory. In many fields of endeavor, proper training may be the prelude to specialized practice through which clumsy or awkward beginners can become capable artists and performers.

Closely connected with motor memory is the kinesthetic sense, or "muscle sense" as it is sometimes called. This provides knowledge of the position of an extremity of the body, or part of an extremity. This may be likened to a "sixth sense" as it is also a guide to the weight of an object, which many persons can gauge very closely simply by lifting or "hefting" the object in question.

However, where motor memory itself is concerned, the long recognized senses of sight, hearing, touch, taste and smell all play individual as well as collective parts in connection with the kinesthetic sense.

As a simple example, take the act of typing. A skilled typist utilizes what is termed the "touch system," which consists of typing without looking at the keyboard. Actually, this does not depend on touch much more than it does on sight or sound. The keys may not be seen but they can be heard clicking away, although this is not sufficient to tell which is which. Also, most of the keys feel so much alike that touch does not differentiate between them.

What the typist does use is a "kinesthetic system" in which the positions of the fingers provide the actual guide. This is supplemented by touch to some degree, as in first finding the right positions for the hands by spreading the fingers across the entire keyboard. Sight figures, too, with the typist watching the typed words as they appear on the paper, where any mistakes are immediately noted. Hence there is sense coordination in typing, but motor memory is the outstanding factor.

The sense of balance, which may also be regarded as an individual function, plays a part in motor memory. The tightrope walker combines it with his kinesthetic sense, his feet scouting the positions that his body muscles require to maintain their equilibrium. A high wire specialist may use a long balancing pole, which provides added stability but also gives other kinesthetic sensations through his hands.

Many analogies could be drawn to describe the operation of the kinesthetic sense and the sense of balance as well. The main point is that motor memory has become of increasing importance in the acquisition of modern skills, many of which are far more exacting than those required in the past.

Music, riding, acrobatics, juggling are still time-honored examples of motor skills but, today, driving automobiles, operating high-speed machinery, piloting airplanes, and many other activities like typing and using adding machines, have become a daily routine.

All this is reflected also in the modern emphasis on sports and athletics, with golfers and bowlers outnumbering those of a few generations ago by ratios of 100 to 1 and even more than 1,000 to 1. Emphasis on tennis, swimming, fencing, skating, and skiing has undergone proportionate increases. In dancing, such innovations as the Twist for a time become practically a universal craze, while the more staid pursuits of painting and handicrafts show a tremendous growth.

It is interesting to note the large number of records that have been set in track events and other sports during recent years. This may indicate that modern generations are developing greater motor skills along with the world's swifter tempo, or that more effective measures are being applied to the cultivation of motor memory—perhaps both. Whatever the case, it stresses the importance of the overall subject.

Progress in Motor Memory

Natural abilities play an important part in the memory of motor skills; however, without teachers or other guidance, motor memory becomes more a matter of trial and error. Repeated practice thereby becomes mere rote and unless inherited genius or keen visualization surmounts such handicaps, further trial may result in worse error. This should be avoided.

As with all efficient memory, a basic ingredient of good motor memory is the best possible health, particularly because the muscles involved require proper nourishment and should be in condition to function well. Fatigue is a pressing problem; unless avoided, it will delay prolonged periods of activity and will affect accuracy. Drugs, alcohol and emotional disturbances may exact similar toll, often impairing strength as well.

In acquiring certain motor skills it is essential to have an instructor and in many other instances this is highly helpful. Some persons think they can learn everything on their own; that by watching dancers, for example, they have learned how to dance. Usually, they make many mistakes, which they have trouble correcting later. At the opposite extreme are those who depend entirely on books, not realizing that some printed explanations are often offered simply as guides for students already proficient in the subject.

Between these extremes are those who wisely combine both methods and, fortunately, today there are many opportunities to read up on skills and then watch persons performing them. This is possible at home with the aid of television, movie projectors, and recordings, as well as books and instruction sheets of an advanced type. But whenever personal instruction is needed or advisable, it should be sought.

Aside from the factors already stressed, those of primary importance to motor memory are: (1) *motivation;* (2) *observation;* (3) *association;* and (4) *repetition,* which may also be defined as *practice.* These include other factors which will be mentioned in their proper places.

Motivation. The motive or purpose behind any skill to be learned must be considered in terms of usefulness to the student. If it fits in with ambition or interests, that may be sufficient. Sometimes the acquisition of a skill may be presented as a challenge to the individual.

Otherwise, more concrete incentives may be needed, usually in the form of rewards. These may consist of the anticipation of a performance to be given before a friend, small groups, or finally before the public. This is why recitals are important in the study of musical instruments; but the same rule may be applied toward the acquisition of other skills.

A strong incentive is needed for the student to maintain a constant attitude, for if it changes, results are quickly affected. Adults often become discouraged quite easily and will give up lessons as well as practice.

Successful performance is rewarding in itself, hence motivation is increased by knowledge of results. These may be quickly noted in the development of motor skills; thus errors can be eliminated early, which is essential. Here teachers prove invaluable and group instruction or demonstration may fulfill a similar function.

Observation. This consists primarily in noting exactly how an action should be performed, as well as keeping watch on its progress during the learning or demonstration process. It therefore requires close attention, which should be undivided, if possible, but not to the point of interfering with relaxation.

Rest periods allow time to reenforce the attention but should not be prolonged to the point of forgetting some vital element of the skill being learned. Such periods may vary according to the individual involved, the nature of the activity, which may be strenuous or tiring in itself, the surroundings, or other environmental conditions.

167

Once adept at a skill, a person may perform it under the most adverse circumstances, as the activity of the muscles appears to be relegated to a subconscious level of the mind. Diversions of the attention may occur then without significantly affecting a performance. Emotional performers, however, may require minimum distractions in order to provide what they feel is perfection, the attunement of their own mood to the combined emotional aura of the audience.

Association. Where a person has no previous knowledge of a skill, trial and error come into play. Organization may shorten the task, which may then be associated with something already known. However, highly similar tasks take longer to learn than those which are dissimilar, due to the possibility of confusion.

Hence, in ballet, as an example, certain stances are named and learned. These are then combined individually into dance effects, thus avoiding conflict. In other forms of dancing, steps may be diagrammed and named. The same applies to various motor skills, such a breakdown allowing for proper organization.

A person can often go through the mental motions of a dance or other action, then later put them into practice through actual motor memory. Sometimes, when learning a motor skill, humming a tune or repeating words may help toward motor memory. This is similar to soldiers counting while they march or perform the manual of arms. Association also plays a part in the "calling" of square dances.

Usually, it is best to discard such mental jogs after eliminating the hesitancy or obstruction which the association device was used to overcome. In contrast, however, there are certain instances of two activities being learned simultaneously as a performance feat, such as singing and dancing, tapping and juggling, or singing while playing the piano.

Repetition. This is the most important adjunct to motor memory, as it includes practice, which in itself is the greatest single factor in producing skilled performance.

Practice, aside from physically strengthening the muscles and creating a motion-memory impression, exposes the learning effort to the experience of trial and error. The detection and correction of errors helps eliminate others which may have occurred in the same trend.

At the outset, it must be recognized that there are individual and physiological limits to a skill which no amount of practice can overcome. What practice does is reduce tasks to the least possible number of movements. It also demonstrates the results of the training program, allowing the learner to adjust as he proceeds, which in itself is rewarding.

Some persons feel that in learning a new movement, a definite physical and mental resistance must be overcome. Much repetition is required for that purpose and, often, the acquisition of a skill may level off and show no further improvement for a time, despite continued practice and other efforts.

One explanation is that we learn in "habit groups" and that this levelling off represents a "plateau" between such groups. It is also attributed to a decline in motivation, such as discouragement. The answer is to keep on practicing, particularly if there is reason to expect improvement. It will usually resume.

This emphasizes the fact that active performance of a task yields superior results to merely watching someone else perform it, no matter how skillfully. It also yields superior recall of the task, indicating that the motor memory is charging up to greater intensity and becoming more and more firmly established.

How far that can go is illustrated by cases where persons have tried swimming, skating, or riding a bicycle after a lapse of many years and have found that they still possess the basic skill—the ability to stay afloat or balance on skates or a bicycle. Persons well schooled in the manual of arms can pick up a gun and go through the drill many years later.

In the case of skating in particular, the muscles may soon ache too painfully to continue; and the same applies to bicycling if attempted too strenuously after a long lapse. But the "know how" persists showing that the function of motor memory is ingrown in these cases, even though the muscles rebel.

Continuous practice in acquiring certain motor skills is less effective than when spaced over increasingly separated time intervals. This holds true even though the total time spent in practice may be considerably less. The intervals apparently improve the motor memory; and there are times when practicing up to a certain point, then waiting a week or so, will show surprisingly superior results.

Another interesting fact is that relatively short periods of practice from day to day may allow the addition of fresh material with considerably less burden. Permanence in the retention of a skill is also furthered if the work is properly distributed over periods of time.

In some skills, abilities are apt to decrease if rest periods are interposed improperly. Here the capable teacher plays a role in setting the time of the practice periods and how widely they should be spread out. Generally, some distribution is better than none in the acquisition of nearly all psychomotor skills.

An unusual feature is that reminiscence may improve a skill without practice, up to a certain point. That is, after a waiting period, if a person first recalls or reviews the material practiced and then repeats its performance, the result may be better than when it was last done.

Still, there is some controversy whether imaginary practice, in the form of "dry runs," can produce improvement. Though there is no strict reason to condemn such dry runs, their extensive use should not be encouraged. Perhaps too much imaginary repetition can cause a hiatus similar to the result of excessive over-practice.

Motor memory, thanks to the physical help supplied by the muscles, is stronger than simple psychic memory, which is all in the mind. But the greater the time lapse, the more need to strengthen the muscles involved and to reestablish the required associations between muscle groups. Once an original position is resumed, recall becomes rapid and actions fall into sequence.

Individual exercises may be invented to develop suppleness and flexibility, with special attention to difficult phases of an activity. Pianists, for example, may go through a "daily dozen" to exercise the fingers and attune the ears. Thinking ahead of the action in order to direct it, is also kept at high efficiency through frequent practice periods. As for regular practice, the point to remember is that there is never—at least in theory—a limit to the refinement of dexterity, though it may approach the infinitesimal.

2. REMEMBERING MUSIC, *OR* MUSICAL MEMORY

Every ambitious musician has the great desire to perform in public, to hear the applause of an enthusiastic audience, and receive the plaudits of the press. To achieve this ultimate goal, the musician must have, not only the talent and the ability to persevere with years of study and dedication, but one more facet is absolutely indispensable, namely, the power to memorize. Memory is the only dependable source of help when a musician plays or sings without the aid of written music, either privately or publicly.

This power is within the realm of achievement for every normal human being. A young child at first memorizes "parrot" fashion but, as adolescence approaches, the mind begins to weigh various things increasingly, so a kind of interpretation and meaning enter this mind. As a result, memorizing takes on various shades of meaning. Unconsciously the student mind forms associations. Complexities begin to take hold and the young adult continues to store knowledge and at the same time expresses more clearly the latent talent that is within the mind. With some musicians this may appear early, as with Mozart, Chopin, Schubert and innumerable other greats of music. Musical talent may develop in later years and be equally important, but its degree of importance depends much upon the capacity of the memory. The basic problem is, then, for the talented musician, how to develop a musical memory or just how to remember music.

To get the general idea of the art of memorizing music there must be a knowledge of the technique of music. In other words, technique is a prerequisite to musical memory training. There must also be a strong feeling of the mood and rhythm of each piece or parts of lengthy works such as sonatas.

Although there is always a certain amount of tenseness during a performance before the public there must be a state of relaxation so that there is complete freedom to think and move. Muscles respond best to thought control when there is complete concentration.

Physical Fitness for Musicians

Co-ordination depends upon a state of physical fitness. This in turn is maintained through good health, which includes a proper diet and sufficient exercise. A musician can not do his best work if he is depressed by insufficient food, or sluggish because of too much to eat just before a concert. The nature of diet depends upon the individual needs. What is helpful to one person may not be good for another. So that there will be no doubts, periodic consultation with a physician as to health and diet is wise.

One of the commoner ailments that an ardent musician suffers from is fatigue. Closely allied are nervous disorders and tension. Sleep is often of great benefit for these complaints especially when they are due to overwork. The musician cannot afford to skimp on sleep and then expect to give a brilliant concert. There must be time for sleep, time for work, time to eat and time to relax. These must be sensibly balanced to obtain the maximum results.

Vision and hearing are very important to the average person for memorizing music. Only the blind or the deaf must manage without one or the other of these two faculties. If one of the senses is missing, these persons often seem to be endowed with some unusual facility in another way. Many of the deaf can feel vibrations or observe much more than the average person who possesses all the senses. With the blind, hearing is often extraordinarily sensitive and keen, as are also their sense of touch and muscle sense. There are and have been musicians among both these classes. Beethoven, the great composer, was deaf. Toscanini's eyesight was so bad he memorized orchestral scores to conduct.

Musicians possessed of both vision and hearing should be intently aware of the need to make the most of these physical gifts. It is very easy to read the written notes wrongly if the eyesight has deteriorated. Sometimes a musician may not be aware that the eyesight has changed to such a marked degree that the notes are being misread. The same can happen with hearing. If it is slightly impaired, the sense of "pitch" can go "off-key." For these reasons it is worthwhile to include a special examination of vision and hearing when you have a medical check-up.

Posture is an important factor for body balance and an aid to good circulation. While seated, the musician should get the habit of sitting straight, not letting the midriff slump. While standing, the weight should be balanced equally upon both feet, keeping the body erect. Slumped shoulders and sloppy positions are not attractive to the viewer, nor are they conducive to a good performance by the musician, who needs the best possible physical condition to draw upon the memory.

The proper environment for the study of music is one which emphasizes quiet, and includes good lighting, comfortable temperature and dress. Noise of any kind is distracting. Conversation of family and friends, TV and radio programs, even the ticking of a clock can disturb, especially when reading music without playing it. A metronome should be discontinued as soon as you have established the tempo of your practice piece. It is possible to stop up the ears but it is not a good habit. If you must practice with noise, the only alternative is to learn to concentrate to the extreme.

One very common hazard to the memorizing of music is mind wandering. It may be due to any number of reasons, among which are laziness, indifference, fatigue, little or no ambition, or a lack of interest in the particular music being studied. If a state of boredom is reached, it is time to stop rather than indulge in thoughts other than your music. If mind wandering becomes a habit, try duets with another musician or ask a friend to listen who is interested in your music. Working with a teacher gets you back on the track. Repeating a passage too many times in succession can cause disinterest. Three times in succession is usually sufficient at one time. Let it rest and try later. Although memorizing by rote, which is repetition, exercises the muscles, it is considered, with few exceptions, a waste of time.

The actual art of memorizing music is greatly helped by a knowledge of harmony, which teaches the analysis of the structure of written music. It is possible to memorize without this basic musical education but it is easier if you know the chord progressions, cadences, variations and innumerable combinations that enable the musician to improvise. Natural improvisers without any knowledge of harmony can play remarkably well, so they are not to be discouraged. Prodigies like Mozart and Beethoven were born with a natural knowledge of harmony, proof of which is the compositions they wrote in their very early years.

One factor in remembering music is the ability to differentiate the tones, to identify them so well that you can name them, play them or reproduce them vocally. This ability is termed "absolute pitch."

Absolute Pitch

Pitch, in music, is that property of a musical tone which is determined by the frequency of vibrations of sound waves as

174

they hit the ear. The higher the pitch or note, the more vibrations per second. For instance A above middle C has 440 vibrations per second by the philharmonic pitch standard. When sounded, the tone is heard by the ear, then registered in the memory.

If you can recall and reproduce consistently a specified tone, either with your voice or upon a musical instrument, you possess *"absolute pitch."* Many people have this talent but do not use it. Fortunately it is not absolutely necessary for a musician, but it is a great asset nevertheless. The harpist finds absolute pitch an advantage because harp strings are continually going out of tune. The string sections of the orchestras are often seen adjusting their strings, utilizing aural memory of pitch as to what is correct. A singer with the capacity of absolute pitch also has to co-ordinate this with the muscular reaction in the throat to produce a particular tone. This applies to mimics too.

To go about acquiring absolute pitch, if it is not well developed in you, a start can be made with the piano. Strike one note and repeat it while you hum it. It is a good idea to associate the note with chords of different keys. Middle C can be used with chord C E G C of the key of C. It can also be used with the chord G B♭ C E, the G and B♭ below middle C. This belongs to the key of F. Then hum the same C with the chord F A C F, the F and A located below middle C. The C sounds different with these chords yet it is actually the same sound with the same number of vibrations. No matter what key it is used in, it never varies. When you can hum or sound a selected note absolutely from memory, you have "absolute pitch" for that note. This can form the basis for almost unconsciously calculating other notes.

There are numerous devices such as the tuning fork, the pitch pipe, chromatic master tuners and others that are an invaluable aid for musicians, choral directors and teachers, so that they can be sure of the pitch, especially where many singers are concerned.

When learning absolute pitch for a note, try to recall it during the day; repeat it. True it with the piano. Repeat this every day, for at least three days, then skip a day, repeat the next day, skip, repeat until you have it. The practice must be continued and more so if the sense of absolute pitch is not particularly natural with you. If you just can't remember the pitch of a note, don't worry. There are many musicians and singers who lack this ability, but once they start with an assist such as the piano, they sustain the right tone relationships in the number they are performing.

Basic Hints for Memorizing Instrumental Music

Start by memorizing short pieces of music. Make an accurate analysis of each piece as you proceed. If it is new to you, read over the entire work. Establish in your mind the key in which it is written. Check the difficult passages and try to play them. If any are too difficult, vary the fingering. Learn all the difficult parts first. If still too difficult, wait until another practice period. If you are advanced in music and studying a longer work, such as a sonata, learn it in parts.

Musical marks of expression such as *legato, pianissimo* and so on, should be observed and used as you practice. These associate the moods in your mind as you learn the passages. This helps you to remember the music audibly even though you may not always visualize the notes.

Dissimilar phrases must be analyzed carefully. Mentally check the difference in the notes. The left and right hand of piano and organ music may have relatively the same change of notes. This may require a change of fingering. If so, you can mark it on your music so that you can have it for future reference. Never slight these changes.

If the piece of music you are memorizing is reasonably short, play it over during each practice period after you have rehearsed the difficult phrases. On very lengthy works each section must be learned, one at a time, in sequence, then put together. If you discover that you can memorize easier by separating any piece into parts, do so. Students with a thorough background of harmony can analyze and memorize more rapidly. Lacking a knowledge of harmony, memorizing is a much slower process unless you have some elements of genius or are a prodigy. If the practice begins to tire or bore you, leave it and return to it another day.

Interpretation should be stressed after you have mastered the technical difficulties. This means rhythm, tonal expression and the very mood of the music as written by the composer.

When you repeat your music for memorizing get the habit of listening to it. If you forget, look at the written page. After you have accurately memorized your piece, do not play it for a few days or a week. When you return to it, if you think you cannot remember it accurately, look at the written notes, then put them aside and try to play from memory. If you have forgotten anything, re-read and practice until the weak spots are clear. Do not play it again for a few days unless you feel the urge to do so. In time the music will be part of you. Whenever you do not play it for a long period of time, rehearse it as a refresher for your memory.

As soon as you finish learning one piece of music, start on another. It is possible to learn several at one time. It seems to accelerate interest. However, some minds absorb only one type of musical mood at a time; others need variety. If in doubt, consult a teacher. Musical talent varies and upon this hinges your capacity to memorize.

Regular, set hours must be planned for intensive practice. Mornings are considered most advantageous by many, but any time of the day or night is good if you feel you work best then and are rested and ambitious. Allot as many practice periods per day as you can manage. Three hours a day or more have been the minimum crowded in by many a successful musician. One hour at a time is considered sufficient. The first fifteen minutes, which are the most valuable, should be given to limbering up exercises such as scales and the difficult passages of the piece you are memorizing. The next fifteen minutes can be spent on that new piece of music. After analyzing it again, play it over a couple of times, then repeat, individually, the difficult phrases you worked on during the first fifteen minutes. Now play the entire piece again paying attention to expression. You may want a little relaxation or a breather for a few minutes after the first half hour. The second half hour can be devoted to music previously memorized or to another piece you intend to memorize. If you wish to continue with the music you worked on during the first half hour, and have not tired of it, you may do so. The time you save by intelligently planning your practice periods makes it possible to increase your repertoire just that much faster.

Silent practice may be helpful too. Many instrumentalists can visualize and hear their memorized music just as many singers can think out their words and melody. In order to visualize correctly, association of a particular chord with some difficult phrase need only be recalled. Sometimes the easier chord phrases are neglected and in turn are not so vivid in the memory. Writing or copying the music may also cause a more indelible impression in your memory. However, the actual physical repetition of the pieces after careful study and practice is the most important element in making the music more and more a part of you.

Memory Tips for Singers

Singers are in a category all their own. There are some with beautiful voices who can sing to an accompaniment without any studied knowledge of harmony and the theory of music, yet they have been able to earn a very comfortable living. They have good memories; that is, they can remember a melody by hearing it, and the words become a part of them at the same time that the rhythm is mastered. These are exceptional singers.

Another group of singers have a good musical education. They study harmony, theory, voice, piano or organ. They may study composition, acting and languages. It is obvious that a good memory is not only obligatory for most of this study, but it can save time. From this same student group come musicians who perform professionally as entertainers. Among them are instrumentalists who sing to their own accompaniment: pianists, accordionists, guitarists, organists and the numerous others. They have the ability to sing the words of songs without any obvious conscious thought of the melody notes. They concentrate mainly on the instrumental work. Many are natural improvisers whose study of harmony has given them a tremendous scope for chord association and sequences.

Choir work is often a starting place for singers. Here they have plenty of time and help to study and analyze songs and voice culture. Oratorios are lengthy and laborious, but the use of the written work during rendition is a wonderful aid for the memorizing of the oratorio. A conscientious singer practically has it memorized for the first public rendition. The use of the music folio is as a prompter. After a few such appearances, the singer has all the confidence necessary to sing without "book." This is an easy way to outgrow severe stage fright and nervousness. At least it is an easing off process so that visual memory does not fail you.

A singer wants to remember the melody and the words "by heart," a practice which has become more and more popular with the revival of many old time songs. To do this, your first step is to read or review *Basic Hints for Memorizing Instrumental Music*.

Next, read the words of the entire song so that the general theme or story is understood. Don't try to memorize at this point, just get a good concept of the song. Decide whether it is sad or gay and just what it is about. It will express a mood of one kind or another. Mood has much to do with memory. The words tell a story, present pictures or scenes that you can recall. These are your cues, or links.

Notice if the song is divided into parts, such as verses and chorus or an actual variation of the theme in the music itself. The parts can be studied separately. Concentrate on the first part or verse, then the second, and so on.

Study the tempo, where it changes, if it does. Hum the tune while you tap out the time with your foot or hand. If you can work with a metronome close by, use it long enough to establish correct timing, then discontinue it. The tapping too should be eliminated after you have perfect timing. Many entertainers who sing popular songs have a natural habit of swaying or using their hands to mark the timing or rhythm of the climactic portions of the songs.

If you play your own accompaniment, play over the music in strict tempo.

Play the music a second time observing the modulations which add to the expression of the mood of the song.

At this time, the singer should practice the tone quality of each note sung. This can be done while you sing through the entire song. If this is done without accompaniment, it is wise to strike occasional notes on the instrument to test the accuracy of your own vocal tones. It is easy to sing "off-key" if you are not gifted with "absolute pitch."

Take a short rest period.

After the rest, read the words of the song again, thinking the melody as you proceed.

Now repeat and hum the tune in time.

Go over any difficult parts. Vocalize as much as you want until you have mastered each part.

Having analyzed each part of the song thoroughly you should be able to retain it more readily in your memory. Observe rest intervals and repeat the study and practice until the song is part of you. Then, and then only, will you give an effective personalized interpretation of the music and the message of the words.

If visualizing written words helps you to memorize, be sure to write them in the same way that they appear on the music page. That is, line for line, comma or pause, and so on. This helps to keep the music in mind too. After all, the music and the words belong together.

Many songs, unlike poetry, are tied together from part to part, forming natural links; therefore it is safe to memorize certain parts and then put them together. This is helpful if some passages are difficult and require special study. Once learned they can be added to the rest of the song, remembering the links or bridges.

Singers who have the gift of aural memorizing do not need the visualization of the words and music. This is the presentation which confronts blind people. There are many excellent blind singers who have been born with a perfect sense of timing and a wonderful ability to remember words and music that they hear. Teachers, friends and family help them so that the music can be repeated until they memorize a complete song. Recordings and Braille are invaluable for them. T V sound and radio also add to their education.

There are individual ways of memorizing that each singer discovers, just as a unique style emerges while study and application progress. Great opera singers memorize lengthy and strenuous works. Not only must they remember words and music, they must remember exactly where to take their deep breaths for lengthy and difficult phrases. They must also act and take direction from the director. All this is a test of memory. Here motor memory takes over in many of the functions.

Children should be encouraged to memorize music. Singing games that tell stories such as the old favorite "Farmer in the Dell" and counting songs like "One Little Indian, Two Little," are attractive to young beginners. The old phrase *"Every Good Boy Does Fine"* helps a child remember the lines of the treble staff while the word *"FACE"* supplies the letters for the spaces. Ofttimes a parent should sit with the child during practice periods to help bridge a difficult study period. Children, and teenagers too, need bolstering by occasional words of praise. Also conducive to intensive study are examinations, which in turn sharpen the memory. Adults must consciously force themselves to practice and memorize. For additional incentive and assurance they can work with groups of musicians or consult with teachers.

Lapse of memory can happen. For children it is frequently due to a lack of confidence. With adults it is more likely the result of incorrect or insufficient memorizing. To help avoid memory lapses when performing in public, try to think of the rhythm or mood of the piece rather than the actual notes. There are, of course, some people who have memories that actually recall the notes on every page. Entertainers can often start their number if they remember the name of the first chord formation.

Whether you intend to pursue music as a profession or just for your own personal pleasure, it is a most rewarding achievement to be able to perform from memory, "without book."

3. REMEMBERING THE INTERNATIONAL MORSE CODE

Many persons are somewhat familiar with the International Morse Code, which is used not only in radio telegraphy but for flag signals, whistle blasts and light flashes. The letters are coded in the form of short "dots" and long "dashes" which can even be given as finger taps, by making dots light and dashes heavy.

Like any alphabet, the International Code must be learned somewhat by rote until it becomes a matter of motor memory. Once proficient in "sending," a person rapidly gains ability at "receiving." But the early problem is to keep the code in mind while trying to transcribe the letters into dots and dashes.

Systems have been used with "key words" in which certain letters represent dots and dashes, but these require almost as much study as the International Code itself, because it is a case of superimposing one code on another. What is needed is a method that catches the rhythm of the dots and dashes. There are two ways of doing this: by syllables and by words.

The syllabic system is the more compact, so it will be given first, in its improved form; but before studying it, go on to the word system to see which of the two you prefer.

The Syllabic System

Each letter of the International Morse Code is represented by a word beginning with the same letter: A is Against; B is Barbarian; C, Continental; and so on. But these words are broken into syllables, long ones of three or more letters representing dashes; the short ones, dots.

The list follows with dots (·) dashes (–) and key words:

A ·– A-gainst (Against)

B –··· Bar-ba-ri-an (Barbarian)

C –·–· Cont-i-nent-al (Continental)

D –·· Dahl-i-a (Dahlia)

E · Eh (Eh!)

F ··–· Fu-ri-ous-ly (Furiously)

G ––· Gal-lant-ly (Gallantly)

H ···· Hu-mi-li-ty (Humility)

I ·· I-vy (Ivy)

J ·––– Ju-ris-dic-tion (Jurisdiction)

K –·– Kang-a-roos (Kangaroos)

L ·–·· Li-ber-i-a (Liberia)

M –– Mount-ains (Mountains)

N –· Nob-le (Noble)

O ––– Off-ens-ive (Offensive)

P ·––· Pa-tri-mon-y (Patrimony)

Q ––·– Queen Guin-e-vere (Guinevere)

R ·–· Re-becc-a (Rebecca)

S ··· Sa-la-mi (Salami)

T – Team (Team)

U ··– Un-i-form (Uniform)

V ···– Ve-ry va-ried (Very varied)

W ·–– Wa-ter-loo (Waterloo)

X –··– Hex-a-go-nal (Hexagonal)

Y –·–– Youth-ful and fair (Youthful)

Z ––·· Zinc Vit-ri-ol (Vitriol)

It is possible to link some of these with such phrases as: "*Gallantly* and *furiously,* he fought *against* the *barbarian* at *Waterloo*"; "They have *jurisdiction* over *kangaroos* in the *Liberian mountains*"; "The *team* wore *uniforms* that were *very varied*."

These may be helpful in the preliminary work of learning the actual word list, but the latter must be gone over so frequently that each key word springs to mind when required. If you want the letter "K" you will then think of "kangaroos," not just as a word but as "KANGG-a-ROOOS," which practically shouts "DASH-dot-DASH."

Similarly "L" for "Liberia" will bring out "Li-BEER-i-a," as "Dot-DASH-dot-dot" and "U" for "uniform" will be "Un-i-FORM" signifying "Dot-dot-DASH." The more exaggerated this singsong procedure, the better.

In American Morse, which is used in ordinary telegraphy, some of the letters differ from the International Code, and in several, spaces are included in a letter, these being equal to a dot in length. One letter, L, is simply a long dash.

Special words can be used for these, with long and short syllables, the syllable "Blank," "X" or "No" being used to indicate a space. The list follows:

C $\cdot\cdot$ $\cdot$ Ca-sa-BLANK-a (Casablanca) "Blank" for space.
F $\cdot\-\cdot$ Fo-rest-er (Forester)
J $\-\cdot\-\cdot$ Jack-a-dand-y (Jack-a-dandy)
L $\-\-$ Llewellyn (One long syllable for long dash)
O $\cdot$ $\cdot$ O-X-en (Oxen, as *three* syllables) "X" for space.
P $\cdot\cdot\cdot\cdot\cdot$ Po-pu-la-ri-ty (Popularity)
Q $\cdot\cdot\-\cdot$ Quo-ta-tion-al (Quotational) with "QU" being pronounced as simply "K" the "Quo" is a short syllable. (Like "Ko")
R $\cdot$ $\cdot\cdot$ Re-NO Ci-ty (Reno City) "No" for space.
X $\cdot\-\cdot\cdot$ Ex-ter-i-or (Exterior)

Y ·· ·· Yo-gi BLANK-et-ed (Yogi blanketed) "Blank" for space.

Z ··· · Zo-di-ac NO-va (Zodiac Nova) "No" for space.

Mental pictures will help with the last two, as a Hindu yogi wearing a blanket for "Y" (Yogi blanketed) and a new bright star flashing high in the sky for "Z" (Zodiac Nova).

In many forms of communication, American Morse is not used, so its special letters should be totally disregarded unless you have definite need for them; otherwise, they will cause confusion.

In transcribing words into the International Code, think in dots and dashes (sounded as "*di*" and "*da*"). Thus you would spell out "FEW" as Dot-dot-dash-dot Dot Dot-dash-dash, which would be written ··—· · ·—— but if you should forget, say "F," you can get it from your key-word "Furiously" or Fu-ri-OUS-ly, forming the Dot-dot-DASH-dot.

The Word System

Here, whole words are used to represent dots and dashes. Each one-syllable word is a dot; any multiple syllable word is a dash. These are formed into phrases, with the initial letter of the first word representing that letter of the alphabet, thus:

A ·— All alone

B —··· Beetles are big bugs

C —·—· Curiosity kills care-less cats

D —·· Devil may care

E · Ease

F ··—· Friends can provide fun

G ——· Gamblers squander cash

H ···· He hi ho hum

I ·· I am

J ·——— Jobs require special training

K —·— Kittens act crazy

L ·—·· Live happily at home

M —— Monday morning

N —· Never quit

O ——— Organ grinder's monkey

P ·——· Put pictures around rooms

Q ——·— Quartets vocalize old melodies

R	·—·	Ring wedding bells	X	—··—	X-rays show you skeletons
S	···	Safe at home	Y	—·——	Yesterday will never return
T	—	Terrific	Z	——··	Zebras always have stripes
U	··—	Use no substitutes			
V	···—	V is for victory			
W	·——	We never wander			

These phrases take longer to memorize than single words, though some of them are quite catchy and will stay in mind immediately. The memorization may also be done more rapidly by substituting any phrases of your own that may seem more natural, but which have the correct number of syllables in each word. Examples: For "F"—"Fun is always good"; or for "R"— "Red robins hop."

The important point is that when the list is once learned, you can practically write off code letters from it. Dots and dashes can be transcribed immediately from the key phrases, as there is no trouble distinguishing multi-syllable words from those with single syllables.

For the special letters in American Morse, the following phrases can be used, the word "Not" or "No" indicating a space:

C	·· ·	Cats do NOT bark	R	· ··	Reap NO wild oats
F	·—·	Far better now	X	·—··	X indicates the spot
J	—·—·	Johnny comes marching home	Y	·· ··	Youth does NOT give up
L	——	Lemonade	Z	··· ·	Zoo bars will NOT bend
O	· ·	Oh, NO, now!	&	· ···	And NO one wants it
P	·····	Put your best foot first			
Q	··—·	Quick hands lighten work			

These, of course, are learned only if you intend to use the American Morse code.

In transmitting Morse, the dash is equal to two—or even three

—dots in duration; the interior space (used only in American Morse) is equal to a dot in duration; the space between letters is equal to two dots; between words to three dots; between sentences to five dots or more, as extra prolongation does not matter in this case. A simple way to practice is with finger taps, using the forefinger alone for the light "dots" and the first two fingers for the heavy "dashes," which can include a brief pause to simulate the actual length of a dash. At the same time, calling off a dot or dash as "*di*" and "*da*" respectively is extremely effective in fixing the impressions.

Numerical Characters

Figures are transmitted by special code characters, as are some punctuation marks. In the International Code, these are:

1	·————	Dot (1) plus dashes (4)	6	—····	Dash (1) plus dots (4)
2	··———	Dots (2) plus dashes (3)	7	——···	Dashes (2) plus dots (3)
3	···——	Dots (3) plus dashes (2)	8	———··	Dashes (3) plus dots (2)
4	····—	Dots (4) plus dash (1)	9	————·	Dashes (4) plus dot (1)
5	·····	Dots (5)	0	—————	Dashes (5)

Period ·· ·· ··   Interrogation ··——··

Comma ·—·—·—   Exclamation ——·——

The figures are easily remembered by their progression. Dots run from 1 to 5, with dashes being added to give five units to each character, thus signifying "figure" which can be identified with "five." Beginning with 6, dashes run from 1 to 5, being followed by enough dots to give five units to each character.

For "period" you can think of a "dot" doubled and repeated twice, with spaces to indicate this. For "comma" you have a "dot" with a "dash" for a "tail"—repeated twice.

187

For the interrogation mark, think of two dots representing an inverted question mark, as in Spanish (¿), followed by the sentence represented by two dashes "Blank–Blank," and finishing with two dots for a question mark (?), giving the whole character.

For the exclamation, think of two tall exclamation points, each a double dash above a dot. These have been knocked over and broken, in opposite directions, so they are lying in the position: Dash–dash–dot–dot–dash–dash (— — · · — —).

With American Morse, the figures and punctuation marks run:

1 · — — ·	6 · · · · · ·	Period · · — — · ·
2 · · — · ·	7 — — · ·	Comma · — · —
3 · · · — ·	8 — · · · ·	Interrogation — · · — ·
4 · · · · —	9 — · · —	Exclamation — — — ·
5 — — —	0 ———	

These are somewhat irregular in their formation, but if 1 (· — — ·) and 9 (— · · —) are "pegged" as "opposites" it is not too hard to recall the rest. With 2, 3 and 4 there is a definite sequence; three dashes for 5 and six dots for 6 are easy. Double two of the six dots into dashes for 7 and transform one pair of dots back to a dash for 8. For 0 you use a very prolonged dash, trailing like the figure it represents, "0000000000000."

The period, like a 1 with double dots at beginning and end; the comma, two dots, each with a dash as a tail; the interrogation, like a 9 (— · · —) with a period; and the exclamation point, like a tall one knocked down, all have features which aid in their recollection.

4. MEMORY OF ART—FORM—SCULPTURE

Though closely allied to the recognition of faces and the identification of pictures, memory for art, form, and sculpture includes the ability at reproduction of the things remembered, as drawings, paintings, or sculptures.

Knowledge of forms is therefore of prime importance. Forms consist of places, objects, and faces; these must be recalled in relation to one another. Unfortunately, memory of form, like that of color, is too often left to chance, even in art education.

While some persons are remarkably gifted where memory of form is concerned, the ability can be cultivated to a high degree. The human face is easier to remember than objects such as animals or flowers. Any oddity is helpful and its transcription through caricature further strengthens the recollection.

This is in keeping with the linking of associations through exaggeration, a fundamental of memory development. The formula for remembering faces can thereby be applied to animals, giving them human expressions, or to objects, by making them distorted or grotesque.

Close recall of shape and color is important in mechanics, natural sciences, and industry. It is valuable in the design of textiles, bronzes, wall paper, in fact, all phases of the art of ornamentation. Training in recognition of form is therefore essential in many fields and memory of such training will not injure individuality of style and expression. Memory consists of stored observation and is to be cultivated for manipulation by the intelligence.

Interest is a necessary motive for memory of form, as well as other factors to be discussed. Such interest, if lacking, can be provided by encouraging curiosity, group competition, or through the devising of games and experiments.

Observation requires strong emphasis on *attention* and later *concentration,* for features to be effectively registered and reproduced.

Perception is developed in children along with elementary visual training. A child may first draw an entire object, such as a house, and then be taught to include only what is seen, not what is imagined or might exist. From such art training, the perspective sense is to be developed.

A child may be taught lines, angles and curves, but abstract forms lack interest where reproduction from memory is concerned. Once trained in elementary art, children from 12 to 15 years of age can draw simple details of the human face from memory; and often, exact reproduction can be learned in a few days.

Graduated series of shapes may then be drawn from memory in an attempt at form development. Starting with straight lines, in proper length and proportion, the student draws shapes of gradually increasing difficulty, then goes into shading, modeling, effect and full relief from real objects.

Characteristics that must be fixed in memory are those of anatomic construction, proportions, outline, shape, and color. These should be observed when studying an object and later visualized, closing the eyes as needed to regain the image. If this proves difficult, give attention to one detail, then another, until all is managed.

Association is another basic step. Associate hand movements with the actual outlining of drawings or feeling objects to be sculptured. In drawing, it is a good plan to look at an object and retain the image in memory while drawing it with the hand.

Another procedure is to draw the object in mind, following the form with a pointing finger, then shut the eyes, look away from the object, open the eyes and draw again. If unable to do so, try big lines first; then details or parts.

In observing dimensions, position, form, modeling, and color, the following points should be noted:

Dimensions, or proportions: Compare parts and choose one, keeping it in mind as a unit of measure.

Position. Imagine horizontal and vertical lines passing through the most noticeable parts. These serve as mental landmarks.

Form or shapes. Visualize the object as included in a square, circle or some other single form or element; then compare imaginary relationships.

Modeling. Compare tones resulting from varying light and

shade. Use one part as the unit of comparison for darkest or lightest.

Color. Observe and compare light and shade of colors along with other values and contrasts. From these choose a unit of comparison.

Repetition provides practice that can be gained in no other way. Work can be redrawn mentally, as well as on paper. In the latter case, the presence of a critical instructor is valuable where corrections are concerned. Modeling and drawing of simpler forms should be repeated often.

Here, again, it should be noted that if full details cannot be recalled, big lines should be sought first; then, details or parts. If form or color is not grasped, make an abstract of shadows. All such factors go hand in hand with memorization.

In sculpture, repeated use of the hands, with attention to simple detail, constant practice while visualizing form, all serve the same purpose of helping to impress the material into the memory.

COLOR MEMORY

Despite the important part that color plays in art, it falls into a category that is very much its own and not comparable with others. The reason is that the appreciation of color, and therefore a memory for colors, depends upon the limitations of the individual. There are many degrees of color blindness and lesser variations even in the average normals.

Some capable pen-and-ink artists have been color-blind, their interest in art being, in a sense, a compensation for their inability to appreciate color. Naturally, they should be made aware of this before they take up mixing oils, as they are apt to accomplish very little with color while dwelling in a world which they see as lights and shades.

It is therefore a good plan to have color vision checked and to know one's limitations before proceeding with color study. Any attempt at color memory is also hopeless for persons who are unable to identify the very things they are trying to remember. Without color recognition, there can be no color memory.

Assuming that a person's color vision is normal and that he intends to use it in art, interest and observation should be applied, along with practice exercises toward the use and memorization of color, just as in other phases of art. With color, however, a special procedure is required, such as along the following lines.

First, learn to match to flat tints of complementary colors on gray tinted papers. Use oils, as they can be mixed rapidly and accurately.

Next, use three tints, less definitely related than those first matched.

Later, work with a series of tints, increasing them in number and complexity.

Repeat, over and over. Then advance to bits of still life or fragments of pictures to be learnt.

Color recognition and memorization can be carried into many specialized fields. It is important in industry, as a good human eye is still superior to other ways of matching colors. This applies in fields of textiles, carpets, decorative painting, wall papers, and others.

Identifying colors by name also demands constant recognition as well as memorization of the terms themselves. Some of the nomenclature is self-descriptive, including such terms as "shocking pink" or "stratosphere blue." Others demand specialized recognition, as "turquoise," referring to the gem of that name, or "canary," signifying the color of the bird. The term "Wedgwood blue" has come into vogue as indicating the particular blue shade found on that long-famous brand of chinaware.

New names for colors come and go with fashions, frequently with the same speed. How far any one should go in learning these short-lived terms is a matter of personal choice. But they certainly offer a fertile field in the application of memory devices, with many opportunities for odd associations.

5. REMEMBERING GEOGRAPHY

Perhaps the simplest and most effective way of remembering plans, maps, and geography in general is by the picturization method, as when the outline of a country or the course of a river is noted to resemble some easily recognized object. The great possibilities of this method have been sadly neglected, largely because it has been confined chiefly to cases of the most obvious sort.

Often the more exaggerated or far-fetched a mental image, the easier it is to visualize and thereby to remember. Not only that, the links do not have to be confined to picture forms only. Historical data, comparative facts, word and letter play, even local products, can be worked into the memory theme.

Picturization is, of course, the ultimate in map memory, because the maps themselves form shapes. This method is one of the earliest known to man, for the ancients mapped the heavens by the shapes suggested from stellar formations and charted their courses from them long before they gained a working knowledge of physical geography.

It should be noted that many of these formations were far-fetched; that legend was woven into various constellations, which in turn were linked with others and translated into action scenes. So we are applying what is, in a sense, a natural memory method in conjunction with the artificial aids provided by our modern map makers.

Since many of the geographical patterns are the result of accidental associations, the simplest procedure is to begin with the more obvious pictures, then graduate to the more complex. While this means taking them at random, geographically speaking, the similarities of the pictures and patterns will in themselves forge helpful links.

Thus we start with the classic example of:

Italy and Sicily. Most school children are taught to note how Italy resembles a man's boot about to kick a crude football in the form of Sicily. If other geographical formations were that obvious, it would be helpful indeed. But you would have to go far to find another like it!

So let's go far, clear to the other side of the world and study the case of:

New Zealand and Australia. Here we find the very same boot, in the form of New Zealand, but it has completed its kick, which is a very high one. What is more, the kicker has broken his leg (forming the North and South Islands of New Zealand) because he kicked something much larger than a football, the whole continent of Australia.

That brings us to:

New Guinea, Australia, and Tasmania. Here is a neat and easily remembered picture. Study the island of New Guinea and you will note that it is shaped very much like a guinea hen, with its head stretched toward Asia, screaming a warning as it flies up from its nest, which happens to be Australia. The guinea hen is excited because an egg has fallen from its nest and is dropping down below Australia. The "egg" is the island of Tasmania.

Reverting to the original picture, we have:

Sicily and Sardinia. Follow the upward course of the kicker and one football, Sicily, will bring you to another, Sardinia, an island of almost the same size. Here, history forms a link, as both Sicily and Sardinia were the "footballs" of contending nations, ancient and modern. The picture can be carried farther with:

Corsica and Sardinia. Think of Sardinia as a large stone with a smaller stone, Corsica, balanced on it as in the game of "Duck on the Rock." This forms a mental picture that is hard to lose.

194

Other recognizable shapes include:

South America. This continent forms an elephant's head, with its trunk pointing directly downward and finally curling inward. It is appropriate as South America is the one equatorial continent where elephants are *not* found, so it *needs* an elephant's head.

If you picture yourself at Central Park Zoo in New York City, stroking an elephant's trunk straight downward, you will have another good geographical link, for the west coast of South America, as represented by the trunk, runs southward almost on a line with New York. But why stroke the elephant's trunk? Because it is *chilly* up north and it is *Chili* down along the western coast of South America!

South America also looks like a cornucopia, or "horn of plenty," or in more modern form, an ice cream cone, with the ice cream representing the hottest part.

The Atlantic coast of Europe can be recalled by forming a series of graphic pictures, as follows:

The Spanish Peninsula. This represents an excellent profile of Columbus gazing west toward the New World. His face is formed by *Portugal;* his long, flowing hair is *Spain.*

The French Coast. Here is a rough profile of a bearded face representing William the Conqueror with his head tilted well back so his eye is on England, the country he intends to invade.

Denmark and Adjacent Countries. The Danish peninsula, Jutland, represents the head of a bird *jutting* up from the Belgian, Dutch, and German coasts.

Norway and Sweden. Shaped like a huge dragon with mouth open wide to devour the bird within its jaws.

The English Coasts. The west coast of England roughly resembles a rugged, leering face staring westward, while the east coast has the general look of a determined bulldog.

Such outlines, though crude, serve as natural guides; and having drawn them from memory, they can be checked against an actual map and corrected, so that each time they will be remembered more precisely. Cities, rivers, and other features can be localized in relation to such outlines, with one feature helping the other.

This works quite effectively with the map of the United States, when remembering the:

Shapes of States. One writer on this subject has commented that the happiest of American school children are those living either in Wyoming or Colorado, since they find it so easy to draw maps of their home states. That is quite understandable, as both those states are perfectly rectangular in shape.

There is a difference in the location of their capitals, Denver being a little northeast of the center of Colorado, while Cheyenne, appropriately pronounced "Shy Anne," is huddled down in the southeast corner of Wyoming, as far away as possible from the frightening geysers and grizzly bears of the Yellowstone National Park, which occupies the northwest corner.

Often, however, the odd shapes of states make them easier to remember, as well as forming links with others. Florida, for example, is shaped like a pistol, the peninsula being the handle. Tallahassee, the capital, is midway in the strip running westward; here, history is the link, because its site was chosen as the meeting place of two parties coming from opposite directions.

This picture can be carried farther: The pistol is pointed directly at Louisiana, which is shaped like the letter "L" with its capital, Baton Rouge, on a direct line with Tallahassee. With Florida and Louisiana properly placed, it is easy to picture the intervening states, Alabama and Mississippi. Both are roughly upright rectangles, but each has a "step down" to allow for the "squeeze" from Florida and Louisiana. The capitals of Alabama and Mississippi, namely Montgomery and Jackson, are similarly located in their respective states.

In shaping a state like Florida, size as well as other features can be kept in mind by using initials for "key" cities as part of a skeletal structure on which the outline may be imposed. Taking Florida as a simple example:

Draw a horizontal line, marking it with three letters, equally spaced: P T A. These stand for Pensacola, Tallahassee and the Atlantic Coast. Now draw a downward line, slanting slightly to the right. It starts just above the horizontal line and crosses it near the right end.

At the top of the line put G for the Georgia border; at the bottom put M for Miami. Where the lines cross, put J, which stands for "junction" but, more important, represents Jacksonville. Each line is approximately 400 miles long, giving a fair idea of the dimensions of the state.

Now draw a line from T (Tallahassee) to M (Miami) and at the midpoint put the letters S T which stand for St. Petersburg and Tampa. With these guides, you can draw in the outline of Florida, with a line curving down and to the left from M (Miami) shaped like a key and ending with a K for Key West.

New York can be pictured as a lion with upraised head and flowing mane, one paw extended downward to snare a fish that is swimming toward it in the form of Long Island. Here, you can draw a line from A (Albany) leftward to B (Buffalo) representing four units of 70 miles each.

Then draw a line from A two units straight downward to N; and another from A running 2½ units straight up to C, which stands for Canada. The line CAN (an abbreviation for Canada) will then end at N, for New York City. If you place an S for Syracuse, midway between A and B, then run a line one unit in length straight up to a W for Watertown, and another one-unit line straight down to a B for Binghamton, you will have the lion's height from head to haunches and can outline the state in almost exact proportions.

What about states that do not give the appearance of objects, real or fanciful? Most of them respond to the skeletal system, too. Take Missouri as one example: It is named after the Missouri River, which wiggles its way down the western border of the state, then cuts across the middle, to show its authority.

The crossover begins at Kansas City, which is easy to remember because it is in Missouri instead of Kansas. After 150 miles it reaches Jefferson City, the capital, which is in the geographical center of the state, where it belongs. It then keeps on another 150 miles to St. Louis and there joins the Mississippi River, which has been wangling down the eastern border of the state in the same lazy fashion.

Together, the two rivers head on south, always working toward the east enough to give the state the appearance of a rhombus rather than a square. They even carry a little portion of the state along with them and deposit it in the southeast corner for good measure.

Other states can be constructed in similar ways. With Massachusetts, you can draw a vertical line representing 50 miles as the north to south measurement at the center of the state. Draw a horizontal line three times that length with the letters B-W-S-P representing Boston, Worcester, Springfield, Pittsfield, with approximate 50 mile intervals. On a line with Boston run another vertical line two units long (100 miles) from N for *New*buryport to N for *New* Bedford.

Then add a line extending from New Bedford to the right, 50 miles to Hyannis; then an angle to the right and up, 50 miles to Provincetown, remembering them by the letters H-P for "homing pigeon" or whatever phrase seems appropriate.

Delaware looks like an old-fashioned slipper with a curled toe, the buckle near its center being the letter D for Dover, the capital, as well as Delaware. The "panhandles" of Texas, Oklahoma, and West Virginia are features that help in further shaping of those states. The more individualistic these pictures, the better.

Global Memory

The memorization of world localities comes into the general category of topical memory systems and forms an intriguing subject in its own right. Its importance has increased proportionately to the speed of modern air and space travel, so the concept itself has come a long way from a century ago, when remote portions of the globe were less known and actually less accessible than the moon and the neighboring planets are today.

Nevertheless, most of the older memory methods can still be applied to global study and it is interesting to check back to the system used by William Stokes, whose highly popular "mnemonical globe" sold by the thousands during the period of 1868 and later. (See above illustration.)

A description of the globe and its remarkable merits ran as follows:

"An outline of the human face and head is seen upon the globe. Noting on what portion of the face or head the various geographical places are located, fixes their relative positions easily and indelibly upon the memory, and renders the study of geography not only interesting but fascinating. A child will, as an amusement, teach himself more geography in a couple of hours with this globe than the most indefatigable schoolmaster could thrash into him in a twelvemonth.

"With the Mnemonical Globe, beating a child will be found of no service, as he will not object to take pains. Even adults, who have either never known much of geography, or who have let their geographical knowledge evaporate, will find that they can fix in memory the position of places upon the globe by this plan with remarkable ease and speed. Those who study the Mnemonical Globe will find that occasionally a little playful pleasantry with the geographical names will enliven the proceedings, and will produce and strengthen mental impressions.

"Picturing the meaning conveyed by the sound of a name in conjunction with its given locality upon the face or head is by no means an unamusing or unprofitable performance; in fact, quite the reverse. A little verbal distortion or substitution is also within the scope of mnemonical license."

On the face formed by the globe, Europe represents the center of the forehead, remembered by the phrase "You're up." The Sahara Desert is between the eyes, one of which is in the Atlantic Ocean, while the other "sees red" from the general location of the Red Sea.

Above the left ear is "the bit" of China, signifying Tibet, while the ear itself follows the contour of the Indian peninsula to where it has been struck by a "mad rascal"—signifying Madras—and, just below it, there is a "seal on" in the shape of Ceylon. The right ear is represented by Mexico.

The bridge of the nose is remembered by thinking of a coin balanced there, the coin being the obsolete English guinea, which links with the modern Republic of Guinea, giving the picture a decidedly modern twist. The mnemonical globe placed the center of the face at St. Helena, midway between Africa and South America; while the mouth was near Gough Island, just south of the tiny volcanic isles of Tristan da Cunha.

Now, a century later, Stokes' Mnemonical Globe has been given its one needed touch, an eruption of the supposedly extinct volcanic summit of Tristan da Cunha, which caused the inhabitants to abandon the islands. So we can picture the great global face as blowing tobacco smoke from between its smiling lips, which spread from Cape Town well toward Rio de Janeiro.

Such concepts as the mnemonical globe still have merit in their appeal to the imagination; but modern students will find many other features that will serve as memory jogs where maps are concerned. The bulge of Africa, for instance, fits roughly into the concave coasts of North and South America. Greenland is a wedge between the widespread northern coasts of North America and Europe.

Comparative Geographical Areas

One difficulty in visualizing continents, countries, and other geographical divisions, is that of judging their comparative sizes when they are in widely separated parts of the world. The size of the United States in relation to North America does not help with other continents, as their areas vary greatly. What is needed in each case is a basis for comparison; and that is as simple to remember as A, B, C, D, E.

Those letters are utilized as follows:

"A" is for Australia. If you place the continental United States (without Alaska) upon Australia, it will just about fit. The shapes are not just the same, but they are near enough, especially if you turn Australia upside down.

"B" is for Brazil. It is actually larger than the continental United States (without Alaska) but by lopping a little off around the edges, it can be brought rather close to the same size and shape. It forms a good basis of comparison between the United States and other South American countries, as Brazil occupies just about half that continent.

"C" is for China. Again a close comparison, as the area of China proper is about that of the United States, Australia, or Brazil. If outlying territories are included, China becomes much larger; but by adding Alaska to the U.S.A., the sizes again strike a fairly close balance.

"D" is for Desert; and that means the Sahara Desert of Africa. It is just about big enough in size and shape to cover Australia, Brazil, China, or the United States.

"E" is for Europe. Here we must add Alaska to the United States in order to come fairly close. To simplify it, just let Alaska balance up Norway, Sweden, Finland and the British Isles. The United States will then come fairly close to equalling the rest of Europe in size, as will Australia, Brazil, China and the Sahara Desert.

Such pictured comparisons are as good as a mental yardstick where measuring continental areas is concerned. By looking at maps and imagining one transposed to another portion of the world, it is easy to gain a correct idea of proportions.

The Caribbean Islands. Pegging the islands of the West Indies is simple, if you start by picturing Cuba as an alligator swimming eastward, squarely into the pincer grip of a crablike monster formed by the island of Hispaniola. The pincers extend from the country of Haiti; the rest of the monster is formed by the Dominican Republic.

If you picture the monster as much longer, but partly submerged as it comes up out of the sea, you can include Puerto Rico (to the east) as part of its body and to that append a long, curving tail like a lobster's, that swings southward forming the Leeward and Windward Islands down to the coast of South America.

Jamaica, just south of the western end of Cuba, must also be fitted into the picture. It looks like some small creature that was lucky enough to get away, either from the alligator or the sea monster, or both.

Another way to picture Cuba is in the shape of one of its principal products, a long, slender tobacco leaf, with its tip appropriately extending westward beyond Havana. How long is that tobacco leaf? Just think of Havana cigars being smoked clear from Florida up to Washington, D. C., a distance of about 750 miles and you will have a good idea of how far Cuba would stretch along the Atlantic seaboard.

The Caribbean and the Mediterranean. An interesting comparison may be made between the Caribbean and Mediterranean Seas. They are approximately the same size (about 1,000,000 square miles) with the Caribbean about 10 per cent the larger.

Picture Central America as corresponding to the Spanish Peninsula, which is appropriate as it was once part of New Spain (which included Mexico). Tilt Cuba's eastern section to form an extension of Florida, and it represents Italy, with Jamaica as Sicily. Hispaniola is the equivalent of Greece and Puerto Rico for Crete. The Leeward and Windward Islands of the Caribbean then correspond to the Asiatic coast of the eastern Mediterranean.

Each sea has an isthmus bisected by a canal; Panama for the Caribbean, Suez for the Mediterranean. Each also is the division between two continents, which makes the resemblance all the more remarkable. The only difference is their location, the Isthmus of Panama being near the southwest of the Caribbean, while the Isthmus of Suez is at the southeast of the Mediterranean. But even that ties in with the fact that South America and Africa "bulge" in opposite directions, so that Panama and Suez have to be "left" and "right" respectively.

Other Resemblances. Many graphic pictures can be formed from seas as well as continents and countries. Just as the Scandinavian Peninsula resembles a monster about to swallow Denmark, so does the Baltic Sea look like a creature trying to devour Finland, its jaws being the Gulf of Finland and the Gulf of Bothnia.

The Caspian Sea, in Asia, has the appropriate shape of a sea horse, while Hudson Bay, in northern Canada, looks like a closed right fist, back upward, with its forefinger pointing directly down toward the Hudson River, which was discovered by the same famous explorer.

The Peloponnesus, or lower peninsula of Ancient Greece, has been likened to the palm and outstretched fingers of a left hand, with Attica (above the Isthmus of Corinth) as the thumb. Modern France takes on the shape of a pig's head with its snout in a bucket formed by Spain and Portugal.

Section C · Recreational

1. MEMORY GAMES

Anagrams

Anagrams are words or phrases of different meanings that have just one thing in common. Each is composed of the same letters, differently arranged. Thus, PAL is an anagram of LAP. Other anagrams sometimes may form three words, as ACRE, CARE, RACE; and there are still other letter combinations that can be made into four or more.

As a game, "Anagrams" offers fun along with practice at word formation based on word recognition and word memory. Each player is given a list of a dozen—or more—letter groups, such as the following:

A E G R T	*A E L P T*	*A E H L S*
A C H M R	*O P R S T*	*A E R S T*
E L M N O	*A B E L T*	*D E I R V*
E P R S U	*E E H R T*	*A C E R T*

A time limit is set, during which each player tries to form words from these. At the finish, each receives 5 points for the first word formed from a group; and 10 points for the second word thus formed, since that completes the anagram. As an example: By forming AEGRT into GREAT, a player collects 5 points. If he then forms GRATE, he receives 10 more, for a total of 15.

Some of the groups, like ACERT, allow the formation of more than two words. Any additional words thus formed count 5 points each. Looking for these "extras" adds to the zest of the game.

Sufficient time should be allowed to make the competition keen. One method of play is to continue until one player has formed at least one word from each group. He may then call, "Done!" and the scores are added.

The first player to finish would not necessarily be the winner, as another might have been busy forming 10 point anagrams, while the first was rushing through to complete a full list of 5 point single words.

Here are some extra groups that form good anagram words:

E O R T V	*E I L M S*	*E E L S T*
A D M N O	*A E H R S*	*E O R T W*
A E M S T	*C N O R S*	*A E K S T*

Others may be formed from 3 or 4 letter words, which offer many choices; also, longer anagrams of 6 or more letters are of frequent occurrence.

Words formed from the 5 letter groups given here are listed. In playing "Anagrams," plurals and past tenses are allowed; and any question as to the validity of a word should be decided by reference to a dictionary.

Anagrams formed from 5-letter groups:

Original List:

GREAT	PLEAT	LEASH
GRATE	PLATE	SHALE
	PETAL	
CHARM	LEAPT	STARE
MARCH		RATES
	PORTS	TEARS
	SPORT	TARES
		ASTER

LEMON	TABLE	DIVER
MELON	BLEAT	DRIVE
PURSE	ETHER	CATER
SUPER	THREE	CRATE
	THERE	TRACE

Supplementary List:

OVERT	MILES	STEEL
TROVE	SMILE	SLEET
VOTER	LIMES	
		TOWER
DAMON	SHEAR	WROTE
MONAD	SHARE	
NOMAD	HARES	STEAK
	HEARS	STAKE
STEAM		SKATE
MATES	CORNS	TAKES
MEATS	SCORN	
TEAMS		

Concentration

This is one of the more absorbing of memory games. It is played with a standard pack of 52 cards, preferably by two persons, as each can then take immediate advantage of the other's mistakes; but it can be played by three or more.

The entire pack of cards is dealt face down, spreading over the table so that all cards are completely in sight, forming irregular rows. One person begins by turning two cards face up. If they are the same in value (as two Fives) he removes them and turns up another pair anywhere in the layout. He takes them also, if they match in value and continues on.

But as soon as he turns up two cards that do not form a pair (as a King and an Eight) he must turn them face down again,

207

exactly as they were. The play then moves to the opponent, who turns up two cards in the hope of matching them, removing them and thus continuing his play. The player taking the most cards wins the game.

Skill in "Concentration" lies in remembering cards that have been shown and then turned down. Suppose that after a player has failed to match a King and an Eight, his opponent should turn up a King. If the opponent kept track of the King that was turned down, he can promptly turn it up himself to match his own King, thus taking the two as a pair.

Naturally, a player seldom misses such an easy chance. But frequently three or four plays may be made before a turned down card is matched. That means keeping track, not just of one card but half a dozen or more, from various portions of the layout, as smart players jump around a lot to confuse the opposition. At the same time, a player may keep track of certain cards in somewhat systematic fashion.

But the keener a player's observation, the better his memory, the greater his chance of winning. Ability to capitalize on an opponent's slips is often the whole difference in this fascinating game.

Ghosts

This is an excellent memory game, which also serves as a good vocabulary builder. Far from a mere childish pastime, it can grip the attention of keen, intellectual minds, though it forms good juvenile sport as well.

Any number up to a dozen may play, the game narrowing down as it proceeds until it finally becomes a contest between two players. One person begins by naming a letter of the alphabet; the next adds a letter, but the two must form the beginning of a word; a third person adds another letter toward a word; and so on.

With the naming of the third letter, if a complete word is

thereby formed, the player naming it is the loser of that round; and a new round is begun by the next person in the circle.

Suppose for example that there are five players in the game. Player 1 starts with "M" as a letter, having any word beginning with "M" in mind. Player 2 adds "E" producing "ME" and thinking of some simple word like "Met" or "Men."

Note here, that "Me" is actually a word, but having only two letters, it does not count against the player naming it. Player 3, however, is in an immediate dilemma; he must avoid such letters as "N," "T," or "W" as they will form a word. So he thinks a moment and adds "L," making "MEL."

The word that Player 3 has in mind is "Melon" and Player 4 goes along with it, adding "O" and forming "MELO." Player 5 thinks quickly and instead of adding a fatal "N," adds "D." That makes "MELOD" with the word that Player 5 has in mind being "Melody."

It is again the turn of Player 1. He adds "I" making "MELODI" and it looks as though Player 2 will lose. But he thinks of the word "Melodious" and adds an "O" making "MELODIO." From there on, the only letters that can be added are "U" and "S" so that Player 4 would lose with "MELODIOUS."

Here is how the game went play by play. Letters in parentheses represent those that players avoided:

Players:	1	2	3	4	5	1	2	3	4
Letters:	M	E	L	O	D	I	O	U	S
			(N)		(N)	(Y)	(C)		

If a player wishes, he can challenge a letter given by the player just before him. For example: When Player 5 said "D" forming "MELOD" instead of "MELON," Player 1 might have doubted that Player 5 really had a word in mind. If challenged, Player 5 would have announced "Melodious" and Player 1 would have lost the round because his challenge was met. This would have saved Player 4.

On the contrary, if a player tries to get by with an imaginary or impossible word, he loses if challenged. Sometimes a player does this by mistake, confusing a true word with a false one, thus adding a letter that he shouldn't. In any case, if the next player is afraid to challenge and adds another letter, hoping it is part of a real word, he becomes the one who is open to a challenge.

With two or three players, score may be kept, with each player taking a turn at starting the next round. Game can be set at a specified number of rounds or after one player has lost a certain number. As a group game, the loser of each round drops out, becoming a "ghost," from which the game derives its title. Such elimination reduces the participants to two, who play to decide the winner.

To add fun, the ghosts may be given the privilege of asking questions or making comments as the game proceeds. If one of the active players inadvertently replies or speaks to the ghost, he too becomes a ghost. Some play that, in this case, the ghost supplants the active player, adding a further zest to the game.

Guggenheim

This is an intriguing game that not only tests your memory but your ability to use it under exacting conditions. Several persons may participate, while non-players may act as judges and timekeepers.

First, five categories of words are chosen, such as Animals, Birds, Colors, Countries, Foods, Islands, States, Trees, or any other qualification that is not too restricted. Names of authors, generals, presidents, etc., are also good categories.

Next, a simple five-letter word is chosen. All its letters must be different, as in the word SOLAR. If desired, a list of a few dozen such words can be written on slips of paper beforehand; then one of these is drawn at random.

Suppose that Birds, Colors, Foods, Islands, Trees are used, along with the word SOLAR. Each player forms a 5 by 5 square on a sheet of paper, with the categories down the side and the key word across the top, a letter to each column. At the word "Go!" players fill in the squares, using suitable words beginning with the specified letters.

Here is an example of a completed sheet:

	S	O	L	A	R
Birds	Swan	Oriole	Lark	Albatross	Robin
Colors	Silver	Orange	Lavender	Azure	Red
Foods	Sugar	Oats	Lentils	Asparagus	Rice
Islands	Sicily	Orkney	Lemnos	Azores	Réunion
Trees	Spruce	Oak	Larch	Apple	Redwood

A time limit of 15 minutes (or more) is allowed, so that players can write in the words that spring quickly to mind and then try to fill in those that they find more difficult. However, the purpose is not just to complete the list but to include unusual words that the opponents may not have in their lists.

Thus, given added time, a player might drop "Robin" and insert "Rook." Or he might supplant "Red" with "Rose." Or "Rice" with "Rhubarb."

Scoring is usually done on this basis: A player calls off a word and scores 1 point for each player who does not have it. Thus, in a six-player game, if you alone named "Sicily" as an "S-island," you would score 5 points. But if four other players named "Oak" as an "O-tree," you would only score 1 point, since "Oak" would be absent from one list only.

Usually, a double or compounded word is only allowed a half-score. For example: "Redwing Blackbird" instead of "Robin." If that appeared on one list only, it would score 2½ instead of 5 points. The same would apply to "Sea urchin" as a food, under "S." Such a ruling is necessary to prevent players from going

211

after such double words in the hope that no other player will be using them.

There is no penalty for failing to fill any of the squares; the player just does not score for that square. The same applies, of course, if he inserts a fictitious or incorrect word in any square. The most that a player could score with a unique list in a six-player game would be 25 points; but it must be noted that others have the same opportunity, so it is obviously wise to aim for as high a total as possible.

Other rules can be introduced; in fact, it is well to discuss certain categories and their restrictions before the play begins. Afterward, any questions are left to the judges, or may be decided by a vote of the players themselves.

As an exercise in memory training, this game stimulates the visualization of associated words, pictures, maps and various scenes, as well as aiding spelling and classification of objects.

Mixed Proverbs

Much of memory depends on recognizing things that have been learned because they have been heard or quoted often. This is particularly true of proverbs and old sayings, many of which are learned almost by rote.

Hence it is good training as well as fun to put these to the test by playing "Mixed Proverbs." The game is simple: Each player is given a list such as the following and is told to correct or rearrange certain words:

1. A switch in time saves nine.
2. It's always too late to mend.
3. Perseverance is the thief of time.
4. It's a long worm that has no turning.
5. Let barking dogs lie.
6. Better never than late.
7. A rolling stone gathers the moss.

8. He who fights and runs away
   Will not fight another day.
9. Many cooks make light work.
10. Two heads are wiser than one.
11. Ingenuity is the mother of invention.
12. All that glitters is not gold.

Inasmuch as some of these sayings vary in their original form, it is not necessary to get them letter perfect, but merely to correct the glaring errors. In some of these, ideas from other proverbs have been inserted purposely as catches.

In repeating the game, other sayings or slogans can be mixed or twisted in similar tricky fashion; and if desired, one player can propose a "mixed" proverb, challenging another to answer it; the second player can then counter with a tricky proverb of his own.

As a variant, or extension of this game, titles or quotes may be given from familiar songs or poems, each with a mistake that must be corrected, as:

1. Around the World in 90 Days.
2. Half a league, half a league forward.
3. All around the raspberry bush, the monkey chased the weasel.
4. It's the Wrong Way to Tipperary.
5. Humpty Dumpty walked on a wall.
6. In the Evening, by the Starlight.
7. East Side, West Side, up and down the town.
8. Where did you buy that hat?

Corrections to proverbs and supplementary quotations are given below.

Corrections to Proverbs:

(1) *Switch* should be *stitch*. (2) *Always* should be *never*. (3) *Perseverance* should be *Procrastination*. (4) *Worm* should be *lane*. (5) *Barking* should be *sleeping*. (6) Should read: "Better

213

late than never." (7) *The* should be *no*. (8) *Will not* should be *Lives to*. (9) *Cooks* should be *hands*. (10) *Wiser* should be *better*. (11) *Ingenuity* should be *Necessity*. (12) Should read: "All is not gold that glitters," otherwise it refutes itself.

Corrections to Supplementary Quotations:

(1) 90 should be 80. (2) *Forward* should be *onward*. (3) *Raspberry* should be *mulberry*. (4) *The Wrong* should be *A Long*. (5) *Walked* should be *sat*. (6) *Starlight* should be *Moonlight*. (7) *Up and down* should be *All around*. (8) *Buy* should be *get*.

Word List Game

Perhaps one of the simplest stimulating games of memory is the "Word List" game which has frequently been used in contests. As a form of fun for family and friends, it is even better, as the introduction of a time limit puts a premium on quick thinking rather than slow plodding and affords players a chance to catch up in later innings.

To start, you take a simple word like:

Retailer

Each player, working on his own sheet of paper, begins forming words from the letters of the key word. Each word must have three letters or more, as: Let, Rat, Lit, Ate, Rate, Late, Tail, Tale, Later, Trail, Trial, Relate, Trailer—and any others that players may strike upon.

At the end of a time limit, say five minutes, lists are counted and checked. Each person is given 1 point for each word on his list. Another word is taken as a "key" and a second inning is played on the same basis. The player with the highest score at the end of five innings is the winner.

Longer words may be used, or longer time limits allowed, according to the age or mood of the players. In faster company, it is a good plan to give a player 2 points for any words he forms that are not duplicated on another list. This encourages players to go after more difficult words.

A dictionary should be used to check the validity of any odd words.

2. MEMORY MAGIC

Quick Number Trick

Here is a way of *proving* that you have a remarkable memory for numbers, that requires no practice, no system; in fact, nothing beyond familiarity with certain figures, a fact which you do not mention in connection with the stunt.

In an off-hand way, you write down a number of about two dozen figures, such as

41423344250597281869610311011625

Then, while some one holds the list, you call off the figures in correct order, "Four–one–four–two–three—" and so on, naming them exactly. If you wish, you can call them backwards, "Five–two–one–six—" though this is done more slowly and therefore may prove more impressive.

Actually, it is a simple but clever trick. The number given represents the stations on the Eighth Avenue Subway in New York City, starting with 4th, then 14th, 23rd, and up to 96th Street; then 103rd and so on, up to 125th Street. They are written in order, but as the figures of one continuous number.

Calling them off is then a matter of course to any one familiar with the subway and its stations. Riders on other subways would have other numbers they could call off in the same fashion. For example:

2581113153034405256606369

That one would even baffle New Yorkers because it happens to be composed of the stations on a Philadelphia Subway, starting with 2nd Street, 5th, 8th, 11th, and so on to 69th Street.

Instead of subway stations, you can use telephone numbers, those that you constantly have in mind. These could be 7–4796,

8–9589, 2–3634, 5–1793, which would be written as a single number:

$$74796895892363451793$$

All you have to remember is the order in which you took the numbers and if you want to repeat the trick, use another set. Street addresses of friends can also be utilized. Worked with other memory tricks, or actual memorization of numbers by means of a system, this "quick trick" is rendered all the more effective.

Over the Telephone

Here is a neat trick of pretended mind reading that is simply an application of the "Figure Alphabet" on a two-person scale. You tell your friends that you know a remarkable mind reader, or mystic, who can read thoughts in terms of numbers anywhere up to 10,000. Such a number is chosen, say 3821 and you tell some one to call the mind reader, whose name is Professor Mafanti, and ask him to name the number.

So the call is made to the home or apartment that the professor is visiting, or wherever else he may be, and when called to the phone, the fabulous mind reader concentrates deeply and gives the correct number.

The trick is in the name. There is no Professor Mafanti; the man at the other end is your friend who knows the figure alphabet. You simply coin "Mafanti" or MaFaNTi from the figures forming the chosen number, 3821. (M–3, F–8, N–2, T–1)

You refer to Professor Mafanti as a noted Italian, but if people had picked the number 7450, you would have told them to ask for Professor Carlos, the brilliant Brazilian psychic. The name "Carlos" or CaRLoS gives the number (K–7, R–4, L–5, O–S).

Giving the "professor" a foreign background helps the stunt in two ways. It accounts for the oddity of the name you may be forced to coin; and it enables your friend to disguise his voice with an appropriate accent.

To handle more difficult numbers as 4586, which would utilize the key letters R–L–V–J you can add "ini" to the name, so instead of saying "Professor Ralvaj," you would term him "Professor Ralvajini" which sounds like a stage name and makes the trick all the more impressive. Your friend simply ignores the "ini."

Similarly, a "ski" can be added, making the "professor" a Russian; or by tacking on "opolis" he becomes a Greek. These, or any other artifices, should be planned beforehand, so there will be no confusion when they are used.

To make the trick most effective, have several of your friends write down numbers of three figures each; then add them all together so the mind reader can give the grand total, when every one concentrates upon it.

Once the numbers are added, you have people check them over to make sure the total is correct; and this gives you more time to think up a good name for the pretended "professor," which you announce in due course.

The Paired Cards

An old but clever memory stunt with playing cards. Twenty cards are dealt into ten face down pairs. While your back is turned, three or four people each choose a pair, look at the two cards and remember them. Each then drops his pair on any others and the pairs are all gathered into one face down heap.

You then deal the cards in *random* fashion, face up on the table, one here, another there, until you finally have four cross-rows of five cards each, with pairs well separated. You ask a person to point out the cross-rows in which his cards appear, but without indicating the cards themselves.

Despite that restriction, you immediately pick out his two cards;

not only that, you repeat the test with other persons until you have successfully discovered each chosen pair.

The stunt depends upon four "key" words: THIGH, LINEN, ATLAS, GOOSE. After gathering the face down pairs, you picture those words as if they were printed in huge letters on the table, forming four rows:

T H I G H
L I N E N
A T L A S
G O O S E

Now deal the paired cards face up, thus: A card on the "T" in THIGH; the next on "T" in ATLAS. A card on "H" in THIGH; the next on the other H. A card on "I" in THIGH; the next on the "I" in LINEN. A card on "G" in THIGH; the next on "G" in GOOSE. A card on "L" in LINEN; the next on "L" in ATLAS. Continue thus, with "N's," "E's," "A's," "S's" and finally the two "O's" in GOOSE, as the last pair of cards can go nowhere else.

Haphazard though this deal may look, the cards are still paired according to your imaginary letters; and because of the special "key" words used, none are combined exactly the same, so far as the rows are concerned. The paired letters and their rows run thus:

H–H; 1–1. I–I; 1–2. T–T; 1–3. G–G; 1–4. N–N; 2–2. L–L; 2–3. E–E; 2–4. A–A; 3–3. S–S; 3–4. O–O; 4–4

Thus, if a person says his cards are in Rows 2 and 4, you look for the matching letters in LINEN and GOOSE and pick out the two cards appearing at the letter "E" positions. If both are in Row 3, you take the two cards representing the "A's" in ATLAS. This is continued until all chosen pairs are identified.

Simply be sure that the pairs are not separated before they are gathered and that the heap is not shuffled or cut before you begin dealing your face up rows. The rest is then routine.

Paired Objects

This is a modern version of the "card pairing" test, in which various small objects are used instead of playing cards. Take 20 objects, such as a ring, a match-pack, a pen, a pencil, a dime, a nickel, a key, a knife, a cigarette, a dollar bill, a lipstick, a compact, a handkerchief, a glass, etc. You can use two that are similar, as a bright penny and a dull one; or two match-packs of different colors; or a large glass and a small one.

Let people pair these as they come along, so there are 10 pairs of objects on the table. You turn your back and each person points to a pair which he wants as his own, but without telling you. That done, you turn to the table and begin separating all the pairs, until you have formed five haphazard rows. You then have each person name the row or rows in which his pair happens to be. Immediately, you pick the two chosen objects.

It is simply a case of placing each pair on its proper letters, as with the pairs of cards, using the THIGH, LINEN, ATLAS, GOOSE formula. For convenience, here is another set of code words that will work just as well, so you can switch from one to the other, when repeating either test. These "keys" are: SANTA, TIMID, MORON, REEDS. Picture them as:

```
S   A   N   T   A
T   I   M   I   D
M   O   R   O   N
R   E   E   D   S
```

These paired letters and their rows run:

A–A; 1–1. T–T; 1–2. N–N; 1–3. S–S; 1–4. I–I; 2–2. M–M; 2–3. D–D; 2–4. O–O; 3–3. R–R; 3–4. E–E; 4–4

One of the earliest of these four-word codes consisted of the Latin words: MUTUS, DEDIT, NOMEN, COCIS, which may be translated, "The mute gave a name to the cook." This makes a convenient connected sentence for anyone who understands

219

Latin. Since these four words work in the "pair" trick, they can be used as an alternate.

Triple Memory

This is an elaboration of the "Paired Cards" already described, but in this case 36 cards are used and are dealt in 12 groups of three each, all face down. Persons are allowed to look at individual groups while your back is turned, so that several people each have three cards in mind.

The trios are gathered into one big pile, which you deal face up in six rows of six cards each, apparently hit or miss. But when a person points to the rows where his cards appear, you immediately find the three cards.

A code of six words is used: THRONE, SENDER, DOLLAR, SANCHA, DULUTH, STUCCO. You picture these arranged thus:

```
T    H    R    O    N    E
S    E    N    D    E    R
D    O    L    L    A    R
S    A    N    C    H    A
D    U    L    U    T    H
S    T    U    C    C    O
```

These form the following combinations of letters and rows:

T's, 1–5–6. H's, 1–4–5. R's, 1–2–3. O's, 1–3–6. N's, 1–2–4. E's, 1–2–2. S's, 2–4–6. D's, 2–3–5. L's, 3–3–5. A's, 3–4–4. C's, 4–6–6. U's, 5–5–6

When a person names the rows that his cards are in, counting from the top row down, simply spell the key words mentally and find the three letters common to the rows in question. (Example: O, in THRONE, DOLLAR, STUCCO.) Those cards will be the three the person remembered.

220

The "Whodunit" Test

In this stunt, you play the part of a detective, with results that will greatly impress the average audience. Your "props" consist of two sets of cards: One, a list of articles, written in red; the other, a list of places written in blue.

Two typical lists would be:

Articles		Places	
The Diamonds	The Door Knob	The Freezer	The Hayloft
The Culprit	The Fingerprints	The Lake	The Bowling Alley
The Victim	The Poison	The Station Wagon	The Pine Tree
The Knife	The Bullet	The Tunnel	The Zoo
The Will	The Butler	The Toll Booth	The Ball Park
The Bowling Ball	The Racehorse	The Steeple	The Dressing Room
The Bloodstains	The Teeth	The Elevator	The TV Studio
The Revolver	The Missing Heir	The Red Barn	The Airliner
The Treasure	The Key	The Furnace	The Post Office
The Map	The Wig	The Night Club	The Barber Shop

Mix these groups separately and take one from each pile, observing what they are. Hand the two cards to a friend, saying: "The red card is the clue the detective is looking for; the blue card is the place where he found it. Keep those until I ask for them."

The remaining cards are distributed in the same fashion; then you announce: "From now on, I'll be the detective. Call out any clue and I'll tell you where I found it."

A person refers to a red card and asks, "Where did you find the diamonds?" You answer, "In the steeple," and a reference to the blue card proves that you are right. Another asks, "Where did you find the bowling ball?" You answer, "In the furnace." Right again. As fast as more clues are called, you give the correct answers.

Most people would have trouble remembering two or three of these when trying it as a game, but you go through twenty or more, making it appear as a remarkable feat of rapid memory.

Actually, it is a simple case of pairing objects, one of the easiest forms of association, with no extra word link or peg systems required, as the cards are specially suited to quick picturization. As you hand out each pair, note what they say and visualize accordingly.

It's easy to picture diamonds glistening from a steeple; or a bowling ball bouncing from a furnace when you open the door. Close your eyes just long enough to set the impression and the more ridiculous it turns out, the easier you will find it will be to recall.

When people call out "clues" later, they are actually giving you "cues," as each picture will jump immediately to mind. Often, in forming them, you can add an odd touch that helps; for instance, if a pair of cards read BUTLER and BALL PARK, you could picture a dignified butler eating a hot dog while watching the ball game.

Like all associations of this type, these efface themselves when you form a new set of pictures, provided that you allow a sufficient interval between, which you can determine after several trials. The two lists can be increased to include other articles (red) and places (blue) if desired.

Aside from its entertainment interest, this stunt affords good practice in visualized associations, which is highly helpful to memory training.

Apple, Egg, and Orange

This impresses people as a cross between a mind reading stunt and a memory trick, but it actually belongs in the latter class. It requires a list of code words, but you do not have to memorize them, as you can refer to the list during the demonstration. You must, however, remember the way in which the code is utilized.

An apple, an egg, and an orange are placed on the table. Three people assist in the test; while your back is turned, one takes the apple, another the egg, and the third the orange. They can either hide them or simply choose them mutually, each person keeping one in mind by agreement with the other assistants.

That done, you pour some lumps of sugar from a partly filled bowl. You give one lump to one person (whom we will term X), two lumps to the second person (Y), and three lumps to the third person (Z). These are for your reference only, as they have no bearing on the locations of the apple, egg or orange; at least, not yet.

Now you announce: "While my back is turned, I want the person who chose the apple to take *just as many* lumps of sugar as I gave him. The person who chose the egg is to take *twice* as many lumps as I gave him. The person who chose the orange must take *four times* as many lumps as I gave him."

The persons do as stated, either hiding the lumps or putting

223

them back in the bowl so that you can not see how many were taken by each person. Nevertheless, after a moment of concentration, you point to X, Y, Z in order and announce who chose the apple, who picked the egg, and who took the orange.

Now for the solution of this perplexity:

Actually, the lumps of sugar provide the needed clue; not those that the persons took or replaced in the bowl, but those that are still on the table. At the start, there are exactly 24 lumps. You must see to that beforehand, but do not mention the number when you first pour the lumps from the bowl.

In addition, you have a little list, composed of the following key words with their corresponding numbers:

1. *CAMEO*	5. *GENOA*
2. *REASON*	6. *ROTATE*
3. *LADRONE*	7. *KOREA*

The numbers refer to the remaining lumps; the vowels (A, E, O) represent "Apple," "Egg," and "Orange," in whatever order they appear. Thus, if there is only one sugar lump left, the first person, X, will have the apple; the second person, Y, the egg; the third person, Z, the orange.

If five lumps are left, your key-word, GENOA, will tell you that X has the egg, Y has the orange, and Z has the apple. Note that there is no "key" for 4, as that exact number of lumps can not be left over. The six words listed represent the only possible combinations.

A plate of crackers or a dish of nuts can be used instead of a bowl of sugar lumps, provided that you have the exact number required, 24, at the start of the stunt.

A Mighty Memory

In this "test" of what appears to be a mighty memory, you use a set of cards numbered from 1 to 50, or more if so desired. On each card is a number of eight figures, which, of course, is somewhere in the millions.

You state that you have memorized all these numbers individually; and that all any one has to do is call out the smaller number of the card itself, whereupon with due concentration you can remember the large number appearing on that card.

For example: After persons have taken cards at random, one announces: "I have card Number 47. What is the big number?" Slowly, deliberately, you state: "6-5-1-6-7-3-0-3" and that number, 65,167,303, proves to be correct. This is repeated with other cards, always with success.

Actually, you do remember the big numbers, but not in their entirety. Instead, you use a simple, but deceptive code, based on the index number of the card. When a person calls that number (example, 47) you mentally add 9 (making 56) and reverse the total (65) to begin your big number.

As you call off those two figures "6-5" mentally, add them and call off the resulting digit for your next figure. Thus, 6 and 5 would be 11, so you take the figure at the right and announce "1" as the next figure of your big number, thus making it "6-5-1."

Now add the second and third figures (5 and 1) to get the fourth figure (6) making "6-5-1-6." Then add the third and fourth (1 and 6) to get the fifth figure (7) making "6-5-1-6-7." The fourth and fifth figures (6 and 7) total 13, but you merely keep the 3 which makes "6-5-1-6-7-3." The 7 and 3 total 10, but you keep only the 0, making "6-5-1-6-7-3-0." Finally, you add the 3 and 0, completing your number with the eighth figure (3) making 65,167,303.

As another example: Card Number 8 would give you 8 plus 9, or 17, which is reversed to form the starting figures "7-1." Adding those two, then the next two, and so on, as just described, you would "build" the number "7-1-8-9-7-6-3-9" or 71,897,639.

Two simple exceptions are required, both being logical and therefore easily remembered:

a) Never begin a big number with a 0. Thus, if some one states he has Card Number 31, your addition of 9 gives you 40, which reversed is 0-4. You drop the 0 and give "4" as your first figure. Having nothing to add but 4 itself, it becomes your second figure, making "4-4" as your start. From then on, the big number would add up "4-4-8-2-0-2-0-2" or 44,820,202.

b) After adding 9 to the card number, do not reverse the total if it would bring you back to the original number. That occurs in cases like Card 23, where adding 9 makes 32, which, reversed, is 2-3. Here, you would simply retain 32 and announce your first two figures as "3-2." The big number would then add up "3-2-5-7-2-9-1-0" making 32,572,910.

Making up the cards is easy and is worth the time required, as it will familiarize you with the adding process. The card number can be printed in one color ink, with the big number in another color beneath it. It is best to print the numbers the wide way on the card, to allow room.

You can go up to 60, 70, or even 100 cards if you want, as the principle is the same throughout. With cards 92 and up, you would get off to a three figure start. (Example 95 plus 9 equals 104; reversed, "4-0-1," which builds to "4-0-1-5-6-1-7-8" or 40,-156,178.)

Number Memory

Here is an entertaining way to demonstrate your prowess as a memory expert and at the same time put to use one of the simply learned systems described in this book.

Ask a group of friends to call off figures from 0 to 9 inclusive, giving you time to write them down, one by one. A blackboard is best for this, but as one is seldom available you can use a large card and a heavy pencil, which will do quite well.

Suppose the figures finally form the number:

$$83061179504247581346290 7$$

You give the card to some one and let him call for any figure, as the third from the left, the ninth from the left, etc. You give these correctly as "0" and "5" or whatever other figure he may request.

To show your phenomenal memory, you call off the figures in *reverse order,* starting from the right: 7-0-9-2-6 and so on, until you reach the first figure, in this case, 8.

Again, you name a few random figures as requested; then you reel off the whole number from left to right: 8-3-0-6 and so on, finishing with the final 7. You then ask for a pencil and with it you write something on a slip of paper, which you fold and hand to your friend.

That done, you have him add all the figures in the long number, which in this example would come to 102. After he has finished, you have him open the folded slip; and there is that very total: "102."

All you need for this rather surprising demonstration is a working knowledge of the "A to Z Code" described elsewhere, as it is ideally suited to the rapid memorization of 20 or so figures. However, you should have the positions of the 5th figure (E), the 10th (J), the 15th (O), the 20th (T) well fixed in mind. You can remember these from the coined word EJOT.

As you write down the original figures, make them large and plain. This gives you time to picture them the "A to Z" way. (Two squares of ARROWS, 8; BIRDS on a triangular perch, 3; a CAT going over a fence, 0, etc.) After you have completed your slowly written list, you can let someone call for figures: If he asks for the 17th from the left, you count "E–J–O, Five— ten—fifteen—and two more, P and Q," giving you QUARRY, which you have pegged as 1.

Often, you can count to such a figure faster than your friend can, which makes the demonstration all the more effective. Don't worry if you make one or two slips; just check them, get them right, and do a little more concentration. Then start naming figures from right to left, slowly, one by one.

You do this by going through the alphabet backward from your final letter (in this case, X for XYLOPHONE). Take your time, making a big show of it, while you make each picture all the stronger; and if any are wrong, correct them.

A few more random figures, as called for; then you proceed to give the entire number in proper order, left to right. By now, with your stronger impressions and any necessary corrections, you should have it letter perfect in the full sense of the term. But don't reel off the figures too rapidly.

Instead, announce them slowly, impressively, as though doing some real concentration, which you are, but for a special purpose. As you name each figure and your friend responds, "Correct," add it mentally to those you have already given. That enables you to write the total at the finish and have the folded paper opened for a grand climax.

Memorizing a Pack of Cards

In this great feat, a person goes through a pack—or group—of playing cards, noting them one by one; then later calls them off in exact order. Though it requires practice, it is not difficult to acquire, as it depends upon a system which can be mastered by combining patience and imagination.

The system is an adaptation of the Figure Alphabet, with some special features. First take the word CHASED and use four of its letters C, H, S, D to represent the suits of a pack of cards, Clubs, Hearts, Spades, Diamonds (CHaSeD) in that order. You then prepare a suitable list, as follows:

	CLUBS	HEARTS	SPADES	DIAMONDS
ACE	Cat	Hut	Soda	Date
2	Cane	Hun	Sun	Den
3	Comb	Home	Seam	Dome
4	Car	Hour	Sore	Door
5	Coal	Hail	Sail	Dial
6	Coach	Hedge	Sash	Ditch
7	Cook	Hawk	Sock	Duck
8	Calf	Hive	Safe	Dive
9	Cap	Heap	Soap	Dub
10	Case	House	Sauce	Doze
JACK	Crack	Hack	Shack	Deck
QUEEN	Cream	Heroine	Screen	Dream
KING	Club	Heart	Spade	Diamond

Study the list and you will see that the first letter in each word represents the *suit* of the card, all Clubs beginning with C, Hearts with H, Spades with S and Diamonds with D.

From 1 (Ace) up to 10, each word has a letter or letter formation which corresponds with the Figure Alphabet: T or D for 1 (as in CaT or SoDa); N for 2; M for 3; and so on, with S or Z (as in CaSe and DoZe) representing 10.

From there on, special words are used, designed particularly for the purpose of remembering certain cards. With JACK, the key words are CRACK, HACK, SHACK and DECK because they begin with the proper letters for each suit and sound somewhat like the word "Jack." The same applies to QUEEN, as CREAM, HEROINE, SCREEN and DREAM have similar sounds.

With KING, the simple and effective course is adopted of letting each represent the suit itself, in the form of a wooden Club, a human Heart, a garden Spade, or a glittering Diamond (or Diamonds), as all these picture well.

All these words have been chosen because they are different from those given in the Figure Alphabet and therefore will not conflict with it, though the numerical values (up to 10) are the same.

Anyone may substitute key words of his own choice for those in the list; and it is also allowable to stretch the picturization, so that DOZE represents a man dozing; HOUR, an hourglass; SEAM, a folded cloth, or strip of metal; CLUB, a wooden stick or a men's club; and so on.

To remember a pack of cards in order, you must first know the list perfectly, though you can try out the trick and practice it by referring to the printed list while working with a pack of cards.

As you go through the pack, think of each word, picture it, and link it to the next. Take sufficient time to forge these mental links, and if need be, go through the pack again, to make sure that you have them right. Take this example:

7 D, 6 D, K C, 7 H, Q H, 10 S, 9 C, J D, 5 D, 10 D, K D, 2 D,
5 S, 3 C, 4 H, 5 C, 2 C, J C, 9 D, 10 H, 10 C, Q C, 4 S, 3 D, 7 S,
8 S, 8 C, 2 H, A C, 4 C, A D, J H, K H, A S, Q S, 9 S, 3 S, J S,
9 H, 3 H, 8 H, 6 S, 2 S, 7 C, A H, K S, Q D, 5 H, 8 D

The picture links could run: A *duck* in a *ditch* swings a *club* at a *hawk*, saving a *heroine* who is pouring some *sauce* over a *cap*. This is on a ship's *deck*, beside a sun *dial* where a man is *dozing*. Beside him are some *diamonds* which roll into a *den*. *Sail* is hoisted and the man waves a *comb* at an *hour* glass, which is filled with lumps of *coal*. These are thrown at a *cane* which falls into a huge *crack* from which a *dub* golfer emerges and starts toward a *house*. He finds a *case* filled with bottles of *cream*, which he pours on a *sore* wrist. Above is a *dome*, where a *sock* dangles toward a big *safe*. Inside is a *calf* which is hauled out by a bearded *Hun*. Watching is a *cat*, which hops into a *car*, where it eats a *date*. Along comes a *hack* with a driver who slaps his chest to prove himself big *hearted*. He pours a *soda* through a *screen*, on to a cake of *soap*, which is used to wash the *seam* of a cloth which is hung on a *shack*, beside a *heap* of junk where a man sings "*Home*, Sweet Home." Bees come from a *hive* and he pulls down a window *sash* to stop them, while the *sun* shines on a *cook*, who runs into a *hut*. He finds a *spade* and starts to dig, but falls asleep and has a *dream* to be wakened by a sudden *hail*, forming a stream into which he *dives*.

By recalling these pictures and translating them into the cards they represent, the entire list can be called off in order.

Combination Card List and Figure Alphabet

Anyone already familiar with the Figure Alphabet can combine it with the Card List (once the latter has been learned) and form associations that way, thus remembering the exact position of every card in the pack.

Taking the list above, pictures would run thus: 1. A DUCK wearing a HAT. 2. A HEN in a DITCH. 3. A HAM being pounded with a CLUB. 4. A HAWK pecking at a person's HAIR. 5. A HEROINE charging up a HILL. 6. A bottle of SAUCE hanging on a HOOK.

These associations are all so obvious that it is easy to form your own list; and if the link system is used as well, the whole result can be double-checked. Individual experiment furnishes the best test for these methods.

Naming Missing Cards

In the foregoing list, three cards of the pack were purposely left out, so that only 49 are given. If you run through the list, you will find it difficult indeed to note which cards they are. Yet it is possible to name those cards after running through the pack just once.

What you do is form your links, in this case, DUCK, DITCH, CLUB, HAWK and so on; but mutilate each picture as you visualize it, either by word or image. For instance, you could think of the *duck* being a "Lame Duck." The *ditch* would be slimy and full of mud. The *club* could be gnarled and clumsy. The *hawk* could have metal claws.

Among later pictures, the *diamonds* could be scattered; the *crack* could be jagged; the *sore* wrist bandaged. The big *hearted* cabby could be thumping the right side of his chest; he could break the neck off the *soda* bottle. The *seam* of the cloth could be ripped.

These are all good in your regular linkage, as they strengthen the associations by making them more vivid; but they serve an even more important purpose. After going through the pack, lay it aside, and start thinking of cards suit by suit, from Ace up to King, bringing to mind the pictures just formed.

With Clubs, you would think of a CAT (Ace) with a bobbed tail; a CANE (two) that is broken; a COMB (Three) with missing teeth; a CAR (Four) with a flat tire; a lump of COAL (Five) that turns to powder. You would then come to COACH (Six) and find that it has no mutilation. You know instantly that it is one of the missing cards, as you could not have pictured it.

Going through the Hearts, you would come to a plain HEDGE, telling you that the Six of Hearts is missing. With the Diamonds, the same would be true of DOOR, giving you the Four of Diamonds. Check back on the list and you will find 6C, 6H, 4D absent.

This excellent method was devised by H. Adrian Smith, noted memory expert and authority on mnemonics. With its aid, you can discover missing cards more rapidly than you can remember the order of the pack, because you do not need to clinch the links of the entire sequence. The individual pictures are what count.

Memorizing Card Hands

A hand of 13 cards can be rapidly memorized by the picture system. Suppose you hold:

Clubs: Ace, Queen, Eight.

Hearts: Nine, Five.

Spades: Ace, Eight, Three, Two.

Diamonds: Queen, Ten, Nine, Five.

Think of a CAT drinking CREAM with a CALF.

Picture a junk HEAP on which HAIL is falling.

Think of SODA poured into a SAFE where a SEAM is showing in the SUN.

Picture a DREAM as you DOZE as a DUB plays a golf ball from a sun DIAL.

As the hand is played, a check back on these pictures will enable you to recall any cards you have already used.

About Some Prodigious Memories

GEORGE PARKER BIDDER

As "The Calculating Boy," George Parker Bidder might have remained a mere mental freak, if his father, a stonemason in Devon, England, had fully controlled his son's career. Born in 1806, little George was scarcely six years old when his older brother taught him to count up to 10 and then up to 100. This so intrigued George that he began toying with peas, marbles, and finally a bag of shot, laying the pellets into squares and counting them to find the total.

In this way, he invented processes of his own, different from formal arithmetic and soon he was astonishing people with his facility at multiplication. His favorite haunt was the blacksmith shop in his home village of Moreton Hampstead and when some one told him that ten "hundreds" made a "thousand" his talent became unbounded. That was when George's father stepped into the scene and took the precocious child on tour to show off his ability at a profit.

So limited was George's early education that he had to be taught to tell time and be told what a year was, in order to make calculations involving hours and minutes. He knew nothing about inches, feet and other measurements, but when those were explained to him, along with square and cubic measures, they opened new channels for his fantastic forte at figures.

The rest of his education was totally neglected, but his youthful fame brought Sir John William Herschel, the noted astronomer and discoverer of the planet Uranus, to Moreton in the year 1817. In studying the Calculating Boy in his native habitat, Herschel and others were impressed with his intelligence. They put him in school until his father insisted on taking him out for another tour. Finally, George was placed with a private tutor between times.

Though no freak himself, young Bidder was never stumped by freakish questions. Once he was asked:

"If a flea springs 2 feet, 3 inches every hop, how many must it take to go around the world, the circumference being 25,020 miles? Also, how long would it require for the journey if it took 60 hops every minute?"

To that, George Bidder replied in prompt style:

"It would take 58,713,600 hops, requiring one year, 314 days, 13 hours and 20 minutes."

Here was a question that George answered in 80 seconds: "Suppose a city to be illuminated with 9,999 lamps, each consuming one pint of oil every 4 hours, how many gallons would they consume in 40 years?" The answer was, "109,489,050 gallons."

Another that George answered at the age of 10 was:

"What is the compound interest on 4,444 pounds for 4,444 days at 4½ per cent per annum?" The solution, given within two minutes, was, "2,434 pounds, 16 shillings, 5 pence and one farthing."

In 1818, a friendly contest was held between George Bidder and the American calculator, Zerah Colburn, who was then nearing the end of his meteoric career. One year later, George began attending classes at the University of Edinburgh and soon gave up his public demonstrations, though his powers—unlike Zerah's —did not dwindle.

Instead, George Bidder studied engineering and rose high in that profession. Years later, he was elected to parliament, where his wonderful memory, his power of instantaneous calculation and his quick perception caused him to be dreaded by opposing lawyers. One appealed to the House of Lords that "Mr. Bidder should not be allowed to remain in the room because nature has endowed him with qualities that did not place his opponents on a fair footing."

In describing his methods of calculation, Bidder stated:

"If I am asked the product of 89 times 73, the answer, 6497, comes immediately into my mind. I multiply 80 by 70, 80 by 3, 9 by 70 and 9 by 3."

It was just that simple. But it works better if those figures, 5600, 240, 630, 27, can be visualized as a column and held as a retentive image—like chalk on a blackboard—until the addition can be completed mentally. Apparently, George Bidder was gifted with a sort of *photographic* memory before photography itself was known. Bidder put it more fully when he stated:

"In mental arithmetic, you begin at the left-hand extremity and you conclude at the unit, allowing only one fact to be impressed on the mind at a time. You modify that fact every instant as the process goes on; but still the object is to have one fact and one fact only; stored away at one time. . . . The last result in each operation, alone, is registered by the memory, all the previous results being consecutively obliterated until a total product is obtained."

The notion that child prodigies "grow old while still young" did not apply with George Parker Bidder. He lived to the age of 72 years and how well he retained his calculating faculties can be appreciated from these comparative instances:

When Bidder was 11 years old, Sir John William Herschel gave him this question: "Light travels from the sun to earth in 8 minutes and the sun being 98,000,000 miles off, if light would take 6 years and 4 months traveling from the nearest fixed star, how far is that star from earth, reckoning 365 days and 6 hours to each year and 28 days to each month?"

To which Bidder answered correctly:

"40,633,740,000,000 miles."

A few days before his death, some 60 years later, Bidder was asked:

"If 36,918 pulses or waves of light, which occupy only one inch in length, are requisite to give the impression of red; taking the velocity of light at 190,000 miles per second, how many of its waves must strike the eye and be registered in one second to give the color red?"

Before the questioner could start to work it out with paper and pencil, Bidder told him:

"The number of vibrations will be 444,433,651,200,000."

The remarkable mnemonic faculties of George Parker Bidder, rather than being entirely unique or individualistic, were shared to a definite degree by other members of his family. One of his brothers had a tremendous store of historical dates and could quote almost any Biblical text, with chapter and verse. Another brother was a capable mathematician who became a professional actuary.

Bidder's son, George Jr., became a noted calculator in his own right and was popularly known as the "Younger Bidder." He inherited his father's ability at visualizing figures and regarded it as a necessary function in mental mathematics. Two of his daughters were similarly gifted, so that the Bidder talent manifested itself through three generations.

JEDEDIAH BUXTON

Arithmetical prodigies have run the gamut from outright imbeciles with "adding machine" brains to budding geniuses, whose first symptoms of mental greatness have been their precocity at figures. Usually, their one factor in common has been the lightning like rapidity of their calculations; but Jedediah Buxton, whose mentality fell between those two extremes, was just a plodder, mathematically as well as socially.

It was Buxton's ability at working things out the slow way that won him fame; and his case is particularly interesting in that it evidenced a highly retentive memory as much as a mathematical mentality.

Born at Elmeton, near Chesterfield in Derbyshire, England, in 1707, Jedediah was no scholar, for although his grandfather, John Buxton, was vicar of the parish, and his father, William Buxton, the schoolmaster, Jedediah never learned to read or write. Even his penchant for figures did not show strongly until he was 12 years old, and then in a peculiar way.

Time, to Jedediah, was something to be reduced to minutes; and distance, to hair-breadths. He talked constantly in such terms and soon people were proposing him problems as:

"If a body has three sides measuring 23,145,789 yards, 5,642,732 yards, and 54,695 yards, how many cubical eighths of an inch does it contain?"

Buxton mulled over that one for five hours while working with a group of laborers; then gave the right answer. Given long

239

figures to multiply or square, he would sometimes work on them for weeks, making many other calculations in the meantime, for he could resume any problem wherever he left off and converse on any other subject while engaged with figures.

After walking over a field in two or three directions, Buxton could tell the number of square inches it contained, as exactly as if it had been measured. He put this to practical use by surveying the entire township; but meanwhile, in a more facetious mood, he kept exact count of all the glasses of beer that he had drunk at local taverns since he was 12 years old.

Once, Buxton became "drunk with reckoning" as he styled it, when he worked on the problem: "In 200,000 million cubic miles, how many grains would there be of eight different kinds of corn and pulse and how many hairs one inch long?" Jedediah started by actually counting the various grains and hairs required to fill a cubic inch; and then went on from there, returning to his mental task at irregular intervals.

Buxton married, raised a family of several children and was happy with life in his native heath. At the age of 50, he walked to London, hoping to see the king, which was his only urge outside of family and figures. His Majesty was absent, but the Fellows of the Royal Society entertained Buxton and he returned the favor by demonstrating his powers as a calculator.

In London, he was taken to see the tragedy of *Richard III,* at Drury Lane, but instead of being impressed by the splendor of the surroundings or the dramatic quality of the play, he mentally counted the words spoken by Garrick and the other actors and announced the totals afterward. Similarly, at dances, he spent his time in counting the steps taken.

Back in Chesterfield, Buxton occupied himself at intervals in calculating the exact value that a farthing would attain if doubled 140 times. His answer came to a number of English pounds that required 39 places of figures to represent.

Until his death at the age of 65, Jedediah Buxton remained a local celebrity; and when asked to solve a mathematical problem, he would sit down and take off his old brown hat, revealing a linen "thinking cap" underneath. Then, resting his hands and chin upon the knob of his crooked wooden stick, he would tilt his head, listen intently, and finally go to work.

Whether his ability declined in his last few years is not known; but it is generally conceded that Buxton's mnemonical processes set a pattern for attainable achievement that might be applied to other fields as well as mathematics, provided that all other interests were excluded.

ZERAH COLBURN

Until he was six years old, Zerah Colburn was very much like the other children of his age in the little backwoods settlement of Cabot, Vermont. Then, one day in August, 1810, he was playing on the floor of the family carpenter shop, crooning in singsong style. Zerah's father paused to listen, then decided to lay down his hammer and never drive another nail from that day on.

Zerah was reciting snatches of the multiplication table, which he had apparently picked up by listening to the students in the upper grades in the one room school that he had attended for a few months. But instead of stopping at the customary 12 times 12, Zerah kept jumping into higher brackets, giving the answers as he went along. Mr. Colburn promptly called in the neighbors and they were amazed at the speed with which young Zerah could perform the most complex calculations.

Many people came to Cabot to witness the performances of the "boy wonder" and soon his father took him to Montpelier, where Zerah gave a demonstration for the Vermont state legislature. This was followed by a tour of the United States, starting from Boston, where Zerah demonstrated his rapid fire mentality by answering questions like the following:

"How many seconds are there in 2000 years?"

Rapidly, Zerah cracked it down: "730,000 days . . . 17,520,000 hours . . . 1,051,200,000 minutes . . . 63,072,000,000 seconds."

In Portsmouth, New Hampshire, Zerah was asked, "If the distance to Boston is 65 miles, how many steps would it take to get there, assuming that you do three feet to a step?" His correct answer, given within 10 seconds, was, "114,000 steps."

These examples indicate what may have been a visualization process, as they are the sort that could be worked rapidly with paper and pencil. But Zerah's ability displayed itself in more extensive fields. Early in 1812, his father took him to London. There, it was announced:

"Zerah Colburn's singular faculty extends not only to the raising of powers, but also to the extraction of the squares and cube roots of a proposed number; and likewise to the means of determining whether it be a prime number, or a number incapable of division by any other number."

At one demonstration, he raised the number 8 to the 16th power, 281,474,976,710,656. He raised some two figure numbers as high as the 8th power, but invariably encountered difficulty as he proceeded. Efforts were made to analyze his methods and, on one occasion, the Duke of Gloucester had him multiply 21,734 by 543, then asked him how he did it.

Zerah's reply was that he had multiplied 65,202 by 181, which amounted to the same thing; but why, or how that simplified the process, he was unable to explain. His method was unquestionably unique, for he was ignorant of the common rules of arithmetic and could not do a simple multiplication or division on paper. In the extraction of roots and mentioning of factors, he gave the answers far too rapidly to be using any of the common methods, which were slow and laborious in contrast.

Within a few years, Zerah's calculating ability began to fade. He went to school in England and showed an aptitude for languages. Returning to Vermont in his early twenties, he became a traveling preacher and finally was appointed professor of languages at Norwich University. In his memoirs, which he wrote at the age of 28, he was able to explain his calculating methods to some extent; and he apparently retained some of his childhood ability, though his facility at figures had greatly waned.

None of Zerah's seven brothers and sisters showed his extraordinary powers; nor did any of his own six children exhibit such proclivities. As a child prodigy, Zerah was evidently one of the type that "grow old" before their time, for in addition to his powers fading at maturity, he died at the age of 35, which to anyone else would have been the prime of life.

JOHANN MARTIN ZACHARIAS DASE

As a man endowed with multiple mental powers, Johann Martin Zacharias Dase was a positive standout. His career is deserving of a lengthy essay in itself, but can be discussed here more satisfactorily and simply in terms of its components. For Dase embodied, in one way or another and in varying degree, many of the faculties found individually in noted prodigies who preceded him.

Dase was born in Hamburg, Germany, in 1824, and attended school when still only two years old. In this way, he resembled the infant wonders who faded so rapidly, as Heinecken, or those who became geniuses in later life, such as Bentham. But Dase adhered to neither pattern. Apparently, his education became neglected or was abandoned, for he has been classed as "stupid" in mature life. It was not until he was 15 years old that Dase began to tour as a youthful calculator.

On this account, Dase has been likened to Buxton, along with the fact that he possessed Buxton's type of memory where prolonged calculations were concerned. But Buxton was a local lad who only once left his home town, whereas Dase had an urge for travel. Besides, Buxton's flair was directed toward trivial calculations, whereas Dase was a man with a mission where mathematics was concerned.

More properly, Dase might be likened to Colburn, who traveled and showed off his ability, yet did not have a full understanding of his actual methods. Dase was criticized for his unwillingness to learn mathematics or to master any language other than his own. But it could be that he was intuitively trying to preserve what he had. Colburn, the linguist, ceased to be Colburn, the calculator; and Bidder emphasized quite clearly how the processes of these arithmetical marvels were at variance with accepted methods.

Dase had Colburn's quality at lightning calculation on certain problems; and with it, a flash of photographic memory that rivaled Magliabechi's, though it was greatly limited. Peas, other small objects could be thrown on a table and Dase would give the total number at a glance. Similarly, he could count cattle in a field, books on their shelves, in an instantaneous fashion which indicated that he retained an exact mental impression of what he saw.

It is recorded that Dase multiplied two numbers of eight figures each in 54 seconds; two of 20 figures each in six minutes; two of 40 figures each in 40 minutes; and two of 100 figures each in 8 hours and 45 minutes. That was certainly combining the respective talents of Colburn and Buxton in their prime!

Dase's mission was to put his talents to good use and at the age of 25, he began making tables of factors and prime numbers from the 7th million to the 10th million. He was still at work on this when he died at the age of 37. That was two years older than Colburn's age at death; but unlike Colburn, Dase retained his calculating ability to the end.

DATAS

In the thriller movie of "The Thirty-nine Steps," the mystery reaches its climax in a London music hall, where a man called "Mr. Memory" is on the stage, answering any question put to him by the packed audience. Many people who have seen the movie have supposed that "Mr. Memory" was a fictitious character. Actually, he was a real-life vaudeville performer whose act provided John Buchan, author of "The Thirty-nine Steps," with a good scene for his story.

The original "Mr. Memory" was a man named William John Bottell and his stage name was "Datas." He is remarkable in the field of memory for two reasons: He was not a child prodigy; and he did not specialize in any one branch. He was a grown-up man who developed a reputation of being able to answer anything that he was asked on any general subject. As such, he sets the pattern for advanced memory work.

Bottell was born in 1875 in the town of Newnham, Kent, England, and had very little schooling, but between selling newspapers, running errands and working in a blacksmith shop, he read up on everything that interested him and remembered it for the same reason. If he couldn't answer anything, he looked it up for his own satisfaction. And so, one day, he happened to impress some strangers in a London cafe with his amazing fund of miscellaneous knowledge.

One of the listeners was a theatrical agent, who promptly signed Bottell to a contract. Then 26 years of age, Bottell became "Datas"

247

and proceeded to bowl over variety audiences for the rest of his career. Not only did he answer thousands of questions that they shouted; he gave them sidelights that they themselves didn't know. He died in 1956 at the age of 82.

Here are some of the comments that Datas made regarding his memorization processes:

"I am asked the date of the Great Fire of London. I give the correct answer, 1666, and immediately there arises before me a panoramic scene of that calamity, from its start in Pudding Lane to its finish in Pie Corner. . . .

"When you are called upon to answer any questions, endeavor to call up some 'mind pictures' for you will find their help of immense value. Remember that failure is the result of a weak mental impression due to lack of concentration on the subject matter you are endeavoring to commit to memory. . . .

"One idea begets another; therefore, when memorizing one idea, kill two birds with one stone, and also memorize the corresponding idea. . . . When you have ideas which are unconnected, you should establish an intermediary idea as a connecting link."

Since the successful Datas act, a wave of memory experts have appeared publicly during the years. Their acts, if anything, have gained in popularity. They demonstrate conclusively that, in many instances, remarkable memorizers are made, not born.

CHRISTIAN FRIEDRICH HEINECKEN

It is difficult to believe the claim that Christian Friedrich Heinecken talked within a few hours after his birth at Lubeck, Germany, on February 6, 1721. Further facts of his brief career are equally incredible, but are more strongly authenticated. At the age of 10 months, he could speak and repeat every word said to him; at one year, he knew the principal events in the first five books of the Bible.

During his second year, this "Infant of Lubeck," as he was known, learned practically all the facts of Biblical history; while in his third year, he gained a general knowledge of world history and geography, while learning to speak Latin and French. In his fourth year, he applied himself to the study of religion and church history.

After being taken to the court of the King of Denmark, where he was pronounced to be the wonder that he unquestionably was, Christian returned home and began to supplement his skill at reading by learning to write. A sudden illness interrupted and the child prodigy calmly predicted his coming death, which occurred on June 27, 1725, when he was less than four and one-half years old.

Among other abilities, the Lubeck infant was credited with a skill at figures, ranking him among the "boy calculators" whose careers, like their powers, proved to be brief.

ANTONIO DA MARCO MAGLIABECHI

One of the greatest of literary prodigies, Antonio Da Marco Magliabechi spent his early years in total ignorance of what was to be his fantastic field of endeavor. He was born in Florence, Italy, October 29, 1633 and his parents were too poor to give him even the most rudimentary education. Unable to read or write, Antonio was apprenticed to a fruit dealer and spent his spare time poring over waste sheets from printed books, which were used for wrapping merchandise.

The boy's peculiar fascination attracted a local bookseller who took him into his shop, where Antonio was able to identify every book on sight. When he learned to read, it became his ruling passion, and coupled with his virtually photographic memory, he retained much of what he read in its entirety.

As a test of this, he was given a manuscript which he read with his remarkable speed and returned to the author, who later pretended that he had lost it and begged Magliabechi to recall what he could of it. Antonio proceeded to write it out in its entirety, without missing a word or punctuation mark.

So vast was his reading and his exact retention that he was consulted by experts for source material on their own subjects, as he could quote innumerable authors by book, word and page. The Grand Duke of Tuscany eventually appointed him librarian and, to absorb vast quantities of literature, Magliabechi adopted tactics that would make our modern "speed reading" into a slow-motion process. By simply dipping in among the chapters of a book, he absorbed the gist of whole pages almost at a passing glance, much to the amazement of onlookers.

So great was his memory of books that once, when the Grand Duke asked him for a certain rare volume, Magliabechi told him, "There is but one copy in the world; and that is in the Grand Signior's library at Constantinople, where it is the seventh book on the second shelf on the right hand as you go in."

How closely Magliabechi's affinity for words resembled a lightning calculator's skill at figures is an open question; but certainly the results were quite as fabulous. From the standpoint of memorization, Magliabechi's work was not only unique but quite unparalleled, as he read and absorbed everything that came his way, regardless of the subject or its comparative importance.

In his old age, Magliabechi spent much of his time in a bed surrounded by books, which he read as incessantly as ever, until he would fall asleep. He retained his remarkable faculties up to the time of his death at the age of 81 years.

PAUL CHARLES MORPHY

Among chess prodigies, the name of Paul Charles Morphy is unique. Not only did he show an almost inspirational knowledge of the game while still a child but as he grew older, he developed into perhaps the greatest chess player of modern times. Yet seldom did he give close study to the game, depending almost entirely upon his intuitive endowments, of which memory was perhaps the most remarkable.

Born in New Orleans in 1837, Paul Morphy came from a family of chess players, his uncle, Ernest Morphy, being the recognized chess master of Louisiana. Though Paul was a precocious child, there was no indication of his extraordinary genius, until his father, Judge Alonzo Morphy, decided to teach him the rudiments of chess. Then it was discovered that the child, by merely having watched the game played, had already learned its fine points and rated as a master in his own right.

According to one account, Paul was by then 10 years of age; and by 12, he defeated the best opposition that local players could offer. Despite that, chess remained his sideline, for he was studying for the law and acquiring four languages in the meantime. He was admitted to the bar at the age of 20 and then made a trip to New York and later to Europe, winning over the chess masters of both continents.

While chess primarily demands keen analysis and foresight, the masters who take on several opponents simultaneously, playing them *while blindfolded,* must possess a remarkable visual memory as well. Morphy was one of the first experts of this type; even as a child he played games blindfolded. In some of his contests with Louis Paulsen, another chess prodigy, *both* played blindfolded.

Since then, other child prodigies have appeared in the chess world; some of these have played simultaneous games and blindfold chess has become a regular exhibition. But one of the most amazing things about Morphy was the retentive quality of his practically photographic memory. Fantastic though it may seem, Morphy claimed that he could remember *every move* in *every game* of the hundreds that he had played throughout his championship career!

What is more, the facts seem to back the claim. Some 400 of Morphy's games have been preserved play by play, because he was able to record or dictate them afterward. Thus memory was the factor that preserved these great games for posterity. It is also worthy of note that Morphy frequently reviewed a game after finishing it, thus strengthening the memory process. So it is as a memory master that Morphy should be remembered, as much as a chess master.

Morphy retired from public tournaments at the age of 23 and gave up the game entirely some ten years later, feeling that it handicapped his professional career as a lawyer. He died in New Orleans in 1884.

ROBERT PASFIELD

The case of Robert Pasfield, who lived about the year 1600, is a remarkable instance of natural memory extended through an artificial device created to fill a specific purpose.

Pasfield was the servant of John Bruen, a highly educated man of Cheshire, England. Bruen went to many religious meetings and took copious notes of the sermons, which in that day were filled with scriptural passages from which each minor topic stemmed.

Afterward, Bruen would use his notes to repeat the discourses that he had heard, which greatly impressed Pasfield, who could quote heavily from scripture but could neither read nor write. Soon Pasfield was attending meetings and coming back with complete sermons in his mind, quoting them in full.

His method was this: He formed a leather girdle, so long that it went twice about his waist. He divided it into sections, each representing a book of the Bible. He fixed knotted thongs for chapter divisions, with smaller knots for groups of verses.

Pasfield wore this when he went to meeting and as he listened to the sermon, he found the knot corresponding to each new text and fingered it during that portion of the discourse, while noting what was said.

His familiarity with the scriptures enabled him to find the knots in their right order later, and from them Pasfield repeated details of the sermon as fully as Bruen did from his written notes.

After Pasfield's death, Bruen kept the much knotted belt, which he called the "Girdle of Verity," and it still stands as a unique memory device. The advantage of such a memory aid was well summed by Dr. Edward Pick, noted mnemonics authority of the late nineteenth century, when he stated:

"*Comparison* is the easiest way and surest means of facilitating remembrance, if you always take *the known* as starting point for the unknown."

Selective Bibliography

ALIU, SALVIO (Prof. Sas Richard). *La Magia de la Memoria* . . . Barcelona: Editorial Sintes, 1952. 3 v.

ANONYMOUS. *Acronyms Dictionary* . . . Detroit: Gale Research Co., 1960.

BARLOW, FRED. *Mental Prodigies; an Enquiry into the Faculties of Arithmetical, Chess and Musical Prodigies, Famous Memorizers, Precocious Children and the Like, with Numerous Examples of "Lightning" Calculations and Mental Magic.* New York: Philosophical Library, 1952.

BARTLETT, FREDERIC C. *Remembering; a Study in Experimental and Social Psychology.* New York: The Macmillan Co., 1932.

BEROL, FELIX. *The Complete Mnemotechnical Dictionary.* Rev. and Suppl. by William Berol. New York: [Auth.] 1918.

BROTHERS, JOYCE D., EAGEN, EDWARD P. F. *10 Days to a Successful Memory.* Englewood Cliffs, N. J.: Prentice-Hall, 1957.

BYRNE, BRENDAN. *Three Weeks to a Better Memory.* Introduction by James A. Farley. Philadelphia: J. C. Winston Co., 1951.

CAMERON, DONALD E. *Remembering.* New York: 1947. (Nervous and Mental Disease Monographs, no. 72)

CATTERSON-SMITH, R. *Drawing from Memory and Mind Picturing.* London: I. Pitman & Sons, Ltd., 1921. (*Ed. by* F. Morley Fletcher)

CHILTON-DIDIER. *Audio-Visual Language Courses.* Philadelphia: Chilton Co., 1962. Twenty-five Lessons each, *including* Teaching Guide, Textbook and Four Records.

Cooke, James F. *How to Memorize Music*. Bryn Mawr, Pa.: T. Presser Co., 1948.

Deese, James. *The Psychology of Learning*. New York: McGraw-Hill Book Co., Inc., 1958 [1952].

Fletcher, Allan L. *How to Train and Improve Your Memory*. Garden City, N. Y.: Halcyon House, 1948.

Furst, Bruno. *The Practical Way to a Better Memory*. New York: Grosset & Dunlap, 1944.

———. *Stop Forgetting; How to Develop Your Memory and Put It to Practical Use*. Garden City, N. Y.: Doubleday & Co., 1958 [1949].

Gates, Arthur I. *The Improvement of Reading. A Program of Diagnostic and Remedial Methods*. New York: The Macmillan Co., 1959 [1927, 1935, 1947].

Hamilton, F. Stephen. *Mastering Your Memory*. New York: Crown Publishers, 1947.

Harris, Albert J. *How to Increase Reading Ability. A Guide to Developmental and Remedial Reading Methods*. 4th ed., rev. New York: David McKay and Co., Inc., 1961.

Hunter, Ian M. L. *Memory, Facts and Fallacies*. Harmsworth, Middlesex, England: Penguin Books, Ltd., 1957.

Laird, Donald A., Laird, Eleanor C. *Techniques for Efficient Remembering*. New York: McGraw-Hill, 1960.

Lecoq De Boisbaudran, Horace. *The Training of the Memory in Art and the Education of the Artist*. Translated from the French by L. D. Luard, with an Introduction by Selwyn Image . . . London: Macmillan Co., Ltd., 1911.

Leedy, Paul D. *Reading Improvement for Adults*. New York: McGraw-Hill.

Logan, Arthur I. *Remembering Made Easy*. New York: Arco Publishing Co., 1959 [1955].

Lorayne, Harry. *How to Develop a Super-Power Memory*. New York: F. Fell, 1957.

Mackinnon, Lilias. *Music by Heart*. London, New York: Oxford University Press, 1938.

MEYER, LESTER. *High-Speed Math Self-Taught*. Abridged and rev. Maxwell Marxe. New York: Pocket Books, Inc., 1959 [1947].

NUTT, ROBERT H. *How to Remember Names and Faces. How to Develop a Good Memory*. New York: Simon & Schuster, 1951 [1941].

REGNAULT, JULES [Prof. Magus]. *Les Calculateurs Prodiges. L'Art de Jongler Avec Nombres (Illusionnisme et Calcul Mental)*. 2nd ed. Paris: Payot, 1952 [1943].

ROBINSON, FRANCIS P. *Effective Study*. Rev. ed. New York: Harper & Bros., 1961 [1941, 1946].

ROTH, DAVID M. *Roth Memory Course*. Cleveland: Ralston Publishing Co., 1955 [1918].

RUSSELL, A. H. *Rapid Calculations*. 6th ed., rev. & enl. London: Gregor Publishing Co., Ltd., 1946 [1925].

SHEFTER, HARRY. *Faster Reading Self-Taught*. New York: Washington Square Press, Inc., 1961 [1960].

SHINN, FREDERICK G. *Musical Memory and Its Cultivation. Also an Investigation into Forms of Memory Employed in Pianoforte Playing, and a Theory of Such Forms* . . . London: Augener Ltd., 1898.

SLOANE, T. O'CONOR, THOMPSON, J. E., LICKS, H. E. *Speed and Fun with Figures*. New York: D. Van Nostrand Co., Inc., 1939.

SMITH, H. ADRIAN. *Card System Deluxe*. Colon, Mich.: Abbott's Magic Novelty Co., 1937.

STICKER, HENRY. *How to Calculate Quickly*. New York: Dover Publications, Inc., 1955 [1945].

TRACHTENBERG, JAKOW. *The Trachtenberg Speed System of Basic Mathematics*. Translated and adapted by Ann Cutler and Rudolph McShane. Garden City, N. Y.: Doubleday & Co., Inc., 1960.

WALDHORN, ARTHUR, ZEIGER, ARTHUR. *Word Mastery Made Simple*. New York: Made Simple Books, Inc., 1960 [1955, 1957].

WALDMAN, JOHN. *Rapid Reading Made Simple*. Garden City, N. Y.: Doubleday & Co., Inc., 1958.

———. *Ibid*. New York: Made Simple Books, Inc., 1960 ("Junior Series").

WEINLAND, JAMES D. *How to Improve Your Memory*. New York: Barnes and Noble, 1957.

YOUNG, MORRIS N. *Bibliography of Memory*. Philadelphia and New York: Chilton, 1961.

ZUFALL, BERNARD. *Zufall's Memory Trix*. Jamaica, L. I.: Bruhn Bros., 1940. 6 v.

Index

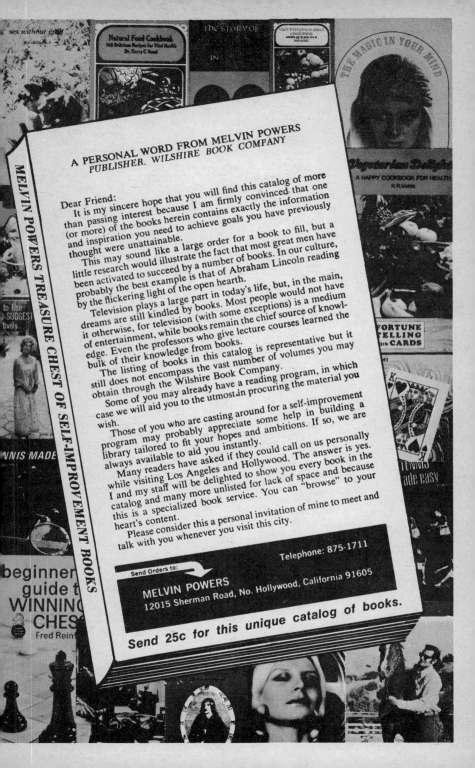

Melvin Powers
SELF-IMPROVEMENT
LIBRARY

ASTROLOGY

_____ASTROLOGY: A FASCINATING HISTORY *P. Naylor*	2.00
_____ASTROLOGY: HOW TO CHART YOUR HOROSCOPE *Max Heindel*	2.00
_____ASTROLOGY: YOUR PERSONAL SUN-SIGN GUIDE *Beatrice Ryder*	2.00
_____ASTROLOGY FOR EVERYDAY LIVING *Janet Harris*	2.00
_____ASTROLOGY MADE EASY *Astarte*	2.00
_____ASTROLOGY MADE PRACTICAL *Alexandra Kayhle*	2.00
_____ASTROLOGY, ROMANCE, YOU AND THE STARS *Anthony Norvell*	3.00
_____MY WORLD OF ASTROLOGY *Sydney Omarr*	3.00
_____THOUGHT DIAL *Sydney Omarr*	2.00
_____ZODIAC REVEALED *Rupert Gleadow*	2.00

BRIDGE & POKER

_____ADVANCED POKER STRATEGY & WINNING PLAY *A. D. Livingston*	2.00
_____BRIDGE BIDDING MADE EASY *Edwin Kantar*	5.00
_____BRIDGE CONVENTIONS *Edwin Kantar*	4.00
_____COMPLETE DEFENSIVE BRIDGE PLAY *Edwin B. Kantar*	10.00
_____HOW TO IMPROVE YOUR BRIDGE *Alfred Sheinwold*	2.00
_____HOW TO WIN AT POKER *Terence Reese & Anthony T. Watkins*	2.00
_____TEST YOUR BRIDGE PLAY *Edwin B. Kantar*	3.00

BUSINESS STUDY & REFERENCE

_____CONVERSATION MADE EASY *Elliot Russell*	2.00
_____EXAM SECRET *Dennis B. Jackson*	2.00
_____FIX-IT BOOK *Arthur Symons*	2.00
_____HOW TO BE A COMEDIAN FOR FUN & PROFIT *King & Laufer*	2.00
_____HOW TO DEVELOP A BETTER SPEAKING VOICE *M. Hellier*	2.00
_____HOW TO MAKE A FORTUNE IN REAL ESTATE *Albert Winnikoff*	3.00
_____HOW TO MAKE MONEY IN REAL ESTATE *Stanley L. McMichael*	2.00
_____INCREASE YOUR LEARNING POWER *Geoffrey A. Dudley*	2.00
_____MAGIC OF NUMBERS *Robert Tocquet*	2.00
_____PRACTICAL GUIDE TO BETTER CONCENTRATION *Melvin Powers*	2.00
_____PRACTICAL GUIDE TO PUBLIC SPEAKING *Maurice Forley*	2.00
_____7 DAYS TO FASTER READING *William S. Schaill*	2.00
_____SONGWRITERS' RHYMING DICTIONARY *Jane Shaw Whitfield*	3.00
_____SPELLING MADE EASY *Lester D. Basch & Dr. Milton Finkelstein*	2.00
_____STUDENT'S GUIDE TO BETTER GRADES *J. A. Rickard*	2.00
_____TEST YOURSELF — Find Your Hidden Talent *Jack Shafer*	2.00
_____YOUR WILL & WHAT TO DO ABOUT IT *Attorney Samuel G. Kling*	2.00

CHESS & CHECKERS

_____BEGINNER'S GUIDE TO WINNING CHESS *Fred Reinfeld*	2.00
_____BETTER CHESS — How to Play *Fred Reinfeld*	2.00
_____CHECKERS MADE EASY *Tom Wiswell*	2.00
_____CHESS IN TEN EASY LESSONS *Larry Evans*	2.00
_____CHESS MADE EASY *Milton L. Hanauer*	2.00
_____CHESS MASTERY — A New Approach *Fred Reinfeld*	2.00
_____CHESS PROBLEMS FOR BEGINNERS *edited by Fred Reinfeld*	2.00

Melvin Powers
SELF-IMPROVEMENT
LIBRARY

_____CHESS SECRETS REVEALED *Fred Reinfeld*	2.00
_____CHESS STRATEGY — An Expert's Guide *Fred Reinfeld*	2.00
_____CHESS TACTICS FOR BEGINNERS *edited by Fred Reinfeld*	2.00
_____CHESS THEORY & PRACTICE *Morry & Mitchell*	2.00
_____HOW TO WIN AT CHECKERS *Fred Reinfeld*	2.00
_____1001 BRILLIANT WAYS TO CHECKMATE *Fred Reinfeld*	2.00
_____1001 WINNING CHESS SACRIFICES & COMBINATIONS *Fred Reinfeld*	3.00

COOKERY & HERBS

_____CULPEPER'S HERBAL REMEDIES *Dr. Nicholas Culpeper*	2.00
_____FAST GOURMET COOKBOOK *Poppy Cannon*	2.50
_____HEALING POWER OF HERBS *May Bethel*	2.00
_____HERB HANDBOOK *Dawn MacLeod*	2.00
_____HERBS FOR COOKING AND HEALING *Dr. Donald Law*	2.00
_____HERBS FOR HEALTH How to Grow & Use Them *Louise Evans Doole*	2.00
_____HOME GARDEN COOKBOOK Delicious Natural Food Recipes *Ken Kraft*	3.00
_____NATURAL FOOD COOKBOOK *Dr. Harry C. Bond*	2.00
_____NATURE'S MEDICINES *Richard Lucas*	2.00
_____VEGETABLE GARDENING FOR BEGINNERS *Hugh Wiberg*	2.00
_____VEGETABLES FOR TODAY'S GARDENS *R. Milton Carleton*	2.00
_____VEGETARIAN COOKERY *Janet Walker*	2.00
_____VEGETARIAN COOKING MADE EASY & DELECTABLE *Veronica Vezza*	2.00
_____VEGETARIAN DELIGHTS — A Happy Cookbook for Health *K. R. Mehta*	2.00
_____VEGETARIAN GOURMET COOKBOOK *Joyce McKinnel*	2.00

HEALTH

_____DR. LINDNER'S SPECIAL WEIGHT CONTROL METHOD	1.00
_____GAYELORD HAUSER'S NEW GUIDE TO INTELLIGENT REDUCING	3.00
_____HELP YOURSELF TO BETTER SIGHT *Margaret Darst Corbett*	2.00
_____HOW TO IMPROVE YOUR VISION *Dr. Robert A. Kraskin*	2.00
_____HOW YOU CAN STOP SMOKING PERMANENTLY *Ernest Caldwell*	2.00
_____LSD — THE AGE OF MIND *Bernard Roseman*	2.00
_____MIND OVER PLATTER *Peter G. Lindner, M.D.*	2.00
_____NEW CARBOHYDRATE DIET COUNTER *Patti Lopez-Pereira*	1.00
_____PSYCHEDELIC ECSTASY *William Marshall & Gilbert W. Taylor*	2.00
_____YOU CAN LEARN TO RELAX *Dr. Samuel Gutwirth*	2.00
_____YOUR ALLERGY—What To Do About It *Allan Knight, M.D.*	2.00

HOBBIES

_____BLACKSTONE'S MODERN CARD TRICKS *Harry Blackstone*	2.00
_____BLACKSTONE'S SECRETS OF MAGIC *Harry Blackstone*	2.00
_____COIN COLLECTING FOR BEGINNERS *Burton Hobson & Fred Reinfeld*	2.00
_____400 FASCINATING MAGIC TRICKS YOU CAN DO *Howard Thurston*	3.00
_____GOULD'S GOLD & SILVER GUIDE TO COINS *Maurice Gould*	2.00
_____HOW I TURN JUNK INTO FUN AND PROFIT *Sari*	3.00
_____HOW TO WRITE A HIT SONG & SELL IT *Tommy Boyce*	7.00
_____JUGGLING MADE EASY *Rudolf Dittrich*	2.00
_____MAGIC MADE EASY *Byron Wels*	2.00

_____ SEW SIMPLY, SEW RIGHT *Mini Rhea & F. Leighton*		2.00
_____ STAMP COLLECTING FOR BEGINNERS *Burton Hobson*		2.00
_____ STAMP COLLECTING FOR FUN & PROFIT *Frank Cetin*		2.00

HORSE PLAYERS' WINNING GUIDES

_____ BETTING HORSES TO WIN *Les Conklin*		2.00
_____ HOW TO PICK WINNING HORSES *Bob McKnight*		2.00
_____ HOW TO WIN AT THE RACES *Sam (The Genius) Lewin*		2.00
_____ HOW YOU CAN BEAT THE RACES *Jack Kavanagh*		2.00
_____ MAKING MONEY AT THE RACES *David Barr*		2.00
_____ PAYDAY AT THE RACES *Les Conklin*		2.00
_____ SMART HANDICAPPING MADE EASY *William Bauman*		2.00

HYPNOTISM

_____ ADVANCED TECHNIQUES OF HYPNOSIS *Melvin Powers*	1.00
_____ CHILDBIRTH WITH HYPNOSIS *William S. Kroger, M.D.*	2.00
_____ HOW TO SOLVE YOUR SEX PROBLEMS	
WITH SELF-HYPNOSIS *Frank S. Caprio, M.D.*	2.00
_____ HOW TO STOP SMOKING THRU SELF-HYPNOSIS *Leslie M. LeCron*	2.00
_____ HOW TO USE AUTO-SUGGESTION EFFECTIVELY *John Duckworth*	2.00
_____ HOW YOU CAN BOWL BETTER USING SELF-HYPNOSIS *Jack Heise*	2.00
_____ HOW YOU CAN PLAY BETTER GOLF USING SELF-HYPNOSIS *Heise*	2.00
_____ HYPNOSIS AND SELF-HYPNOSIS *Bernard Hollander, M.D.*	2.00
_____ HYPNOTISM *(Originally published in 1893) Carl Sextus*	3.00
_____ HYPNOTISM & PSYCHIC PHENOMENA *Simeon Edmunds*	2.00
_____ HYPNOTISM MADE EASY *Dr. Ralph Winn*	2.00
_____ HYPNOTISM MADE PRACTICAL *Louis Orton*	2.00
_____ HYPNOTISM REVEALED *Melvin Powers*	1.00
_____ HYPNOTISM TODAY *Leslie LeCron & Jean Bordeaux, Ph.D.*	2.00
_____ MODERN HYPNOSIS *Lesley Kuhn & Salvatore Russo, Ph.D.*	3.00
_____ NEW CONCEPTS OF HYPNOSIS *Bernard C. Gindes, M.D.*	3.00
_____ POST-HYPNOTIC INSTRUCTIONS *Arnold Furst*	2.00
How to give post-hypnotic suggestions for therapeutic purposes.	
_____ PRACTICAL GUIDE TO SELF-HYPNOSIS *Melvin Powers*	2.00
_____ PRACTICAL HYPNOTISM *Philip Magonet, M.D.*	1.00
_____ SECRETS OF HYPNOTISM *S. J. Van Pelt, M.D.*	2.00
_____ SELF-HYPNOSIS *Paul Adams*	2.00
_____ SELF-HYPNOSIS Its Theory, Technique & Application *Melvin Powers*	2.00
_____ SELF-HYPNOSIS A Conditioned-Response Technique *Laurance Sparks*	3.00
_____ THERAPY THROUGH HYPNOSIS *edited by Raphael H. Rhodes*	3.00

JUDAICA

_____ HOW TO LIVE A RICHER & FULLER LIFE *Rabbi Edgar F. Magnin*	2.00
_____ MODERN ISRAEL *Lily Edelman*	2.00
_____ OUR JEWISH HERITAGE *Rabbi Alfred Wolf & Joseph Gaer*	2.00
_____ ROMANCE OF HASSIDISM *Jacob S. Minkin*	2.50
_____ SERVICE OF THE HEART *Evelyn Garfield, Ph.D.*	3.00
_____ STORY OF ISRAEL IN COINS *Jean & Maurice Gould*	2.00
_____ STORY OF ISRAEL IN STAMPS *Maxim & Gabriel Shamir*	1.00
_____ TONGUE OF THE PROPHETS *Robert St. John*	3.00
_____ TREASURY OF COMFORT *edited by Rabbi Sidney Greenberg*	3.00

MARRIAGE, SEX & PARENTHOOD

_____ ABILITY TO LOVE *Dr. Allan Fromme*	3.00
_____ ENCYCLOPEDIA OF MODERN SEX & LOVE TECHNIQUES *Macandrew*	2.00
_____ GUIDE TO SUCCESSFUL MARRIAGE *Drs. Albert Ellis & Robert Harper*	3.00
_____ HOW TO RAISE AN EMOTIONALLY HEALTHY, HAPPY CHILD, *A. Ellis*	2.00
_____ IMPOTENCE & FRIGIDITY *Edwin W. Hirsch, M.D.*	2.00
_____ NEW APPROACHES TO SEX IN MARRIAGE *John E. Eichenlaub, M.D.*	2.00
_____ SEX WITHOUT GUILT *Albert Ellis, Ph.D.*	2.00
_____ SEXUALLY ADEQUATE FEMALE *Frank S. Caprio, M.D.*	2.00

_____ SEXUALLY ADEQUATE MALE *Frank S. Caprio, M.D.*	2.00
_____ YOUR FIRST YEAR OF MARRIAGE *Dr. Tom McGinnis*	2.00

METAPHYSICS & OCCULT

_____ BOOK OF TALISMANS, AMULETS & ZODIACAL GEMS *William Pavitt*	3.00
_____ CONCENTRATION—A Guide to Mental Mastery *Mouni Sadhu*	3.00
_____ DREAMS & OMENS REVEALED *Fred Gettings*	2.00
_____ EXTRASENSORY PERCEPTION *Simeon Edmunds*	2.00
_____ FORTUNE TELLING WITH CARDS *P. Foli*	2.00
_____ HANDWRITING ANALYSIS MADE EASY *John Marley*	2.00
_____ HANDWRITING TELLS *Nadya Olyanova*	3.00
_____ HOW TO UNDERSTAND YOUR DREAMS *Geoffrey A. Dudley*	2.00
_____ ILLUSTRATED YOGA *William Zorn*	2.00
_____ IN DAYS OF GREAT PEACE *Mouni Sadhu*	2.00
_____ KING SOLOMON'S TEMPLE IN THE MASONIC TRADITION *Alex Horne*	5.00
_____ MAGICIAN — His training and work *W. E. Butler*	2.00
_____ MEDITATION *Mouni Sadhu*	3.00
_____ MODERN NUMEROLOGY *Morris C. Goodman*	2.00
_____ NUMEROLOGY—ITS FACTS AND SECRETS *Ariel Yvon Taylor*	2.00
_____ PALMISTRY MADE EASY *Fred Gettings*	2.00
_____ PALMISTRY MADE PRACTICAL *Elizabeth Daniels Squire*	2.00
_____ PALMISTRY SECRETS REVEALED *Henry Frith*	2.00
_____ PRACTICAL YOGA *Ernest Wood*	2.00
_____ PROPHECY IN OUR TIME *Martin Ebon*	2.50
_____ PSYCHOLOGY OF HANDWRITING *Nadya Olyanova*	2.00
_____ SEEING INTO THE FUTURE *Harvey Day*	2.00
_____ SUPERSTITION — Are you superstitious? *Eric Maple*	2.00
_____ TAROT *Mouni Sadhu*	4.00
_____ TAROT OF THE BOHEMIANS *Papus*	3.00
_____ TEST YOUR ESP *Martin Ebon*	2.00
_____ WAYS TO SELF-REALIZATION *Mouni Sadhu*	2.00
_____ WITCHCRAFT, MAGIC & OCCULTISM—A Fascinating History *W. B. Crow*	3.00
_____ WITCHCRAFT — THE SIXTH SENSE *Justine Glass*	2.00
_____ WORLD OF PSYCHIC RESEARCH *Hereward Carrington*	2.00
_____ YOU CAN ANALYZE HANDWRITING *Robert Holder*	2.00

SELF-HELP & INSPIRATIONAL

_____ ACT YOUR WAY TO SUCCESSFUL LIVING *Neil & Margaret Rau*	2.00
_____ CYBERNETICS WITHIN US *Y. Saparina*	3.00
_____ DAILY POWER FOR JOYFUL LIVING *Dr. Donald Curtis*	2.00
_____ DOCTOR PSYCHO-CYBERNETICS *Maxwell Maltz, M.D.*	3.00
_____ DYNAMIC THINKING *Melvin Powers*	1.00
_____ GREATEST POWER IN THE UNIVERSE *U. S. Andersen*	4.00
_____ GROW RICH WHILE YOU SLEEP *Ben Sweetland*	2.00
_____ GROWTH THROUGH REASON *Albert Ellis, Ph.D.*	3.00
_____ GUIDE TO DEVELOPING YOUR POTENTIAL *Herbert A. Otto, Ph.D.*	3.00
_____ GUIDE TO HAPPINESS *Dr. Maxwell S. Cagan*	2.00
_____ GUIDE TO LIVING IN BALANCE *Frank S. Caprio, M.D.*	2.00
_____ GUIDE TO RATIONAL LIVING *Albert Ellis, Ph.D. & R. Harper, Ph.D.*	3.00
_____ HELPING YOURSELF WITH APPLIED PSYCHOLOGY *R. Henderson*	2.00
_____ HELPING YOURSELF WITH PSYCHIATRY *Frank S. Caprio, M.D.*	2.00
_____ HOW TO ATTRACT GOOD LUCK *A. H. Z. Carr*	2.00
_____ HOW TO CONTROL YOUR DESTINY *Norvell*	2.00
_____ HOW TO DEVELOP A WINNING PERSONALITY *Martin Panzer*	2.00
_____ HOW TO DEVELOP AN EXCEPTIONAL MEMORY *Young & Gibson*	3.00
_____ HOW TO OVERCOME YOUR FEARS *M. P. Leahy, M.D.*	2.00
_____ HOW YOU CAN HAVE CONFIDENCE AND POWER *Les Giblin*	2.00
_____ HUMAN PROBLEMS & HOW TO SOLVE THEM *Dr. Donald Curtis*	2.00
_____ I WILL *Ben Sweetland*	2.00
_____ LEFT-HANDED PEOPLE *Michael Barsley*	3.00
_____ MAGIC IN YOUR MIND *U. S. Andersen*	3.00

_____ MAGIC OF THINKING BIG *Dr. David J. Schwartz*	2.00
_____ MAGIC POWER OF YOUR MIND *Walter M. Germain*	3.00
_____ MENTAL POWER THRU SLEEP SUGGESTION *Melvin Powers*	1.00
_____ ORIENTAL SECRETS OF GRACEFUL LIVING *Boye De Mente*	1.00
_____ OUR TROUBLED SELVES *Dr. Allan Fromme*	3.00
_____ PRACTICAL GUIDE TO SUCCESS & POPULARITY *C. W. Bailey*	2.00
_____ PSYCHO-CYBERNETICS *Maxwell Maltz, M.D.*	2.00
_____ SCIENCE OF MIND IN DAILY LIVING *Dr. Donald Curtis*	2.00
_____ SECRET OF SECRETS *U. S. Andersen*	3.00
_____ STUTTERING AND WHAT YOU CAN DO ABOUT IT *W. Johnson, Ph.D.*	2.00
_____ SUCCESS-CYBERNETICS *U. S. Andersen*	2.00
_____ 10 DAYS TO A GREAT NEW LIFE *William E. Edwards*	2.00
_____ THINK AND GROW RICH *Napoleon Hill*	3.00
_____ THREE MAGIC WORDS *U. S. Andersen*	3.00
_____ TREASURY OF THE ART OF LIVING *Sidney S. Greenberg*	3.00
_____ YOU ARE NOT THE TARGET *Laura Huxley*	3.00
_____ YOUR SUBCONSCIOUS POWER *Charles M. Simmons*	3.00
_____ YOUR THOUGHTS CAN CHANGE YOUR LIFE *Dr. Donald Curtis*	2.00

SPORTS

_____ ARCHERY — An Expert's Guide *Don Stamp*	2.00
_____ BICYCLING FOR FUN AND GOOD HEALTH *Kenneth E. Luther*	2.00
_____ CAMPING-OUT 101 Ideas & Activities *Bruno Knobel*	2.00
_____ COMPLETE GUIDE TO FISHING *Vlad Evanoff*	2.00
_____ HOW TO WIN AT POCKET BILLIARDS *Edward D. Knuchell*	3.00
_____ MOTORCYCLING FOR BEGINNERS *I. G. Edmonds*	2.00
_____ PRACTICAL BOATING *W. S. Kals*	3.00
_____ SECRET OF BOWLING STRIKES *Dawson Taylor*	2.00
_____ SECRET OF PERFECT PUTTING *Horton Smith & Dawson Taylor*	2.00
_____ SECRET WHY FISH BITE *James Westman*	2.00
_____ SKIER'S POCKET BOOK *Otti Wiedman* (4¼" x 6")	2.50
_____ SOCCER—The game & how to play it *Gary Rosenthal*	2.00
_____ TABLE TENNIS MADE EASY *Johnny Leach*	2.00

TENNIS LOVERS' LIBRARY

_____ BEGINNER'S GUIDE TO WINNING TENNIS *Helen Hull Jacobs*	2.00
_____ HOW TO BEAT BETTER TENNIS PLAYERS *Loring Fiske*	3.00
_____ HOW TO IMPROVE YOUR TENNIS—Style, Strategy & Analysis *C. Wilson*	2.00
_____ PLAY TENNIS WITH ROSEWALL *Ken Rosewall*	2.00
_____ PSYCH YOURSELF TO BETTER TENNIS *Dr. Walter A. Luszki*	2.00
_____ TENNIS FOR BEGINNERS *Dr. H. A. Murray*	2.00
_____ TENNIS MADE EASY *Joel Brecheen*	2.00
_____ WEEKEND TENNIS—How to have fun & win at the same time *Bill Talbert*	2.00

WILSHIRE MINIATURE LIBRARY (4¼" x 6" in full color)

_____ BUTTERFLIES	2.50
_____ INTRODUCTION TO MINERALS	2.50
_____ LIPIZZANERS & THE SPANISH RIDING SCHOOL	2.50
_____ PRECIOUS STONES AND PEARLS	2.50
_____ SKIER'S POCKET BOOK	2.50

WILSHIRE PET LIBRARY

_____ DOG OBEDIENCE TRAINING *Gust Kessopulos*	2.00
_____ DOG TRAINING MADE EASY & FUN *John W. Kellogg*	2.00
_____ HOW TO BRING UP YOUR PET DOG *Kurt Unkelbach*	2.00
_____ HOW TO RAISE & TRAIN YOUR PUPPY *Jeff Griffen*	2.00
_____ PIGEONS: HOW TO RAISE & TRAIN THEM *William H. Allen, Jr.*	2.00

The books listed above can be obtained from your book dealer or directly from
Melvin Powers. When ordering, please remit 25c per book postage & handling.
Send 25c for our illustrated catalog of self-improvement books.

Melvin Powers

12015 Sherman Road, No. Hollywood, California 91605

WILSHIRE HORSE LOVERS' LIBRARY

AMATEUR HORSE BREEDER A. C. Leighton Hardman	2.00
AMERICAN QUARTER HORSE IN PICTURES Margaret Cabell Self	2.00
APPALOOSA HORSE Bill & Dona Richardson	2.00
ARABIAN HORSE Reginald S. Summerhays	2.00
ART OF WESTERN RIDING Suzanne Norton Jones	2.00
AT THE HORSE SHOW Margaret Cabell Self	2.00
BACK-YARD FOAL Peggy Jett Pittinger	2.00
BACK-YARD HORSE Peggy Jett Pittinger	2.00
BASIC DRESSAGE Jean Froissard	2.00
BEGINNER'S GUIDE TO HORSEBACK RIDING Sheila Wall	2.00
BEGINNER'S GUIDE TO THE WESTERN HORSE Natlee Kenoyer	2.00
BITS—THEIR HISTORY, USE AND MISUSE Louis Taylor	2.00
BREAKING & TRAINING THE DRIVING HORSE Doris Ganton	2.00
CAVALRY MANUAL OF HORSEMANSHIP Gordon Wright	2.00
COMPLETE TRAINING OF HORSE AND RIDER Colonel Alois Podhajsky	3.00
DISORDERS OF THE HORSE & WHAT TO DO ABOUT THEM E. Hanauer	2.00
DOG TRAINING MADE EASY & FUN John W. Kellogg	2.00
DRESSAGE—A study of the Finer Points in Riding Henry Wynmalen	3.00
DRIVING HORSES Sallie Walrond	2.00
EQUITATION Jean Froissard	3.00
FIRST AID FOR HORSES Dr. Charles H. Denning, Jr.	2.00
FUN OF RAISING A COLT Rubye & Frank Griffith	2.00
FUN ON HORSEBACK Margaret Cabell Self	3.00
HORSE DISEASES—Causes, Symptoms & Treatment Dr. H. G. Belschner	3.00
HORSE OWNER'S CONCISE GUIDE Elsie V. Hanauer	2.00
HORSE SELECTION & CARE FOR BEGINNERS George H. Conn	2.00
HORSE SENSE—A complete guide to riding and care Alan Deacon	4.00
HORSEBACK RIDING FOR BEGINNERS Louis Taylor	3.00
HORSEBACK RIDING MADE EASY & FUN Sue Henderson Coen	3.00
HORSES—Their Selection, Care & Handling Margaret Cabell Self	2.00
HOW TO BUY A BETTER HORSE & SELL THE HORSE YOU OWN	2.00
HOW TO ENJOY YOUR QUARTER HORSE Williard H. Porter	2.00
HUNTER IN PICTURES Margaret Cabell Self	2.00
ILLUSTRATED BOOK OF THE HORSE S. Sidney (8½" x 11½")	10.00
ILLUSTRATED HORSE MANAGEMENT—400 Illustrations Dr. E. Mayhew	5.00
ILLUSTRATED HORSE TRAINING Captain M. H. Hayes	5.00
ILLUSTRATED HORSEBACK RIDING FOR BEGINNERS Jeanne Mellin	2.00
JUMPING—Learning and Teaching Jean Froissard	2.00
KNOW ALL ABOUT HORSES Harry Disston	2.00
LAME HORSE—Causes, Symptoms & Treatment Dr. James R. Rooney	3.00
LAW & YOUR HORSE Edward H. Greene	3.00
LIPIZZANERS & THE SPANISH RIDING SCHOOL W. Reuter (4¼" x 6")	2.50
MORGAN HORSE IN PICTURES Margaret Cabell Self	2.00
MOVIE HORSES—The Fascinating Techniques of Training Anthony Amaral	2.00
POLICE HORSES Judith Campbell	2.00
PRACTICAL GUIDE TO HORSESHOEING	2.00
PRACTICAL GUIDE TO OWNING YOUR OWN HORSE Steven D. Price	2.00
PRACTICAL HORSE PSYCHOLOGY Moyra Williams	2.00
PROBLEM HORSES Guide for Curing Serious Behavior Habits Summerhays	2.00
RESCHOOLING THE THOROUGHBRED Peggy Jett Pittenger	2.00
RIDE WESTERN Louis Taylor	2.00
SCHOOLING YOUR YOUNG HORSE George Wheatley	2.00
STABLE MANAGEMENT FOR THE OWNER-GROOM George Wheatley	3.00
STALLION MANAGEMENT—A Guide for Stud Owners A. C. Hardman	2.00
TEACHING YOUR HORSE TO JUMP W. J. Froud	2.00
TRAIL HORSES & TRAIL RIDING Anne & Perry Westbrook	2.00
TREATING COMMON DISEASES OF YOUR HORSE Dr. George H. Conn	2.00
TREATING HORSE AILMENTS G. W. Serth	2.00
WESTERN HORSEBACK RIDING Glen Balch	2.00
WONDERFUL WORLD OF PONIES Peggy Jett Pittinger (8½" x 11½")	4.00
YOUR FIRST HORSE George C. Saunders, M.D.	2.00
YOUR PONY BOOK Hermann Wiederhold	2.00
YOUR WESTERN HORSE Nelson C. Nye	2.00

The books listed above can be obtained from your book dealer or directly from Melvin Powers. When ordering, please remit 25c per book postage & handling. Send 25c for our illustrated catalog of self-improvement books.

Melvin Powers, 12015 Sherman Road, No. Hollywood, California 91605

Notes

Notes

Notes

Notes

Notes

Notes

Notes

Notes

Notes